An Introduction to Knowledge Engineering

T0202765

S.L. Kendal and M. Creen

An Introduction to Knowledge Engineering

With 33 figures

 Springer

S.L. Kendal
School of Computing & Technology
University of Sunderland
Tyne and Wear
UK

M. Creen
Learning Development Services
University of Sunderland
Tyne and Wear
UK

British Library Cataloguing in Publication Data
A catalogue record for this book is available from the British Library

Library of Congress Control Number: 2006925857

ISBN 10: 1-84628-475-9   Printed on acid-free paper
ISBN 13: 978-1-84628-475-5

© Springer-Verlag London Limited 2007

Apart from any fair dealing for the purposes of research or private study, or criticism or review, as permitted under the Copyright, Designs and Patents Act 1988, this publication may only be reproduced, stored or transmitted, in any form or by any means, with the prior permission in writing of the publishers, or in the case of reprographic reproduction in accordance with the terms of licences issued by the Copyright Licensing Agency. Enquiries concerning reproduction outside those terms should be sent to the publishers.
The use of registered names, trademarks, etc. in this publication does not imply, even in the absence of a specific statement, that such names are exempt from the relevant laws and regulations and therefore free for general use.
The publisher makes no representation, express or implied, with regard to the accuracy of the information contained in this book and cannot accept any legal responsibility or liability for any errors or omissions that may be made.

Printed in the United States of America   (TB/MVY)

9 8 7 6 5 4 3 2 1

Springer Science+Business Media
springer.com

To my wife Janice, who is a better partner than I could wish for, and my daughter Cara, a gift from God.

—Simon Kendal

To Lillian and Sholto—with love.

—Malcolm Creen

Foreword

An *Introduction to Knowledge Engineering* presents a simple but detailed exploration of current and established work in the field of knowledge-based systems and related technologies. Its treatment of the increasing variety of such systems is designed to provide the reader with a substantial grounding in such technologies as expert systems, neural networks, genetic algorithms, case-based reasoning systems, data mining, intelligent agents and the associated techniques and methodologies.

The material is reinforced by the inclusion of numerous activities that provide opportunities for the reader to engage in their own research and reflection as they progress through the book. In addition, self-assessment questions allow the student to check their own understanding of the concepts covered.

The book will be suitable for both undergraduate and postgraduate students in computing science and related disciplines such as knowledge engineering, artificial intelligence, intelligent systems, cognitive neuroscience, robotics and cybernetics.

Contents

1
An Introduction to Knowledge Engineering

Introduction

This chapter introduces some of the key concepts in knowledge engineering. Almost all of the topics are covered in summary form, and they will be explained in more detail in subsequent chapters.

The chapter consists of three sections:

1. Data, information and knowledge
2. Skills of a knowledge engineer
3. An introduction to knowledge-based systems (KBSs).

Objectives

By the end of this chapter, you will be able to:

- define knowledge and explain its relationship to data and information
- distinguish between knowledge management and knowledge engineering
- explain the skills required of a knowledge engineer
- comment on the professionalism, methods and standards required of a knowledge engineer
- explain the difference between knowledge engineering and artificial intelligence
- define KBSs
- explain what a KBS can do
- explain the differences between human and computer processing
- state a brief definition of expert systems, neural networks, case-based reasoning, genetic algorithms, intelligent agents and data mining.

SECTION 1: DATA, INFORMATION AND KNOWLEDGE

Introduction

This section defines knowledge and explains its relationship to data and information.

Objectives

By the end of this section you will be able to:

• develop a working definition of knowledge and describe its relationship to data and information.

What Is Knowledge Engineering?

'Knowledge engineering is the process of developing knowledge based systems in any field, whether it be in the public or private sector, in commerce or in industry' (Debenham, 1988).

But what, precisely, is knowledge?

What Is Knowledge?

Knowledge is 'The **explicit** functional associations between items of information and/or data' (Debenham, 1988).

Data, Information and Knowledge

What is data? Is it the same as information? Before we can attempt to understand what knowledge is, we should at least attempt to come closer to establishing exactly what data and information are.

Activity 1
The following activity introduces you to the concepts of data and information:
1. Read the following descriptions and definitions of 'data' drawn from a
   variety of sources:

   Data (the plural of *datum*) are just raw facts (Long and Long, 1998).

   Data...are streams of raw facts representing events...before they have
   been arranged into a form that people can understand and use (Laudon
   and Laudon, 1998).

   Data is comprised of facts (Hayes, 1992).

   Recorded symbols (McNurlin and Sprague, 1998).
2. Make a note of any factors common to two or more of the descriptions.

Feedback 1
You will have noticed that data is often spoken of as the same as 'facts'—often
'raw' and, in the first quotation, considered to move in a 'stream'. The final quotation from Hayes appears to look deeper in defining data more fundamentally
as recorded symbols.

Hayes actually goes on to insist that data are not facts and that treating them as such
can produce 'innumerable perversions' for example, in the form of propaganda or
lies—which are still 'data'.

You do not need to accept or reject any of the definitions you encounter—simply
be aware that there are no universally accepted definitions of data.

Similarly, in connection to the meaning of the term 'information', we find that
there are many attempts at definitions in the textbooks on information systems
and information technology. In many ways the meanings of the words 'data' and
'information' only become clearer when we approach the differences between
them. The following activity will help you to appreciate this.

Activity 2
This activity introduces you to some definitions of information and its relationship to data.
1. Read the following definitions and descriptions of information. As in the
   last activity look for common denominators.

   That property of data which represents and measures effects of processing
   them (Hayes, 1992).

   By information we mean data that have been shaped into a form that is
   meaningful and useful to human beings (Laudon and Laudon, 1998).

Information is data that have been collected and processed into a meaningful form. Simply, information is the meaning we give to accumulated facts (data) (Long and Long, 1998).

Information is the emergent property which comes from processing data so that it is transformed into a structured whole (Harry, 1994).

Information is data presented in a form that is meaningful to the recipient (Senn, 1990).

Information is data in context (McNurlin and Sprague, 1998).

Information is data endowed with relevance and purpose (Drucker, 1988).

2. Make a note of any similarities between the different descriptions.

Feedback 2

You should have noted that information is commonly thought to be data, processed or transformed into a form or structure suitable for use by human beings. Such words as 'meaning', 'meaningful', 'useful' and 'purpose' are in evidence here.

You may also have noted that information is considered a property of data. This implies that the former cannot exist without the latter.

In the definitions of information you will have seen how the meaning of the word becomes clearer when the differences between it and data are considered. For example, whereas the 'rawness' of data was emphasised earlier, information is considered to be some refinement of data for the purposes of human use.

In addition, the words 'knowledge' and 'communication' have emerged as having a relationship to data and information. What is also worth emphasising at this point is that the interface between data and a human being's interpretation of it is where information—determined by 'meaning'—really emerges.

The two terms are still often used interchangeably and no definition of either will apply in all the situations you might encounter.

Knowledge

In common language, the word knowledge is obviously related to information, but it is clear that they are not the same thing. So, how can we define knowledge in the same flexible way in which we have arrived at working definitions of information and data?

Activity 3
This activity extends your understanding of data and information.

Look at the seven topics described briefly below. Which of them would you consider yourself as 'knowing', and which would you consider yourself as having information about?
(a) A second language in which you are fluent.
(b) The content of a television news programme.
(c) A close friend.
(d) A company's annual report.
(e) Your close friend's partner whom you have yet to meet.
(f) The weather on the other side of the world.
(g) The weather where you are now.

Feedback 3
It is probable—but by no means certain—that you will have been inclined to consider items (a), (c) and (g) as things you can know about and the others as things for which you may have information. Note that the items that you would not describe yourself as possessing knowledge of could actually become known if circumstances were different, e.g. you might come to know your close friend's partner.

It is also worth noting that all of this depends on individual perceptions rather than measurable facts. You may only think you know your close friend. Similarly, your fluency in the second language will always be relatively poorer than that of a native speaker.

Activity 4
This activity brings you closer to a definition by helping you highlight the differences between having information and possessing knowledge.

What would you suggest is the primary characteristic that distinguishes the 'having information' situations from the 'knowing' situations you categorised in the previous activity? You will need to make sure that your description does not simply describe information or data, but must particularly take account of the former.

Feedback 4
You should have been able to identify specific characteristics of knowledge that distinguish it from information similar to those highlighted in the following quotations. According to experts in the field, knowledge is:

the result of the understanding of information (Hayes, 1992)
the result of internalising information (Hayes, 1992)
collected information about an area of concern (Senn, 1990)
information with direction or intent—it facilitates a decision or an action (Zachman, 1987).

Here it has become clear that knowledge is what someone has after understanding information. Often this understanding follows the development of a detailed or long-term relationship with the known person or thing. Such a process can often be accelerated when the need to use the information for a critical decision arises. This application of information to a decision or area of concern is particularly relevant in an organisational situation.

However, it should be clear that data, information and knowledge are not static things in themselves but stages in the process of using data and transforming it into knowledge. On this basis they can be considered points along a continuum, moving from less to more usefulness to a human being, in much the same way as we all move along a continuum from young to old, but at no point can we be defined as either.

Activity 5
Temperature and humidity readings are taken from various locations around one city. These readings are taken four times each day, and the results collated in a central location.

The city is 12 miles in diameter. Readings taken on the periphery of the city can show, over time, how rain or adverse weather conditions start at one side of the city and move across to the other side.

Details of adverse weather can be used to warn weather-sensitive activities such as cricket or tennis matches when to expect a break in play.

Explain how a series of temperature and humidity readings can be transformed from data into knowledge.

Feedback 5

Data. Individual temperature and humidity readings, by themselves, are simply numbers, and therefore represent data.

Information. Information on where the readings have been taken (e.g. at which point in the city) and at what time provides a trend to show how the temperature is currently changing. This information can be used by someone to make a decision.

Knowledge. Knowing how the temperature and humidity are changing AND, knowing about how the weather can affect people living or working in the city will allow decisions to be made concerning the use of umbrellas, warm clothing, running a cricket or tennis match, etc. In this situation, two or more sets of information are related and can be processed to reach a decision.

The movement from data to knowledge implies a shift from facts and figures to more abstract concepts, as shown in Figure 1.1.

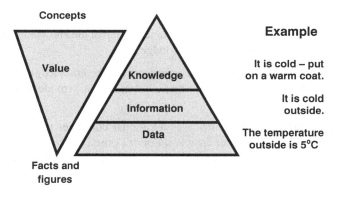

FIGURE 1.1. Data, information and knowledge.

In other words:

It is 5°C—data.
It is cold—information.
It is cold outside AND if it is cold you should wear a warm coat—knowledge.

From a knowledge engineering perspective, it is useful to consider knowledge as something that can be expressed as a rule or useful to assist a decision, i.e.,

IF it is cold outside THEN wear a warm coat.

The perceived value of data increases as it is transferred into knowledge, because the latter enables useful decisions to be made.

Activity 6
Knowledge engineering normally involves five distinct steps (listed below) in transferring human knowledge into some form of knowledge based system (KBS).

Explain what you think should be involved in each of these activities.
1. Knowledge acquisition
2. Knowledge validation
3. Knowledge representation
4. Inferencing
5. Explanation and justification.

Feedback 6
Knowledge acquisition involves obtaining knowledge from various sources including human experts, books, videos and existing computer sources of data such as databases and the Internet.

In *knowledge validation*, knowledge is checked using test cases for adequate quality.

Knowledge representation involves producing a map of the knowledge and then encoding this knowledge into the knowledge base.

Inferencing means forming links (or inferences) in the knowledge in the computer software so that the KBS can make a decision or provide advice to the user.

Explanation and justification involves additional computer program design, primarily to help the computer answer questions posed by the user and also to show how a conclusion was reached using knowledge in the knowledge base.

Knowledge Engineering and Knowledge Management

The terms 'knowledge management' and 'knowledge engineering' seem to be used as interchangeably as the terms data and information used to be. The term 'manage' relates to exercising executive, administrative and supervisory direction, whereas, to engineer is to lay out, construct or contrive or plan out, usually with more or less subtle skill and craft.

The main difference seems to be that the (knowledge) manager establishes the direction the process should take, where as the (knowledge) engineer develops the means to accomplish that direction.

We should therefore find knowledge managers concerned with the knowledge needs of the enterprise, e.g. discovering what knowledge is needed to make decisions and enable actions. They should be taking a key role in the design of the enterprise and from the needs of the enterprise they should be establishing the enterprise level knowledge management policies.

On the other hand, if we were to look in on the knowledge engineers we should find them concerned with data and information *representation and encoding methodologies*, data repositories, etc. The knowledge engineers would be interested in what *technologies* are needed to meet the enterprise's knowledge management needs.

The knowledge engineer is most likely a computer scientist specialising the development of knowledge bases but a knowledge manager may be the chief information officer or the person in charge of the information resource management.

Summary

This section has introduced the concept of knowledge engineering and the relationship between data, information and knowledge.

Self-Assessment Question

Try and think of other systems within your immediate environment that result in data being transferred into information and then knowledge.

Answer to Self-Assessment Question

You might have thought of the following example:
50 litres (*Data*)—e.g. the amount of petrol your car can hold.
Having filled the tank, this can implicitly indicate that you can now travel 320 miles. (*Information*)
With the information above, a map and the addresses of several friends, you can now decide who you can visit within a 160 mile radius (assuming that the next refuelling will take place back at home). (*Knowledge*)

SECTION 2: SKILLS OF A KNOWLEDGE ENGINEER

Introduction

This section introduces one of the most important people in knowledge engineering; namely the knowledge engineer. The knowledge engineer is responsible for obtaining knowledge from human experts and then entering this knowledge into some form of KBS. To undertake these activities, specific skills are required.

Objectives

By the end of this section you will be able to:

• explain the skills and knowledge required of a knowledge engineer
• comment on the professionalism, methods and standards required of a knowledge engineer.

Knowledge Required of a Knowledge Engineer

To begin with, a knowledge engineer must extract knowledge from people (human experts) that can be placed into knowledge based systems (KBSs).

This knowledge must then be represented in some format that is understandable both to the knowledge engineer, the human expert and the programmer of the KBS.

A computer program, which processes that knowledge or makes inferences, must be developed, and the software system that is being produced must be validated. The knowledge engineer may be involved in the development of the program, or this may be delegated to another person.

In developing these systems the knowledge engineer must apply methods, use tools, apply quality control and standards.

To undertake these activities, the knowledge engineer must plan and manage projects, and take into account human, financial and environmental constraints.

Overview of Knowledge Engineers Work

To summarise the above points, knowledge engineering includes the process of knowledge acquisition, knowledge representation, software design and implementation.

To meet the objective of designing a KBS, the knowledge engineer will have to:

* acquire the knowledge from the expert to be used in the system
* use an appropriate method for representing knowledge in a symbolic, processable form.

This means that to deserve the title of knowledge engineer we must really apply professional and rigorous approaches to the development of a product. The engineer will also use various techniques to ensure quality and work to standards.

Knowledge engineering is a multi-stage process, and traditionally a business being tackled by a range of professionals. These include psychologists, computer scientists, software engineers, project managers, systems analysts, domain (or subject) experts and knowledge specialists.

Types of Knowledge

The knowledge engineer will normally be dealing with three types of knowledge:

* *Declarative knowledge* tells us facts about things. For example, the statement 'A light bulb requires electricity to shine' is factually correct.
* *Procedural knowledge* provides alternative actions based on the use of facts to obtain knowledge. For example, an individual will normally check the amount of water in a kettle before turning it on; if there is insufficient water in the kettle, then more will be added.
* *Meta-knowledge* is knowledge about knowledge. It helps us understand how experts use knowledge to make decisions. For example, knowledge about planes and trains might be useful when planning a long journey and knowledge about footpaths and bicycles might be useful when planning a short journey.

A knowledge engineer must be able to distinguish between these three types of knowledge and understand how to codify different knowledge types into some form of KBS.

Activity 7

A knowledge engineer will be involved in the following tasks:
* Advising the expert on the knowledge required for a system
* Acquiring knowledge from the expert
* Encoding the knowledge in some form ready for inclusion in the knowledge base
* Entering the knowledge into a knowledge base on a computer system
* Validating the knowledge in that knowledge base to ensure that it is accurate
* Training users to access and use the knowledge in the knowledge base.

Knowledge engineers are trained in techniques to extract knowledge from experts, in the same way that systems analysts and other specialists are trained to obtain user requirements.

Think of a situation where you have either had to provide knowledge to someone or even had to obtain knowledge from a third party—this will help you answer the following question:

What tools or techniques are available to assist the knowledge engineer in carrying out these activities?

Feedback 7
Advising and obtaining knowledge from the expert can be supporting by some formal elicitation techniques, or use of interviews, questionnaires and similar fact-finding methods.

In addition to standard techniques, software including text editors and specialised knowledge representation languages such as KARL (Fensel, 1996) can assist in the encoding of knowledge for inclusion in a knowledge base.

Specialised programs such as TEIRESIAS (Davis, 1993), help to validate knowledge and check for errors within a knowledge base.

Professionalism, Methods and Standards

Apart from the skills required to place knowledge into a KBS, a knowledge engineer will also normally be expected to:

• be bound by a professional code of conduct
• update their knowledge and skills on a regular basis
• adhere to appropriate rules, regulations and legal requirements.

The following managerial and interpersonal skills are also expected from knowledge engineers. The most important skills are identified at the top of the list.

• Knowledge representation
• Fact finding
• Human skills
• Visualisation skills
• Analysis
• Creativity
• Managerial.

The Project Champion

There are many people involved in the actual building of a KBS. Some of those people, such as the knowledge engineer and the human expert, have been discussed earlier in this chapter.

However, one of the most important people involved in a KBS project from the users perspective is the Project Champion. This is a person who works with the project team, most likely as a user representative. Such a person must:

- be able to convince users that the KBS is needed
- have an appropriate level of authority
- 'get on' with both management and users
- have a personal investment in the project
- believe in the need for the KBS
- be capable of presenting the business benefits to management
- be highly motivated towards the success of the project.

Convincing Management

One of the key activities that takes place at the beginning of a KBS project is convincing management of the need for the system. Obtaining management approval is essential because without appropriate 'buy-in' there will not be the necessary management support, nor the funding required to build and maintain the KBS.

A presentation of the aims of the KBS early in the project will:

- provide an opportunity for management to be made aware of the reality of the project
- allow the knowledge engineer to gauge the real level of support from management.

The aim of the presentation is therefore to obtain management buy-in and the funding for the project. The overall level of support from management will be determined partly by enthusiasm in the meeting and partly by the level of funding obtained.

Example of a KBS Project

The following is an example of how a hypothetical KBS project can start.

The goal of the system was to assist the clinician in the intensive care unit (ICU). The system addressed the following problems:

- The need for interpretation of measurement values with respect to historical information about changes in a patient's status and therapy.
- The difficulty of directly relating measurement values to a therapeutic recommendation.

The system was designed to perform the following tasks in the ICU:

- Predict the initial setting of the mechanical ventilator to assist the patient to breathe.
- Suggest adjustments to treatment by continuous reassessment of the patient's condition.
- Summarise the patient's physiological status.
- Maintain a set of patient's specific expectations and goals for future evaluation.
- Aid in the stabilisation of the patient's condition.

The basic procedure for obtaining information and developing the system is outlined in Figure 1.2.

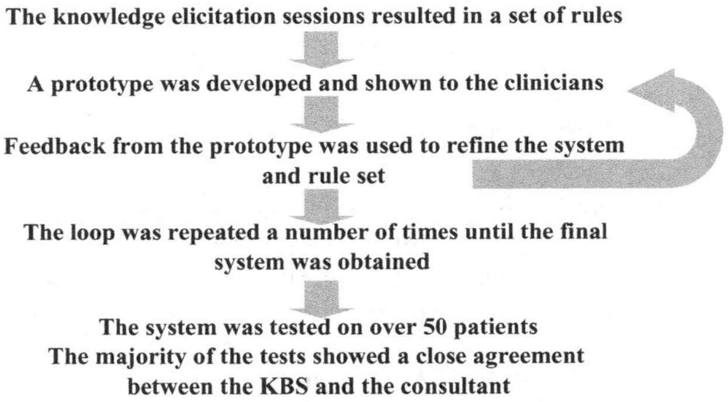

The knowledge elicitation sessions resulted in a set of rules

A prototype was developed and shown to the clinicians

Feedback from the prototype was used to refine the system and rule set

The loop was repeated a number of times until the final system was obtained

The system was tested on over 50 patients
The majority of the tests showed a close agreement between the KBS and the consultant

FIGURE 1.2. Knowledge-based system development process.

One of the main queries in the project was from the experts providing knowledge for the system. Obviously, it was essential that the system provided accurate answers, otherwise patients lives could be at risk. Similarly, experts providing the knowledge did not want to be blamed if an incorrect response was given by the KBS. These concerns can be summarised in Figure 1.3.

The main assurance provided by the knowledge engineer and project manager was that the system was built in accordance with quality assurance standards.

Quality assurance is an essential part of the design of any KBS—especially those designed for such purposes as:

- railway signalling systems
- alarm systems
- detection of gas leaks
- nuclear power station monitoring and control.

FIGURE 1.3. Safety critical systems.

An error in any of these systems could result in significant risk, including loss of life. Attention to quality assurance is therefore essential.

The Project Manager's Dilemma

As well as being skilled in overall project management, a project manager needs some negotiating skills to try and match the expectations of all parties involved in a project.

Stakeholder	Expectation
Users	Want a system that meets their needs
Knowledge engineers	Would like to be left alone to carry out their job
Quality manager	Require the system to conform to their quality control procedures
Senior management	Would like the introduction of the system to go smoothly. They also want the project on time, within budget and working correctly

Balancing the conflicting requirements will be difficult.

Professionalism

One method of trying to ensure high-quality systems development is to employ people who belong to a known profession. Membership of a professional body implies that a certain standard of work will be carried out and that the person will take pride in doing a good job.

Though the word 'professional' is in common usage, most people believe they understand what it means, we need to look more closely at what precisely defines a 'professional'.

Activity 8
This activity helps you focus on precisely what qualities characterise a professional or a professional group.

List the words you might normally expect to use or see used when describing
professionalism.

Feedback 8
You may have thought of such terms as:

- expert   • honesty
- skilled   • ethical
- integrity

The main factors that distinguish a professional organisation are as follows:

- *Expertise*. The individuals within the organisation maintain a current, working
  expertise of a given subject.
- *Self-regulation*. The professional code of conduct and other regulations (such as
  code of practice or code of ethics) are self-imposed and made public. Any individual that wishes to be recognised as a member of the society must voluntarily
  show continuous compliance with such a code.
- *World view*. All of the above conditions maintain a 'world view'. This view
  does not discriminate nor does it compromise the basic moral principles of any
  member of society as a whole.

Professionals are normally recognised as a distinct group of people having established some sort of 'contract' with society. This contract is typically based
upon a code of conduct or a code of ethics. An individual must adhere to
this code in order to become and stay a member of the particular professional
organisation.

In the United Kingdom, a profession is normally granted by Royal Charter. So if
a profession were to be started for KBS development, a charter would be needed.
The two main conditions for the granting of a charter are as follows:

- It should be in the public interest to regulate members within that body.
- The members should represent a coherent group.

Summary

A knowledge engineer requires a variety of skills ranging from the technical to the
managerial.

Self-Assessment Question

Knowledge Engineering: Skills Audit

The skills of a knowledge engineer are listed again in the table below.

Define each of these skills and then consider whether or not you have each skill. Draw up an action plan to acquire the skills you lack or need to improve.

Skill required	Explanation/Definition
Knowledge representation	
Fact finding	
Human skills	
Visual skills	
Analysis	
Creativity	
Managerial	

Answer to Self-Assessment Question

Skill required	Explanation
Knowledge representation	Being able to understand the information being provided by the expert and record this in some appropriate manner
Fact finding	Using tools such as interviews, questionnaires and observations to obtain knowledge from an expert
Human skills	Interviewing skill including how to acquire knowledge from an expert in a friendly and helpful manner
Visualisation skills	Being able to visualise the overall design of the system, prior to committing the ideas to paper
Analysis	Working through data and information to find the most appropriate method of representing it, and identifying links within the data and information
Creativity	Using new ideas or methods of representing data within the structure of the KBS
Managerial	Having good time management and delegation skills to help ensure that the data is recorded on time and within budget

SECTION 3: AN INTRODUCTION TO KNOWLEDGE-BASED SYSTEMS

Introduction

This section introduces some of the software systems used in knowledge engineering and shows how they work compared to human processing.

Objectives

By the end of the section you will be able to:

- explain the difference between knowledge engineering and artificial intelligence
- define knowledge-based systems (KBSs)
- explain what a KBS can do
- explain the differences between human and computer processing
- provide a brief definition of expert systems, neural networks, case-based reasoning, genetic algorithms, intelligent agents, data mining and intelligent tutoring systems

What Is the Difference Between Knowledge Engineering and Artificial Intelligence?

To try and provide a simple answer to this question, consider each of the following life forms:

- Plants
- Fish
- Chimpanzees
- Humans

Now, do the plant and animals in the example above exhibit evidence of intelligence?

Activity 9
We have noted that a knowledge engineer must be able to capture the behavioural skills or knowledge of experts and code these into some KBS. If you
were a knowledge engineer, what particular behavioural skills or knowledge,
in generic terms, would you expect to find in the objects listed below?

If you picture the four objects listed below, this will help you see the different
skills that are displayed by them. Think specifically of the movement (or lack
of) for each object, as well as the communication skills that could be expected.
- A plant
- A fish
- A chimpanzee
- A human.

Feedback 9
The skills may include:

A plant
  - Adapt in time and evolve—an individual plant has no skills but as a species
    they do.
A fish
  - Navigation
  - Visual recognition
  - Avoid danger.
A chimpanzee
  - Language/communication about concrete concepts
  - Use of basic tools
  - Simple problem solving
  - Mimic humans
  - Build mental models.
A human
  - Language/communication about complex concepts
  - Learn from being told
  - Learn from the past experience
  - Identify cause and effect relationships
  - Teach
  - Solve complex problems
  - Design, plan and schedule
  - Create complex abstract models
  - Show initiative.

While we may not consider fish to be intelligent, they do exhibit some complex characteristics that can be considered aspects of intelligence. They navigate around the world, and visually recognise other animals. They can also plan to avoid danger.

All these are all aspects of intelligence, and when applied to computer systems could not be implemented by traditional computing techniques.

Chimpanzees are clearly more intelligent than fish. They have the ability to use language. They use basic tools, sticks and stones. They can solve simple problems, mimic humans and have been shown to build mental models of their environment.

Finally, humans are clearly more intelligent again. They can:

- learn by being told
- learn from past examples and from experience
- teach
- solve complex problems, design, plan and schedule
- create complex, abstract models of the universe.

Further, one common feature that fish, chimpanzees and humans share is that we are all unique individuals. Within the scope of our mental capacity we have individual choice and make our own decisions. This again is evidence of intelligence.

The application of artificial intelligence has tried to emulate all of these characteristics within computer systems. Knowledge engineers have the difficult job of attempting to build these characteristics into a computer program.

By using a range of techniques, including expert systems, neural networks, case-based reasoning, genetic algorithms, intelligent agents and data mining, we can get computer systems to emulate some aspects of intelligent behaviour such as:

- making decisions, diagnosing, scheduling and planning using expert systems or neural networks
- evolving solutions to very complex problems using genetic algorithms
- learning from a single previous example, where this is particularly relevant and using it to solve a current problem using case-based reasoning
- recognising hand writing or understanding sensory data—simulated by artificial neural networks
- identifying cause and effect relationships using data mining
- free will, i.e., the ability to take independent actions—simulated by intelligent agents.

For example, legal systems can suggest suitable fines based on past examples using case-based reasoning—a type of KBS you will encounter later in more detail.

Programs can also process human language including grammar checking, summarisation and translation—all of which use natural language processing techniques (not covered in this book).

Artificial intelligence aims to endow computers with human abilities. Often this involves research into new and novel technologies that might not be immediately usable.

Knowledge engineering, on the other hand, is the practical application of those aspects of artificial intelligence that are well understood to real commercial business problems such as recognising signatures to detect potential fraud.

What Are KBSs?

Knowledge-based systems are computer programs that are designed to emulate the work of experts in specific areas of knowledge.

It is these systems that provide the main focus of this book.

There are seven main types of KBS:

1. *Expert systems.* Expert systems model the higher order cognitive functions of the brain. They can be used to mimic the decision-making process of human experts. Typical example applications include planning, scheduling and diagnostics systems.
   Expert systems are normally used to model the human decision-making process. Although expert systems contain algorithms, many of those algorithms tend to be static, that is they do not change over time. While this provides some certainty in how the system will operate, it does mean that the expert system is not designed to learn from experience.
   It is worth mentioning that expert systems are very often spoken of as synonymous with KBSs. However, expert systems are simply a category of KBS.

2. *Neural networks.* Neural networks, on the other hand, model the brain at a biological level. Just as the brain is adept at pattern recognition tasks, such as vision and speech recognition, so are neural network systems. They can learn to read, can recognise patterns from experience and can be used to predict future trends, e.g. in the demand for electricity.

3. *Case-based reasoning.* Case-based reasoning systems model the human ability to reason via analogy. Typical applications include legal cases, where the knowledge of the law is not just contained in written documents, but in a knowledge base of how this has been applied by the courts in actual situations.

4. *Genetic algorithms.* A genetic algorithm is a method of evolving solutions to complex problems. For example, such a method could be used to find one of many *good* solutions to the problem of scheduling examinations (rooms,

students, invigilators and possibly even equipment) from the millions of *possible* solutions.

The term 'genetic' refers to the behaviour of algorithms. In this situation, the behaviour is very similar to biological processes involved in evolution.

5. *Intelligent agents.* An intelligent agent is, normally, a software program where its goal or overall task is specified but where the software can make some decisions *on its own*

Most agents work in the background (that is they are not seen by the user) and only appear to report their findings. They may work over the Internet looking for important information where the user simply does not have time to sift through all the reports presented to him or her.

Agents often have the ability to learn and make increasingly complex decisions on behalf of their users. The simplest agents simply retrieve information while the most complex learn and use deductive reasoning to make decisions.

6. *Data mining.* Data mining is a term used to describe knowledge discovery by identifying previously unknown relationships in data. Alternative terms for mining include knowledge extraction, data archaeology, data dredging and data harvesting.

The technique relates to the idea that large databases contain a lot of data, with many links within that data not necessarily becoming evident until the database is analysed thoroughly. One of the classic examples of data mining concerns the analysis of sales within supermarkets. Data mining techniques could potentially identify products often purchased at the same time such as nuts and crisps. By placing these items next to each other on the supermarket shelf the sales of both products can be increased as they can now be found easily.

Data mining is used in many different areas of business, including marketing, banking, retailing and manufacturing. The main aim of data mining in these situations is to uncover previously hidden relationships and then use this information to provide some competitive advantage for the organisation.

7. *Intelligent tutoring systems.* The interest in computer-based instructional environments increases with the demand for high-quality education at a low cost. Meanwhile, computers become cheaper, more powerful and more user-friendly. An environment that responds in a sophisticated fashion to adapt its teaching strategy to the specific learning style of a given student/user is highly attractive. For a tutoring system to be intelligent, it must be able to react (teach) continuously according to a student's learning. Most tutoring systems try to use a single teaching method but with various levels of explanations/examples/disclosure of domain materials to react to different student's learning. However, a teacher in practice will use more than one teaching method in teaching a subject according to the type of domain knowledge. In order to be intelligent and effective in teaching, a tutoring system must be able to provide multiple teaching methods. An example is available at: http://www.pitt.edu/~vanlehn/andes.html.

With the exception of intelligent tutoring systems, the systems mentioned above are discussed in greater detail later in this book.

What Can KBSs Do?

A KBS can perform many of the tasks undertaken by humans. However, they do have some limitations, as the examples below explain.

When compared with human expertise—which is often not very accessible since only one or a few people can consult the expert at once—artificial expertise, once captured in some form of KBS, is permanent and open to inspection. Expert systems have been used to capture the knowledge of expert staff who are due to retire and cannot be replaced, for example.

Where human expertise is difficult to transfer between people, the knowledge within any KBS can be re-used and copied around the world. Where humans can be unpredictable, KBSs are consistent. Where human expertise can be expensive and take decades to develop, KBS can be relatively cheap.

On the other hand, humans are creative and adaptable, where KBSs are uninspired and developed for fixed purpose. Humans have a broad focus and a wide understanding. Knowledge-based systems are focused on a particular problem and cannot be used to solve other problems.

Humans can fall back on common sense knowledge and are robust to error. Knowledge-based systems are limited to the technical knowledge that has been built into them. Humans are also very good at processing sensory information. While neural networks can also handle sensory data, expert systems are generally limited to symbolic information.

Summary

There are a variety of KBSs, each designed to attempt to emulate different aspects of human intelligence, knowledge and behavioural skills.

Self-Assessment Question

For each of the four entities listed below, identify the different behavioural skills or knowledge they display that contribute or provide evidence of their 'intelligence'. For one example of each skill, indicate what type of KBS is designed to emulate it.
A plant
A dog
A dolphin
A human.

Answer to Self-Assessment Question

You should have been able to answer approximately as follows:

A plant

- Adapt in time and evolve—genetic algorithms.

A dog

- Navigation-expert systems
- Visual recognition—neural networks
- Avoid danger—neural networks.

A dolphin

- Language—neural networks (used in speech recognition) and natural language processing (not covered in this book)
- Simple problem solving—expert systems
- Build mental models—case-based reasoning-expert systems.

A human

- Reason by analogy—case-based reasoning
- Learn from being told—expert systems
- Learn from past experience—case-based reasoning and neural networks
- Identify cause and effect relationships—data mining and neural networks
- Teach—intelligent tutoring systems
- Solve complex problems—expert systems/genetic algorithms
- Design, plan and schedule—expert systems and genetic algorithms
- Create complex abstract models—expert systems
- Show initiative (or at least emulate individual choice and decision making)— intelligent agents.

References

Davis, R. (1979). Interactive transfer of expertise: Acquisition of new inference rules. *Artificial intelligence*, 12: 121–157.

Debenham, J. K. (1988). *Knowledge Systems Design*. Prentice-Hall: Englewood Cliffs, NJ.

Drucker, P. F. (1988). The coming of the new organisation. *Harvard Business Review*, 66(1):39–48.

Fensel, D. (1995). *The Knowledge Acquisition and Representation Language KARL*. Kluwer Academic Publishers: Amsterdam.

Harry, M. (1994). *Information Systems in Business*. Pitman Publishing: Boston, MA, p. 50.

Hayes, R. (1992). The measurement of information. In Vakkari, P. and Cronin, B. (editors), *Conceptions of Library and Information Science*. Taylor Graham: London, pp. 97–108.

Laudon, K. C. and Laudon, J. P. (1998). *Management Information Systems: New Approaches to Organisation and Technology*, 5th ed. Prentice-Hall: Englewood Cliffs, NJ, p. 8.

Long, L. and Long, N. (1998). *Computers*, 5th ed. Prentice-Hall: Englewood Cliffs, NJ, p. 5.

McNurlin, B. and Sprague, R. H., Jr. (1998). *Information Systems Management in Practice*, 4th ed. Prentice-Hall: Englewood Cliffs, NJ, p. 197.

Senn, J. A. (1990). *Information Systems in Management.* Wadsworth Publishing: Belmont, CA, p. 58.

Zachman, J. (1987). A framework for information systems architecture. *IBM Systems Journal*, 26(3):276–292.

2
Types of Knowledge-Based Systems

Introduction

This chapter builds on the brief introduction to different types of knowledge-based systems from the first chapter and provides you with the opportunity to explore them in greater depth.

The chapter consists of six sections:

1. Expert systems
2. Neural networks (NNs)
3. Case-based reasoning (CBR)
4. Genetic algorithms
5. Intelligent agents
6. Data mining.

Objectives

By the end of the chapter you will be able to:

- describe the characteristics of a knowledge-based system
- explain the main elements of knowledge-based systems and how they work
- evaluate the advantages and limitations of knowledge-based systems
- identify appropriate contexts for the use of particular types of knowledge-based systems.

SECTION 1: EXPERT SYSTEMS

Introduction

This section provides you with an introduction to expert systems and their use within knowledge engineering.

Objectives

By the end of this section you will be able to:

- describe expert systems
- explain the main elements of an expert system and how they work
- evaluate the advantages and limitations of expert systems
- recognise appropriate contexts for the application of expert systems.

What Are Expert Systems?

You already know, knowledge acquisition is the process of acquiring knowledge from a human expert, or a group of experts, and using the knowledge to build knowledge-based systems.

Expert systems are computer programs designed to emulate the work of experts in specific areas of knowledge.

Activity 1

This activity give you direct experience of an expert system.

1. Visit the ESTA (Expert System Shell for Text Animation) web interface at: http://www.visual-prolog.com/vipexamples/esta/pdcindex.html (see Figure 2.1)

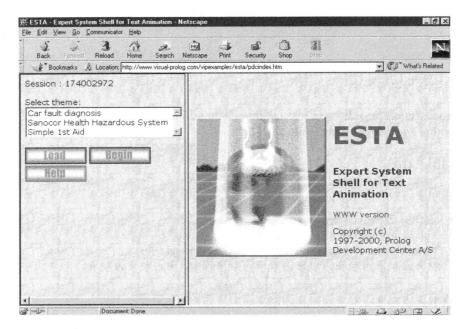

FIGURE 2.1. The expert system shell for text animation web interface.

2. Select **Car Fault Diagnosis** in the **Select theme** box.
3. Press **Load.**
4. Press **Begin Consultation** on the next screen.
5. Work your way through the consultation process during which you will be asked several questions to determine the cause and possible solution of a problem with a vehicle. You can treat this experience this consultation as real as you like. The important thing from your point of view is to consider at each stage how the program is processing the data you provide to it.
6. Choose 'car' as the type of car.
7. Press Continue.
8. Choose 'the car smells of gasoline' as the problem.
9. Press Continue.
10. Choose Yes when asked 'Is the smell only present when the engine is running?'

You will find a free Personal Edition of Visual Prolog 5.2 (the software used to create ESTA) on the web at: http://www.visual-prolog.com/vip/vipinfo/freeware_version.html. You will need to register it online in order to fully activate it.

Definition of an Expert System

The British Computer Society defines an expert system as follows:

An expert system is regarded as the embodiment within the computer of knowledge based component from an expert skill, in such a form that the system can offer intelligent advice or take an intelligent decision about a processing function. A desirable additional characteristic, which many would consider fundamental, is the capability of the system, on demand, to justify its own line of reasoning in a manner directly intelligible to an enquirer. The style adopted to attain these characteristics is rule based programming.

We can see from this definition the main characteristics of an expert system. We can see that an expert system uses knowledge, and therefore must have some way of storing this knowledge. It must have some inference mechanism, i.e., some way of processing knowledge to reach a conclusion. Finally, an expert system must be capable of acting as a human expert; i.e., to a high level of decision-making within a particular area.

The following features are also essential to an expert system:

- Having a highly focused topic, or domain, for the expert systems to solve makes them much easier to develop.
- Being able to justify their own reasoning helps to show why expert systems have made particular recommendations.

Main Elements of an Expert System

The elements of an expert system are as follows:

- A knowledge-based module. This is where the knowledge is stored in a particular representation.
- An inference engine. This is a program that uses the knowledge base (KB) to reach conclusions. Clearly, it must understand the format of the KB with which it reasons.
- An explanatory interface with which the human interacts.
- A knowledge acquisition module that helps when building up new KBs.

Figure 2.2 provides an overview of the elements required in building and using an expert or KB system. It also shows the key elements just outlined above.

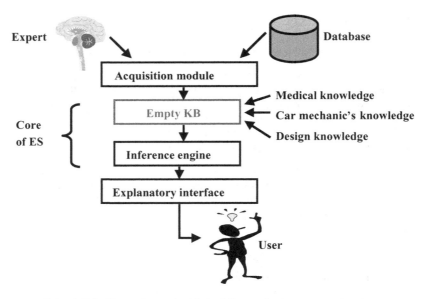

FIGURE 2.2. Elements required in building and using an expert system.

Different Types of Expert Systems

Types of expert systems currently available are noted below. The examples of expert systems (some of which are still interesting for historical reasons) are given in bold letters.

Type of system	Examples
Diagnostic systems	Doctor, technician, car mechanic, etc.
	MYCIN—an interactive program that diagnoses certain infectious diseases, prescribes anti-microbial therapy, and can explain its reasoning in detail. In a controlled test, its performance equalled that of specialists. Since it was designed as a consultant for physicians, MYCIN was given the ability to explain both its line of reasoning and its knowledge. Because of the rapid pace of developments in medicine, the KB was designed for easy augmentation. Although MYCIN was never used routinely by physicians, it has substantially influenced other artificial intelligence (AI) research.
	VM – The ventilator manager program interprets online quantitative data in the intensive care unit and advises physicians on the management of post-surgical patients needing a mechanical ventilator to help them breathe. While based on the MYCIN architecture, VM was redesigned to allow for the description of events that change over time. Thus, it can monitor the progress of a patient, interpret data in the context of the patient's present and past condition, and suggest adjustments to therapy. Some of the program's concepts have been built directly into more recent respiratory monitoring devices.

Type of system	Examples
Identification systems	Materials spillage, bacterial agent identifier, etc.
	DENDRAL – The DENDRAL Project—one of the earliest expert systems—began as an effort to explore the mechanisation of scientific reasoning and the formalisation of scientific knowledge by working within a specific domain of science, organic chemistry. Its performance rivals that of human experts for certain classes of organic compounds and has resulted in a number of papers that were published in the chemical literature.
Decision support systems	Planning, scheduling, designing systems.
	DART – used to assist in deployment of military resources
	XCON – assists in configuring mainframe computers (developed by DEC).

Activity 2

The main elements of an expert system are shown in Figure 2.2. Note that the expert, database and user are outside the expert system itself but are obviously required to build and then query the expert system.

Using the labels provided, can you explain the purpose of each of the main elements of an expert system?

Expert
Database
Acquisition module
Knowledge base
Inference engine
Explanatory interface
User

Feedback 2

Expert—human expert to provide the knowledge for the expert system.

Database—some knowledge acquisition methods use data in databases to automatically generate new rules, e.g. weather data can be used to generate rules that will enable prediction of tomorrow's weather.

Acquisition module—obtains appropriate knowledge from the human expert and the database ready for input to the KB of the expert system.

Knowledge base—retains the knowledge and rules used by the expert system in making decisions.

Inference engine—system that reasons to provide answers to problems placed into the expert system. The inference engine uses knowledge from the KB to arrive at a decision.

Explanatory interface—to provide the user with an explanation on how the expert system reached its conclusion.

User—the human being using the expert system!

Many expert systems are built using a generic 'shell'. An expert system shell consists of the programming components of an expert system but without a KB. Using a shell, a knowledge engineer can quickly enter a new KB and, without the need for any programming, create a complete working expert system.

How Do Expert Systems Work?

The basic components of an expert system are a *knowledge base* or KB and an *inference engine*. The knowledge in the KB is obtained by interviewing people who are expert in the area in question. The interviewer, or 'knowledge engineer', organises the information elicited from the experts into a collection of rules, typically of 'if-then' structure. Rules of this type are called *production rules*. The inference engine enables the expert system to make deductions using the rules in the KB and applying them to a particular problem. The expert system can be used many times with the same knowledge using that knowledge to solve different problems (just like a doctor uses their knowledge many times to diagnose and cure lots of patients).

For example, if the KB contains production rules *if x then y* and *if y then z* and the inference engine is informed that x is true then the inference engine is able to deduce that z is true. For example, the expert system might ask if the patient has a rash and if the answer is affirmative, the system will proceed to infer the condition the patient is suffering from.

Strengths and Limitations of Expert Systems

Expert systems are designed to replace human knowledge in some situations; overcoming not just the problems of *obtaining* that knowledge, but also problems involved with humans *providing* knowledge.

Activity 3
Given the areas in which expert systems can be used, what do you think are the advantages of using an expert system?

What do you see as the disadvantages of using expert systems?

Feedback 3
Some of the advantages of using expert systems are noted below.

Human expertise can be expensive. After an expert system has been built, the only cost is providing the hardware to run the system on.

Human advice can be inconsistent. Human advice may be adversely affected by tiredness, busy diaries, personal problems, etc. Computer advice will always be based on the rules within the expert system, and those rules can be checked by other experts to ensure their validity.

Human knowledge may be lost. That is humans tend to die eventually, or their knowledge may be lost in other ways such as brain disease or simply changing jobs.

Human knowledge can only be accessed in one place at one time—that is where the expert happens to be. However, an expert system can be duplicated as many times as required or accessed online.

In contrast expert systems tend to lack:
• common sense—humans may draw conclusions based on their overall view of the world; expert systems do not have this information
• inspiration or intuition—computers tend to lack these attributes
• flexibility to apply their knowledge outside a relevant domain.
Humans understand the limits of their knowledge and will seek help when confronted by complex or novel situations. Unless programmed specifically, expert systems will not recognise their limitations and fail when confronted with new situations.

Activity 4
This activity helps you evaluate expert systems from the point of view of their limitations.

On the basis of what you have learned so far about expert systems, suggest three main limitations and three main strengths.

Feedback 4
You should have been able to suggest three of the following limitations:
• Narrow knowledge domain, they are developed to solve a very specific problem
• Knowledge acquisition from experts
• Need for commitment from expert(s)
• Cannot generalise
• Cannot apply 'common sense'
• Cost of development and maintenance
• Expert systems think mechanically and lack the power of human creativity
• Expert systems require regular maintenance to update with new knowledge. An expert system responsible for providing advice on legal or tax matters for example, would need frequent re-programming.
• A wide range of sensory experience is available to human experts. Expert systems are largely confined to abstracted symbolic input. The knowledge acquisition process necessary for extracting knowledge from experts is

also problematic. Asking experts to articulate their 'intuition' in terms of a systematic process of reasoning is sometimes compared to extracting a tooth with rusty pliers.

And three of the following strengths:
- Reasoning using previously established rules
- Separation of KB and the inferencing mechanism which allows either to be updated separately
- Explanation capability
- Quick solution—efficiency
- Standard output—consistency
- Replication
- Perform repetitive tasks and free-up human experts
- Provide increased problem-solving abilities to the less expert.

Where Are Expert Systems Used?

There are various important guidelines that help when deciding whether a problem is suitable for an expert system solution.

Expert systems are generally suitable in situations where:

- The problem is important to business—meaning that time or money or both can be saved by using the expert system.
- The expertise required is available and stable. In other words human experts are available who can provide the appropriate knowledge, without ambiguity, to build the expert system rule base.
- The knowledge required is scarce—at least in terms of human experts available to provide answers to queries within that knowledge domain.
- The problem is recurrent—so the expert system will be used over many geographical locations or a long period of time.
- The problem is at the right level of difficulty. In some situations, it may be easier to train more human experts where a limited amount of knowledge is required. Alternatively, extremely complex knowledge domains may require human expertise only.
- The domain is well defined and of a manageable size. Particularly large domains or domains with no easily defined limits are difficult to program due to the large number of rules that are required.
- The solution depends on logical reasoning, not 'common sense' or general knowledge. The knowledge-based system needs definite rules to make decisions as it tends to lack any intuition that humans occasionally use in making decisions.

Current Research in Expert Systems

The following web addresses contain information on research in expert systems:

FuzzyJ ToolKit for the Java (tm) Platform & FuzzyJess at: http://ai.iit.nrc.ca/IR_public/fuzzy/fuzzyJToolkit.html

Legal Information Systems—University of Warwick at: http://www.law.warwick.ac.uk/ltj/2-2h.html

Expert Systems in Corrosion at: http://www.corrosionsource.com/technicallibrary/corrdoctors/Modules/Knowledge/ES.html

Berkeley Expert Systems Technology at: http://best.me.berkeley.edu/

Papers on Expert Systems can be found via Citeseer at: http://citeseer.ist.psu.edu/

Summary

In this section you learned how expert systems are designed to mimic human knowledge in specific domains or knowledge areas. You also discovered that they are not designed to be general purpose problem-solving systems, but do have some advantages over humans.

Self-Assessment Question

Do some browsing on the Internet and find four expert systems. Explain briefly how each is used and the specific advantages each has over human systems in the same context.

Answer to Self-Assessment Question

Examples of the sites you could visit include the following.

Example	Web address
Applied expert systems—production of expert systems for monitoring traffic on networks	http://www.aesclever.com/
Examples of expert system use in agriculture	http://www.manage.gov.in/managelib/faculty/PanduRanga.html
Graduate screening expert system for university—see if you can gain admission	http://www.aiinc.ca/demos/grad.shtml
Example of an expert system to identify the differences between coins	http://www.hf.uio.no/iakk/roger/lithic/expsys.html

SECTION 2: NEURAL NETWORKS

Introduction

This section provides an introduction to NNs and their place in knowledge-based system design.

Objectives

By the end of the section you will be able to:

• describe the characteristics of NNs
• evaluate the usefulness of NNs in particular contexts.

What Are NNs?

Starting with measured data from some known or unknown source, a NN may be trained to perform classification, estimation, simulation and prediction of the underlying process generating the data. Hence, artificial neural networks (ANNs), or neural nets, are software tools designed *to estimate relationships in data*. An estimated relationship is essentially a mapping, or a function, relating raw data to its features.

The general area of ANNs has its roots in our understanding of the human brain. In this regard, initial concepts were based on attempts to mimic the brain's way of processing information. Efforts that followed gave rise to various models of biological NN structures and learning algorithms.

Differences in Human and Computer Processing

The basic features in human and computer processing are shown in Figure 2.3.

Humans are very good at inferring conclusions from limited amounts of data while computers tend to excel at problems where a large number of repetitive or similar operations are required.

Computers are built with many millions of individual switches within a single processor. They can perform millions of operations per second and, assuming that there is no hardware failure, they can carry out these operations with absolute mathematical precision.

In contrast, a human brain has about 10 billion neurons. Each neuron averages several thousand connections. Each can perform hundreds of operations each second only with relatively low reliability. Neurons die frequently and are not replaced.

However, these problems are overcome by the capability for parallel processing that provides the brain with the ability to handle missing or erroneous data.

FIGURE 2.3. Features of human and machine processing.

The Brain
    Pattern recognition
    Association
    Complexity
    Noise tolerant

The Machine
    Calculation
    Precision
    Logic

Structure of Human and Computer Processing Units

A typical human neuron is shown in Figure 2.4.

The features of the individual parts of the neurons are listed in the table below.

Part	Feature
Soma or nucleus	Main body of the neuron
Dendrite	Filaments providing inputs to the cell
Axon	Sends output signals from the cell
Synapse	A junction that allows signals to pass depending on the strength of the synapse

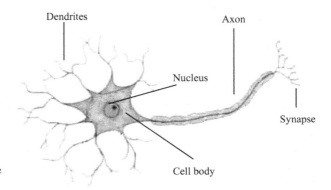

FIGURE 2.4. Structure of a biological neuron.

The state of the neuron is controlled by the signals received from its dendrites. When sufficient signal strength is received, then the nucleus becomes 'excited' and passes this information along axons to other cells.

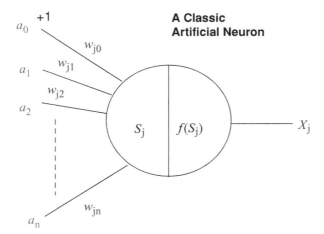

FIGURE   2.5. Artificial neuron.

A biological reason can be simulated using a computer (see Figure 2.5). In Figure 2.5, a_0 to a_n represent the inputs (numbers) into the neuron. The weights attached to each input are shown by w_{j0} to w_{jn} [numerical indicators of the strength of the synapse (S)]. Depending upon the actual inputs and the weights assigned to the inputs, the neuron may or may not fire. If it fires, then the output X_j is produced, which in turn may form an input to another neuron in the system. These inputs, multiplied by the weights, are added together and compared with some threshold value to determine if this neuron should fire. This is then processed by a function (f) to determine the exact output from the neuron.

Activity 5
An artificial neuron applet is available at:
http://icwww.epfl.ch/mantra/tutorial/english/aneuron/html/index.html

Follow the instructions on the page to experiment with inputs ($x1$ and $x2$) and weights ($w1$ and $w2$).

Neurons are not designed to work alone. They are connected together with many others to form a network. A computer neuron will 'fire', that is pass on an electrical signal to other neurons. This may in turn cause other neurons to fire. The 'firing' of one neuron is controlled by the total of the inputs to that neuron within a given period of time. The total input to a neuron is calculated from the number of inputs and the strength of the signal from each of those inputs. Thus, in Figure 2.5 the total input is $(a_0 \times w_{j0}) + (a_1 \times w_{j1}) + (a_2 \times w_{j2}) \ldots (a_n \times w_{jn})$.

The strength of the synapses is determined by the weight given to each one. Varying the weights within the network helps to determine whether or not a particular neuron fires.

Main Elements of NNs

An ANN is either a hardware implementation or a computer program that strives to simulate the information processing capabilities of its biological equivalent. Artificial neural networks are typically composed of a great number of interconnected artificial neurons. The artificial neurons are simplified models of their biological counterparts.

The typical characteristics of ANNs differ very much from what is normally expected of a computer. These new properties include:

- adaptive learning
- self-organisation
- error tolerance
- real-time operation
- parallel information processing.

Learning, in the context of ANNs, means that the network can adopt different behaviour on the basis of the data that is given to the network. Unlike telling the network how to react to each item of data separately, as would be the case in the conventional programming, the network itself is able to find properties in the presented data. Learning can be continued *and adapted* as new data is made available.

As data is given to the ANN, it adjusts weights to reflect the properties of the given data. In most ANN models, the term self-organisation refers to the determination of the connection strengths between neurons. The way the internal structure of an ANN is altered is determined by the learning algorithm used. Several distinct NN models can be distinguished both from their internal architecture and from the learning algorithms that they use.

Error tolerance is an important aspect of an ANN. It refers to the network's ability to model the essential features of the given data. In other words, an ANN is capable of finding a generalisation for the data. This powerful characteristic makes it possible to process new, imperfect and distorted data with NNs.

Activity 6

An ANN applet for the Travelling Salesman problem is available at: http://www.patol.com/java/TSP/index.html.

Follow the instructions on the page to train and test the network.

Activity 7
A NN has been set up to provide processing of information for the purposes of face recognition. On the basis of your experience with the Travelling Salesman network and any other appropriate experience, what allowances might it have to make in order to account for new, imperfect and distorted data?

Feedback 7
You should have realised that the NN would need to make allowances for variations in facial characteristics such as:
• spectacles
• hair length
• makeup
• skin tone.

In addition, variations in the amount of light cast on the face or the angle at which it is viewed would need to be taken account of in determining whether a particular face matched the one on record or not.

Due to the parallel nature of the information processing in ANNs, real-time operation becomes possible. Basically, three entities characterise an ANN:

• The network topology or interconnection of neural 'units'
• The characteristics of individual units or artificial neurons
• The strategy for pattern learning or training.

Decisions are made depending on the importance or weight of each input going into a neuron. As those weights change, then this delays or stops the neuron firing, which in turn affects the decision being taken. In other words, NNs can amend their outputs, based on the experience they gain, by amending the weights assigned to each output in the system.

Each neuron will be given a threshold over and above which it fires, sending a message to the next neuron in the system. For example, the weighted inputs to a neuron could be as follows.

Ability to pass degree:

Works hard	0.2
A level points	0.3
Interested in subject	0.3

The sum of the weighted inputs is 0.8. If the neuron is set to fire at a value of 1, then in this example it will not fire.

The initial value for the weights can be set by randomly generated numbers. Real world examples can then be fed through the neuron (training) and the results checked (testing) to see whether or not the neuron fired at the correct time. For example, if the network indicated that Bill obtained a degree with the input weights above, then it is in error. This means that the weights need to be changed to reflect the real world example. Standard values might therefore be fed into the network to increase or decrease the input values. For example, all values could be increased by 15% or decreased by 10%.

Activity 8
Here are the inputs to a neuron that is being used to predict whether or not a driving test will be passed.

Criteria	True/False (1/0)	Weighting
Hours driving experience > 40	1	0.3
Age > 22	1	0.2
Power steering in car?	1	0.2
Qualified instructor?	1	0.6

The neuron is set to fire, i.e., a pass is expected, where the combined inputs × weights >0.7.

Richard is 23 years old and has just taken his driving test for the first time. He was taught by his father in the family car without power steering (Richard's father is a solicitor). So far he has had 55 hours driving experience. He has just passed his test.

Jennifer is 21 years old. She has been learning to drive for 30 hours with a qualified instructor in a power-assisted car. She has just passed her test.

If the results of the real world data show that the neuron is firing incorrectly, then the weights are adjusted by 10%.

Show whether or not the neuron works for Richard, then Jennifer.

Feedback 8
The relevant weights to use for Richard are:

Criteria	True/False (1/0)	Weighting
Hours driving experience > 40	1	0.3
Age > 22	1	0.2
Power steering in car?	0	0.2
Qualified instructor?	0	0.6

Giving a value of 0.5. As Richard has passed his test, then the weights of the two inputs used appear to be too low (<0.7); they will be increased by 10%. Note that the 10% increase is still not sufficient to predict Richard passing. It would take several instances in which the weights need to be increased in order to end up with a better performing system.

The relevant weights to use for Jennifer are now:

Criteria	True/False (1/0)	Weighting
Hours driving experience > 40	0	0.33
Age > 22	0	0.22
Power steering in car?	1	0.2
Qualified instructor?	1	0.6

The weights applicable to Jennifer have a value of 0.8, which suggests that she should pass her test. As a pass was obtained, then the system was correct in predicting this, no alternation is necessary. If the system predicted a pass and the student failed then the weights would have been reduced (not increased).

The process of amending the weights of inputs will continue until the network provides the correct output for as many different inputs as possible.

Multi-Layer Perceptron

One architecture of NNs is a *multi-layer perceptron*. It learns by applying what is known as the *back propagation algorithm*. A diagram of this type of system is shown in Figure 2.6.

The input layer introduces input values into the network ready for processing. No actual processing takes place at this stage.

The hidden layer(s) contains adjustable weights providing links between processors (neurons). Varying the weights will affect the accuracy of the decision-making performed by the system. The aim of human or computer training is to assign correct weights to each connections so that the NN makes correct decisions.

Normally, two hidden layers are sufficient to solve any problem, however, providing more layers may increase the accuracy of decision making.

The output layer passes the output from the network to the outside world, normally via the explanatory interface.

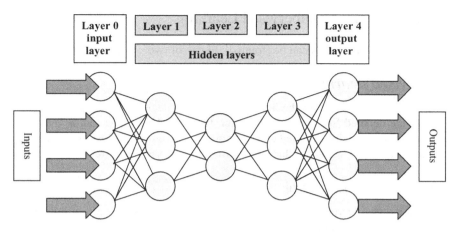

FIGURE 2.6. Learning by multi-layer perceptron.

The Back Propagation Algorithm

There is a difficulty in training a multi-layer perceptron network, i.e., how are the weights adjusted in the middle of the network. Thankfully back propagation, a well-known training algorithm solves this problem. It works in the following way:

1. An error value is calculated for each node in the outer layer.
2. The weights feeding into each node, in this layer, are adjusted according to the error value for that node (in a similar way to the previous example).
3. The error, for each of the nodes, is then attributed to each of the nodes in the previous layer (on the basis of the strength of the connection). Thus the error is passed back through the network.
4. Steps 2 and 3 are repeated, i.e., the nodes in the preceding layer are adjusted, until the errors are propagated backwards through the entire network, finally reaching the input layer (hence the term back propagation).

One minor complication remains—this training algorithm does not work when the output from a node can only be 0 or 1. A function is therefore defined that calculates the output of a neuron on the basis of its input where the output varies between 0 and 1.

A set of training data will be presented to the network one item at a time. Whenever the networks output is incorrect the weights are adjusted slightly as indicated. When all of the training data has been presented to the network once this is called an epoch (pronounced e-pok). An epoch will need to be presented to the network many times before training is complete.

Supervised and Unsupervised Learning

Artificial neural networks can be 'trained', in one of two ways.

Supervised Learning

The system can learn from the accuracy of its past decision-making. Where decisions are deemed 'incorrect' by the user, then the chain of reasoning (i.e., the strength of the weights attached to each input that gave the conclusion) is reduced to decrease the chance of similar inputs providing the same incorrect conclusion.

Unsupervised Learning

In unsupervised learning, the network is provided with inputs but no indication of what the output should be. The system itself must then decide what features it will use to group the input data. This is often referred to as self-organisation or adaption. The goal, then, is to have the network itself begin to organise and use those inputs to modify its own neurons' weights.

Adaptive Resonance Theory

Unsupervised learning is often used to classify data. In this case, the classification is done with a clustering algorithm. Adaptive resonance theory was developed to account for changes in the input data that supervised NNs were not able to handle. Basically, programmers wanted to design a system that could modify itself in response to a changing input environment. If changes are frequent, the ability to adapt is essential for the program. Without this ability to adapt, the system's accuracy begins to decrease rapidly. Creating a network that changes with each input is therefore desirable.

However, as the network is modified to account for new inputs, its accuracy in dealing with old inputs decreases. This problem could be fixed if information from old inputs is saved. The dichotomy between these two desirable network characteristics is called the stability–plasticity dilemma. Adaptive resonance theory was developed to resolve this issue.

The different types of ANN architecture are summarised in Figure 2.7.

The multi-layer perceptron network, descried earlier, is one of the most commonly used architectures.

Radial Basis Function Networks

Radial basis function (RBF) networks are a type of ANN for application to problems of supervised learning (e.g. regression, classification and time series prediction).

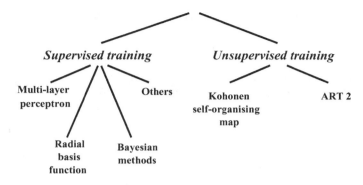

FIGURE 2.7. Different artificial neural network architectures.

Activity 9

This activity will help you visualise a RBF network.

Visit the following URL: http://diwww.epfl.ch/mantra/tutorial/english/rbf/html/

The page contains a Java applet which demonstrates some function approxi-mation capabilities of a RBF network

Follow the instructions on the web page.

Activity 10

This activity provides you with a second opportunity to work with a RBF network.

Visit the following URL: http:// www.mathworks.com/products/demos/nnettlbx/radial/

This is a series of illustrations showing how a neural network toolbox can be used to approximate a function. This demonstration uses the NEWRB function of the Matlab software (available from http://www.mathworks.com/) to create a radial basis network that approximates a function defined by a set of data points.

Self-Organising Maps

Although there has been considerably more progress in supervised learning re-search, Tuevo Kohonen has had some success with his development of a self-organising map (SOM). The SOM (also known as the Kohonen feature map) algorithm is one of the best-known ANN algorithms. Self-organising maps are a data visualisation technique that reduces the dimensions of data through the use of self-organising NNs. In contrast to many other NNs using supervised learning, the SOM is based on unsupervised learning.

The way SOMs go about reducing dimensions is by producing a map of usually one or two dimensions that plot the similarities of the data by grouping similar data items together. So, SOMs accomplish two things, they reduce dimensions and display similarities.

Activity 10

A SOM applet—where data is represented by colour—is available at: http://davis.wpi.edu/~matt/courses/soms/applet.html

Try several iteration settings (e.g. 100, 500 and 1000) and compare the differences in accuracy of colour grouping.

The SOM is a unique kind of NN in the sense that it constructs a topology preserving mapping from the high-dimensional space onto map units in such a way that relative distances between data points are preserved. The map units, or neurons, usually form a two-dimensional regular lattice where the location of a map unit carries semantic information. The SOM can therefore serve as a clustering tool of high-dimensional data. Because of its typical two-dimensional shape, it is also easy to visualise.

The first part of a SOM is the data. The idea of the SOMs is to project the n-dimensional data into something that is better understood visually. In the case of the applet you tried in the activity above, one would expect that pixels of a similar colour would be placed near each other. You might have found that the accuracy of arranging the pixels in this way increased the more iterations there were.

The second components to SOMs are the weight vectors. Each weight vector has two components: data and 'natural location'. The good thing about colours—as in the SOM applet—is that the data can be shown by displaying the colour, so in this case the colour *is the data*, and the *location* is the position of the pixel on the screen. Weights are sometimes referred to as neurons since SOMs are a type of NNs.

The way that SOMs go about organising themselves is by competing for representation of the samples. Neurons are also allowed to change themselves by learning to become more like samples in hopes of winning the next competition. It is this selection and learning process that makes the weights organise themselves into a map representing similarities. This is accomplished by using the very simple algorithm:

```
Initialise Map
For t from 0 to 1
Randomly select a sample
Get best matching unit
Scale neighbours
Increase t by a small amount
End for
```

The first step in constructing a SOM is to initialise the weight vectors. From there you select a sample vector randomly and search the map of weight vectors to find which weight best represents that sample. Since each weight vector has a location, it also has neighbouring weights that are close to it. The weight that is chosen is rewarded by being able to become more like that randomly selected sample vector. In addition to this reward, the neighbours of that weight are also rewarded by being able to become more like the chosen sample vector. From this step we increase t a small amount because the number of neighbours and how much each weight can learn decreases over time. This whole process is then repeated a large number of times, usually more than 1000 times.

In the case of colours, the program would first select a colour from the array of samples such as green, then search the weights for the location containing the greenest colour. From there, the colours surrounding that weight are then made more green. Then another colour is chosen, such as red, and the process continues (see Figure 2.8).

Activity 11
This activity will help you visualise the concept of SOMs.

Nenet (Neural Networks Tool) is a Windows application designed to illustrate the use of a SOM. Self-organising map algorithm is categorised as being in the realm of NN algorithms and it has been found to be a good solution for several information problems dealing with high-dimensional data.
1. Visit the Nenet Interactive Demonstration page at: http://koti.mbnet.fi/~phodju/nenet/Nenet/InteractiveDemo.html.
2. Click on the 'Open the demonstration' link.
3. Proceed through the demonstration, reading the onscreen explanations as you do so.

You may also wish to download and install the demonstration version of Nenet which has the following limitations on the data and map sizes:
• Maximum map size: 6 × 6 neurons.
• Maximum number of data vectors: 2000.
• Maximum data dimension: 10.

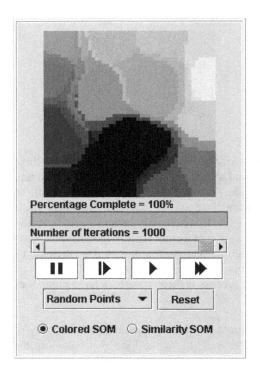

FIGURE 2.8. Self-organising map
after 1000 iterations.

SOMs Reducing Dimensions—What Does This Mean in Practise?

Imagine a new celebrity becomes very famous and their face is shown on television, on large posters and in the press. Having seen their face on several occasions you begin to recognise their features. You won't remember every detail and every pixel of a high resolution photograph but the essential features will be stored in your brain. On seeing a new high resolution photograph your brain will pick out the same essential features and compare them with the details stored in your memory. When a match occurs you will recognise the face in the photograph. By storing only the essential features your brain has reduced the complexity of the data it needs to store.

Why is This Unsupervised Learning?

For many of the things you learn there is a right and wrong answer. Thus if you were to make a mistake a teacher could provide a correct response. This is supervised learning. SOMs group similar items of data together. When picking out the features of a face various features can be chosen, eye colour, the shape of the nose etc. The features you pick can affect the efficiency of the system but there is no wrong or right answer—hence this task is an example of unsupervised learning.

Other examples of SOMs available on the Internet are:

- The World Poverty Map at: http://www.cis.hut.fi/research/som-research/worldmap.html
- WEBSOM—SOMs for Internet exploration at: http://websom.hut.fi/websom/

Using ANNs

In the previous activity, you observed a demonstration of a NN—in the form of a SOM. You should have noted a definite sequence of steps in the process.

Activity 12
This activity helps you recognise the significant stages in the process of applying a NN to data analysis problems.

Write down what you consider to be the main stages in the demonstration of the Nenet software when applied to the example problem illustrated in the demo.

Under what circumstances could one of the stages has been skipped?

Why is this possible?

How is 'Training Length' measured?

Feedback 12
You should have been able to identify the following stages:
- Initialise a new map
- Set initialisation parameters
- Train the map to order the reference vectors of the map neurons (not if using linear initialisation)
- Train the map (again)
- Test the map
- Set test parameters.

Had linear initialisation type been selected, the first training step could have been skipped.

The training process could be run twice. The first step is to order the reference vectors of the map neurons. The linear initialisation already does the ordering and that is why this step can be skipped.

Training length is the length of the training measured in steps, each corresponding to one data vector. If the specified number of steps exceeds the number of data vectors found in the file, the set of data is run through again.

Choosing a Network Architecture

Although certain types of ANN have been engineered to address certain kinds of problems, there exist no definite rules as to what the exact application domains of ANNs are. The general application areas are:
- robust pattern recognition
- filtering
- data segmentation
- data compression
- adaptive control
- optimisation
- modelling complex functions
- associative pattern recognition.

Activity 13
Search the Internet for references to the Hopfield Associative Memory Model.

You will find a page containing some Java applets illustrating the Hopfield model at:http://diwww.epfl.ch/mantra/tutorial/english/hopfield/html/

and the Boltzmann machine at:http://www.cs.cf.ac.uk/Dave/JAVA/boltzman/Necker.html

Run the applets with different parameters.

Figure 2.9 shows how some of the different NN architectures have been used.

| Application | Back propagation | Network model | | Kohonen SOM |
		Hopfield	Boltzmann machine	
Classification	✓	✓	✓	✓
Image processing	✓			✓
Decision making	✓		✓	✓
Optimisation		✓	✓	✓

FIGURE 2.9. The use of well-known neural networks.

Benefits and Limitations of NNs

The benefits of NNs include the following:

- *Ability to tackle new kinds of problems.* Neural networks are particularly useful at finding solutions to problems that defeat convention systems. Many decision support systems now incorporate some element of NNs.
- *Robustness.* The networks are more used to dealing with less structured problems.

The limitations of NNs include:

- *Artificial neural networks perform less well at tasks humans tend to find difficult.* For example, they are less good at processing large volumes of data or performing arithmetical operations. However, other programs are good at these tasks and so they compliment the benefits of ANNs.
- *Lack of explanation facilities.* Unlike many expert systems, NNs do not normally include explanation facilities making it difficult to determine how decisions were reached.
- *Test data.* ANNs require large amounts of data. Some of the data is used for training and some to ensure the accuracy of the network prior to use.

Condition Monitoring

Condition monitoring is the name given to a task for which NNs have often been used, but what is it?

Every car driver listens to the noises made by their car. The noises will change depending upon many things:

- the surface of the road
- whether the road is wet or dry
- the speed the car is going
- the strain the engine is under.

While the car makes a range of normal noises other noises could indicate a problem that needs to be addressed. For example a tapping noise can indicate a lack of oil. If this is not rectified serious and expensive damage could be caused to the engine. Over time car drivers become familiar with the noises their car makes and will mostly ignore them until an unusual sound occurs. When this does occur a driver may not always be able to identify the cause but if concerned will get their car checked by an engineer. This allows maintenance to be carried out before serious damage occurs.

In the example above condition monitoring is something that the car driver is subconsciously doing all of the time—i.e., by listening to the noises the car makes they are monitoring the condition of the car and will initiate maintenance when required.

Just as a car requires maintenance so do many machines. Businesses, factories and power plants depend upon the correct functioning of a range of machines including, large extractor fans, power generators and food processors. Catastrophic failure in a large machine can in some cases cause an entire business to close down while repairs are made. Clearly, this is not an option and thus to prevent this regular maintenance is carried out. But to maintain a machine means shutting it down and even for short periods this becomes an expensive business. There is therefore a

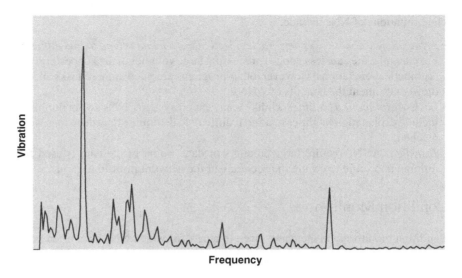

FIGURE 2.10. A vibration spectra.

desire is to maintain the machine when it is required but not on a regular basis. However, how do we know when maintenance is required? One option is to monitor the condition of the machine. By fitting vibration detectors to the machine we can collect vibration spectra (see Figure 2.10).

Collecting vibration patterns is the equivalent to listening to a car however most machines, just like cars, make a range or normal noises. How do we therefore identify when a machine is developing a fault that requires maintenance?

Neural networks have in recent years been applied quite successfully to a range condition monitoring tasks. Neural networks are adept at taking in sensory data, e.g. vibration spectra and identifying patterns. In this case the network can learn which spectra represent normal operation and which indicates a fault requiring attention.

While NNs may appear to be the obvious solution to this task there are other options that could be considered. Interface Condition Monitoring Ltd. (UK) is a company that specialises in undertaking this sort of analysis. With years of experience in this field they decided to try and capture some of their knowledge in order to benefit trainee engineers. Working with the University of Sunderland (UK) they decided to capture this knowledge in an expert system. While the development of an expert system was possible there were some programming hurdles that needed to be overcome. Expert systems, unlike NNs, are not adept at processing sensory information. Thus before the expert system could make decisions the spectra needed to be pre-processed to identify relevant peaks in the spectra. This information was then presented to the expert system in a form it could understand.

This situation highlights one important issue when choosing which AI technology to apply to a given problem. Usually there is more than one way of solving a problem. While choosing the 'best' technology may offer advantages, and make the task easier, business considerations may require the use of an alternative technology.

Further information on condition monitoring can be found at the following websites:

http://www.maintenanceworld.com/preventive-maintenance.html
http://www.pemms.co.uk/Condition_Monitoring.html
http://www.plant-maintenance.com/articles/ConMon21stCentury.shtml
http://www.engineeringtalk.com/guides/condition-monitoring.html.

Current Research in NNs

The following web addresses contain information on research in NNs:

IEEE Computational Intelligence Society at:
http://ieee-cis.org/
Neural Networks Group—University of Edinburgh at: http://www.see.ed.ac.uk/ research/IMNS/neural/
Advanced Computer Architecture Group: Neural Networks at the University of York at: http://www.cs.york.ac.uk/arch/NeuralNetworks/
Papers on Neural Networks can be found via Citeseer at: http://citeseer.ist.psu.edu/

Summary

This section has introduced NNs and explained their use within knowledge-based systems.

Self-Assessment Question

Question 1

Fill in the gaps in the following using either 'neural networks' or 'expert systems'
_____ require humans to update their database of information.
_____ use rules in which to make their decisions.
_____ adjust to inputs and outputs.
_____ continue to expand their own base of information.
_____ emulate human decision making.
_____ learn human thought processes and reasoning patterns.

Question 2

Imagine a NN trained to recognise flowers using 75 sets of data. Another 75 sets of data are used to validate the trained NN. As NNs are trained on a data set the implication is that the bigger the data set the better the training could be. It would therefore be possible for the example problem above to use *all* 150 data items for training. This would leave none for the validation set. However, the NN could be better trained as it would have more data to learn from. Would this be a good idea?

Answer To Self-Assessment Question

Answer 1

Expert systems require humans to update their database of information.
Expert systems use rules and frames in which to make their decisions.
Neural networks adjust to inputs and outputs.
Neural networks continue to expand their own base of information.
Expert systems emulate human decision making.
Neural networks learn human thought processes and reasoning patterns.

Answer 2

It would *not* be a good idea to use all of the data for training. Take a simple analogy: imagine a teacher who tells a small child that '2 + 2 = 4 and 4 + 4 = 8'. If the child correctly answers the question 'What does 2 + 2 equal?' it does not prove that the child has learnt how to add two numbers—they may just be able to recall what the teacher told them. To check if they know how to add we need to give them new, previously unseen problems, such as 3 + 5. In a similar way a NN may learn to remember the inputs it was trained on and the associated outputs. However, we want it to learn how these are connected so that it can solve any problem, i.e., generalise. To test that the NN has learnt to generalise correctly we need to validate the NN using data that was not used in the training process.

SECTION 3: CASE-BASED REASONING

Introduction

This section shows how one form of human reasoning can be used within knowledge-based systems.

Objectives

By the end of the section you will be able to:

• explain the use of CBR in the development of knowledge-based systems
• evaluate the usefulness of CBR systems.

What Is a Case?

A case has two parts:

• Description of a problem or a set of problems
• Description of the solution of this problem.

Possible additional components might be explanations, and comments on the quality of the solution, etc.

Cases represent experiences, i.e., they record how a problem was solved in the past.

What Are CBR Systems?

In CBR, information is stored in a KB in the form of cases, rather than rules. When a new situation is encountered, the CBR system reviews the cases to try to find a match for this particular situation. If a match is found, then that case can be used to solve the new problem (see Figure 2.11).

Case-based reasoning works in a similar way to which humans select a course of action from experience.

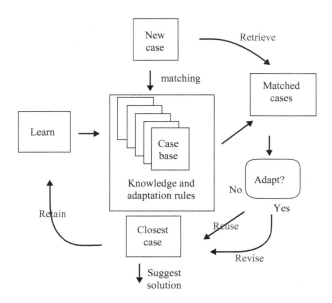

FIGURE 2.11. Case-based reasoning process.

Typical Problems Handled with CBR

Problems handled by the use of CBR tend to be those with a classification and diagnosis feature:

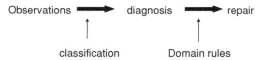

Activity 14
What other examples of classification and diagnosis situations can you think of that would benefit from using a CBR approach to problem solving?

Feedback 14
Situations where CBR can be used include:
• help desks (storage of similar requests from users)
• application of the law (past legal cases setting precedents)
• some diagnosis of illness (e.g. cardiac care) where cause and effect are fairly well established.

For example, a computer technician may encounter a problem with a document failing to print. They may recall a similar situation a few weeks ago, and remember that the cause was a paper jam in the printer. This example will be used to guide them to open the printer and check for blockages before any other diagnostic checks are run.

In CBR terms, this might be described as follows:

Technical Diagnosis of Computer Faults

- Symptoms are observed (e.g. document fails to print) and values are measured (e.g. level of fluid or toner—half full).
- Goal: Find the cause for the failure (e.g. paper jam) and a repair strategy (e.g. open printer and remove blockage).

Case-Based Diagnosis

A case describes a diagnostic situation and contains:

- description of the symptoms
- description of the failure and the cause
- description of a repair strategy.

To perform a diagnosis the following steps must be performed:

- store a collection of cases in a case base
- find case similar to current problem and reuse repair strategy.

Steps in CBR

A CBR program will normally work through the following steps:

- Collect the important features that define each new case presented to the system.
- Retrieve past cases matching these features most closely.
- Select the cases most relevant to the current problem.
- Where necessary, adapt the stored cases to solve the current problem.
- Validate the new solution and store as a new case.
- Where a case match is not found, then find an alternative solution and record both problem and solution.

Where more that one case match is found, the CBR system will need to:

- resolve any ambiguities if multiple solutions are found
- recognise that multiple solutions may sometimes be acceptable.

The CBR system is effectively following important processes or rules to:

- Retrieve the most relevant cases for comparison with the current problem.
- Reuse knowledge from those cases which help in solving the current problem.
- Revise the proposed solution, using the case information.
- Retain details of the current (now hopefully solved) problem as a new case for future reference.

Cases do not need to be understood by the knowledge engineer in order to be stored.

Activity 15
Bearing in mind the steps involved in CBR, draw a diagram to show the CBR process.

Feedback 24
One possible solution is shown in the diagram below.

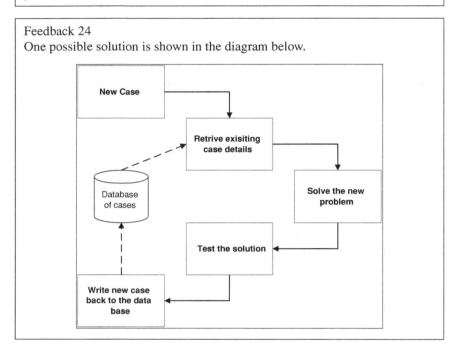

CBR Examples

In the following example, we will look at how a case base containing only two cases deals with a problem with a printer.

The storage of the cases in the case base might be represented by Figure 2.12. Notice that the solution records not only the diagnosis of the cause of the problem but also the action taken.

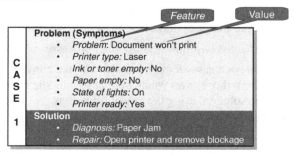

FIGURE 2.12. Case 1.

Figure 2.13 shows the two cases in the case base together for comparison. Each case describes one particular situation and all cases are independent of each other.

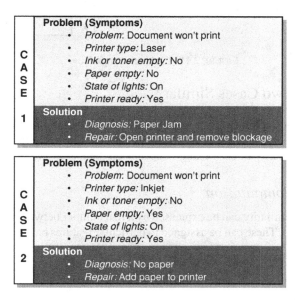

FIGURE 2.13. Cases 1 and 2.

When a new problem has to be solved, several observations of the current situation are made. These observations define the new problem. Not all feature values need to be known.

Note that the new problem is a 'case' without solution component (Figure 2.14).

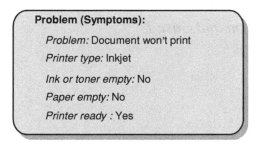

FIGURE 2.14. A problem to be solved.

The new problem is compared with each case in the case base and the most similar case is selected (Figure 2.15).

FIGURE 2.15. Problem comparison.

When Are Two Cases Similar?

Cases are ranked according to their 'similarity' and therefore similarity is the most important concept in CBR. We can assess similarity based on the similarity of *each feature* and similarity of each feature depends on the feature *value*.

Similarity Computation

The degree of similarity can be expressed by a real number between 0 (not similar) and 1 (identical). These can be assigned to particular features based on experience.

- Feature: Problem

Printer type: Inkjet   ◄—— 0.5 ——►   Printer type: Laser

Printer ready: Yes   ◄—— 0.0 ——►   Printer ready: No

However, the *importance* of different features may be different and there is therefore the need to apply weights to features.

High importance: Problem, Paper empty, Printer ready, ...
Low importance: Printer type, ...

Similarity Computation by Weighted Average

Between Problem and Case 1

(see Figure 2.16)

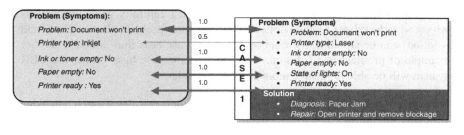

FIGURE 2.16. Similarity computation.

Similarity(new, case 1) = 1/25*[6*1.0 + 1*0.5 + 6*1.0 + 6*1.0 + 6*1.0]
= **0.98**

Note that the 1/25 component is arrived at from

1/total feature weights, i.e., 1/(6 + 1 + 6 + 6).

Activity 16
1. Sketch a diagram relating the problem to Case 2.
2. Conduct a similarity computation for Case 2.
3. Determine which of the cases is more similar to the problem.

Feedback 16
Your diagram should look a little like this:

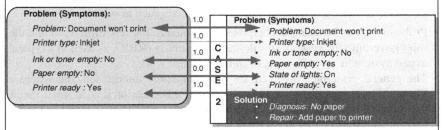

Your calculation should be:

Similarity(new, case 2) = 1/25*[6*1.0 + 1*1.0 + 6*1.0 + 6*0.0 + 6*1.0]
= 0.76

Case 1 is therefore more similar—thus the diagnosis 'Paper jam' would be made.

If the diagnosis is incorrect then a technician must carefully work out what is wrong with the printer. Having done this the new case (problem plus diagnosis and solution) can be stored in the case base and our case base thus contains another example of problem and solution. Over time, as the case base grows, the CBR system will be able to resolve more and more problems.

An example of a CBR system in operation on the Internet is the 3Com Knowledge Base at: http://knowledgebase.3com.com

Advantages of Using CBR

There are a number of advantages of using CBR:

- Reduction in the amount of knowledge acquisition actually needed, because the CBR system searches current cases for solutions rather than inferring solutions from a rule base.
- The CBR system learns over time by adding new cases to the KB. This avoids the need to add new rules or modify existing rules in the KB.

Disadvantages of Using CBR

The main disadvantages of using CBR are as follows:

- Storing of cases in the KB. Care is needed to ensure that cases are referenced correctly with appropriate attributes.
- Ensuring that there is an efficient method for accessing cases, as well as identifying their important attributes for any search.
- Not providing good presentation of information to the user.

When Should CBR Be Used?

Case-based reasoning is generally used in situations such as where:

- Problems cannot be easily decomposed. This means it is very difficult to find the rules governing the system, so rule-based reasoning (RBR), as used in a typical expert system, is less effective, or in fact will not work.
- The general principles involved are not completely understood, but where a library of past experience can be generated. In this situation it is, again, difficult to produce a full set of rules for the knowledge domain. The main reason for the lack of rules may be that the domain is very complex or that contradictory rules apply in different situations.

Differences Between RBR and CBR

There are some important differences between RBR and CBR. In many situations, the two systems provide a direct contrast in approach and use of the KB and the real world.

Activity 17
The table below shows some characteristics of both RBR and CBR. The details about RBR have been entered into the table. Complete the table for CBR, remembering that CBR examples are likely to be the opposite of RBR.

Factor	Rule-based reasoning	Case-based reasoning
Knowledge content – can the knowledge be expressed in small explicit chunks?	Rules are small, independent, explicit pieces of knowledge.	
Domain—is the knowledge domain easy to understand and record?	Yes, rules or heuristics are known and can be written down.	
Does the knowledge exactly match the situation?	In order to fire all rule conditions must exactly match the facts.	

Feedback 17
Information on CBR is given in the third column.

Factor	Rule-based reasoning	Case-based reasoning
Knowledge content—can the knowledge be expressed in small explicit chunks?	Rules are small, independent, explicit pieces of knowledge.	Cases represent large chunks of knowledge. The link between problem and solution is implicit.
Domain—is the knowledge domain easy to understand and record?	Yes, rules or heuristics are known and can be written down.	The domain may not be fully understood but it is still possible to identify solutions to problems.
Does the knowledge exactly match the situation?	In order to fire all rule conditions must exactly match the facts.	Cases maybe applied even if they only partially match the problem.

Current Research in CBR

The following web addresses contain information on research in CBR:

Artificial Intelligence Applications Institute: University of Edinburgh (makers of the AIAI CBR tool) at: http://www.aiai.ed.ac.uk/technology/casebased-reasoning.html
Norwegian University of Science and Technology: Al and Learning Group at: http://www.idi.ntnu.no/grupper/ai/cbr/
Papers on CBR can be found via Citeseer at: http://citeseer.ist.psu.edu/

Summary

In this section you have been introduced to CBR and learned that information in CBR systems is stored in a KB in the form of cases, rather than rules.

You also learned that the use of CBR systems is appropriate where problems cannot be easily decomposed or where the general principles involved are not completely understood, but where a library of past experience can be generated.

Self-Assessment Questions

Question 1

Describe how CBR can be used in searching the Internet for information.

Question 2

The CBR system shown earlier is used to diagnose printer faults. Imagine a new fault occurs which the CBR system incorrectly diagnoses. Explain what happens next.

Later the fault is correctly diagnoses as 'No power' and a solution is provided 'Check electrical supply'. One of the printers symptoms was 'Status lights: Off'. Making up the other symptoms and using the format you saw earlier in the chapter construct a diagram to represent the newly solved problem.

Answers to Self-Assessment Questions

Answer 1

Go to the AskJeeves website and ask the search engine a question. Rather than provide a list of sites straight away that may answer your question, Jeeves sometimes asks additional questions to clarify your initial question.

This website is using two systems to try and determine the answer you need:

- Case-based reasoning—by maintaining a list of frequently asked questions, it may be able to direct you to the appropriate website more quickly by checking this list and the results prepared earlier.
- Firing different search rules to determine the important words within your search criteria. For example, a search for motor vehicles in the twentieth century running on motorways provides all sorts of references from buying cars to computer programming. You need to tell Jeeves exactly which area you are interested in to provide better matches.

Answer 2

After an incorrect diagnosis a technician is asked to investigate and solve the problem. When they have done this the new problem and solution, once it is confirmed, is documented as a new case and added to the case base.

Case 3 should look something like this.

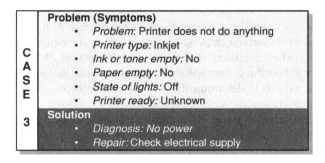

SECTION 4: GENETIC ALGORITHMS

Introduction

This section provides an introduction to genetic algorithms.

Objectives

By the end of the section you will be able to:

• understand how the process of evolution applies to genetic algorithms
• evaluate the value of genetic algorithms in specific problem-solving contexts.

What Are Genetic Algorithms?

An algorithm is a sequence of instructions to solve a problem. Although other knowledge-based systems (such as ANNs) are based on algorithms, many of those algorithms tend to be static, that is they do not change over time. While this provides some certainty in how the system will operate, it does mean that such systems may be limited when trying to determine the solution to a problem.

A *genetic* algorithm is a model of machine learning that derives its behaviour from a metaphor of some of the mechanisms of *evolution* in nature. This is done by the creation within a machine of a *population* of *individuals* represented by *chromosomes*, in essence a set of character strings that are analogous to the base-4 chromosomes in our own DNA. The individuals in the population then go through a process of simulated 'evolution'.

Activity 18
This activity will give you a brief video introduction to genetic algorithms.

Watch the Robot Independence video at: http://www.pbs.org/saf/1303/video/watchonline.html.

You will need to specify the type of media your system can play (either Real Media or Windows Media—the latter is probably your best bet) and your connection speed, 56K (dial-up connection) or 220K (high speed connection, e.g. T-1 or DSL).

Activity 19

This activity will give you the opportunity to visualise genetic algorithms.

Visit the site http://www.rennard.org/alife/english/gavintrgb.html.

Follow the link to the Genetic Algorithm Viewer.

Detailed instructions and explanations are available on the site.

Note that the Java applet and source code can be downloaded from the front page.

When a genetic algorithm is implemented it is usually done in a manner that involves the following components:

- a genetic representation for potential solutions to the problem
- a way to create an initial population of potential solutions
- an evaluation function that plays the role of the environment, rating solutions in terms of their 'fitness'
- genetic operators that alter the composition of children
- values for various parameters that the genetic algorithm uses.

The actual process is cyclical and repeats until an optimum solution is obtained:

1. Evaluate the *fitness* of all of the individuals in the population.
2. Create a new population by performing operations such as crossover, fitness-proportionate reproduction and mutation on the individuals whose fitness has just been measured.
3. Discard the old population and iterate using the new population.

One iteration of this loop is referred to as a *generation*. The first generation (generation 0) of this process operates on a population of *randomly generated individuals*. From there on, the genetic operations, in concert with the fitness measure, operate to improve the population.

Example of Genetic Algorithms

Let's say we have a pool of random letters and 'space' characters, strung into series of length 37. We are attempting to assemble the following sentence out of this primordial soup of letters and spaces:

```
jackdaws love my big sphinx of quartz
```

All we know about this sentence is that it is 37 characters in length, is composed up of the letters a–z and spaces, and that we have a function called *fitness(string)*, which accepts our test strings and returns a fitness value, i.e., tells us how many of the characters are correct.

First we make a set of 37 character random strings of letters. For this example, we'll just use a set of four strings. In practice, hundreds or thousands would be applied to the task.

Here are the four random strings, matched up against the actual sequence, as well as their fitness values:

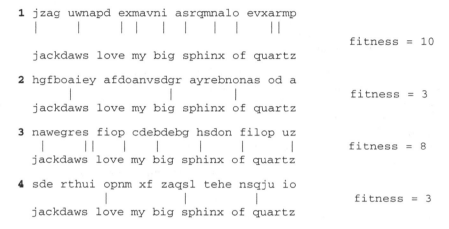

When each member of the population is evaluated we can see that strings **1** and **3** have the best fitness score. Strings **2** and **4** can therefore be discarded.

Incidentally, the average fitness for this first population is $(10 + 3 + 8 + 3)/4 = \textbf{6}$

We then *crossover* portions of the genetic material from each of the remaining members of the population to generate the next generation. We can generate a new string combining **1** and **3** by taking the first letter from String **1** followed by three letters from String **3** then another from **1** and three from **3** and so on.

Repeating the process but this time taking the first letter from String **3** and the next three letters from String **1** will give us two new strings.

```
jawe resa fi p cmdebs hsnon o fila mp
```

```
nzagguwn apdoexmdvni asromnaio e xar_
```

(The '_' character is used here to indicate the presence of a space at the end of the string.)

Another way of combining the genes would be to take the first half (approximately since there are only 37 characters in the string) of **1** and combine it with the second half of **3** then vice versa for the second string.

```
jzag uwnapd exmavniebg hsdon filop uz

nawegres fiop cdebd asrqmnalo evxarmp
```

After crossing over the genes in this way, we apply, consistent with the analogy of genetics, a small element of *mutation*. In this case the 11th character of the second new string has been changed to a space and the 3rd character of the fourth has been changed to a 'c'.

We now have a new population of four strings and can evaluate them against our goal string.

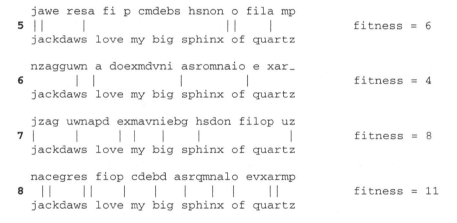

```
     jawe resa fi p cmdebs hsnon o fila mp
5    ||      |                 ||     |                    fitness = 6
     jackdaws love my big sphinx of quartz


     nzagguwn a doexmdvni asromnaio e xar_
6        | |            |            |                     fitness = 4
     jackdaws love my big sphinx of quartz


     jzag uwnapd exmavniebg hsdon filop uz
7    |      |      | |   |    |              |              fitness = 8
     jackdaws love my big sphinx of quartz


     nacegres fiop cdebd asrqmnalo evxarmp
8    ||    ||    |    |   |   |  |     ||                   fitness = 11
     jackdaws love my big sphinx of quartz
```

The average fitness score for our new population of strings has increased to

$$(6 + 4 + 8 + 11)/4 = \mathbf{7.25}$$

This process of selection, crossover and mutation continues until a reasonable solution to our problem has been found.

Though there may be many better ways of solving the small-scale problem of the example, for extremely complex situations where the string is merely a model or representation of something else—such as a series of possible components in a very complex organic molecule—the application of genetic algorithms becomes a very efficient solution strategy.

It must also be emphasised that many of the applications of genetic algorithms are to problems where it is sufficient to reach an *adequate* solution. For example, generating one possible examination timetable would be a typical application of genetic algorithms. If you imagine several thousand students all sitting examinations over a 2-week period there would be many billions of possible examination timetables. However, the vast majority of these would involve one or more clashes, where a student would need to take two or more examinations at the same time. Clearly this is impossible. The goal would be too find an examination timetable with no clashes. Further no student would like to sit five examinations in 5 days (nor two in the same day) therefore an ideal timetable would be one where all examinations are evenly spread out. Given the immense difficulty in finding this one *ideal* timetable (assuming it exits), from among the many billions of *possible* timetables, we may be willing to accept any of the *very good* timetable solutions available, i.e., any timetable where there are no clashes and no student has two examinations in 1 day (though they may have three or four in 1 week). This is where genetic algorithms excel. They are very good at finding one of the many hundred of *good* solutions to such a problem.

Complex problems *can* be solved using other techniques, but it is in the *rapid* development of set of good solutions where genetic algorithms are particularly useful.

Other Examples of Genetic Algorithms

You will find examples of actual genetic algorithms on the Internet at:

http://ai.bpa.arizona.edu/~mramsey/ga.html
http://ai.bpa.arizona.edu/~tong/gaoi/

You will even find a genetic algorithm applied to playing jazz solos at:

http://www.it.rit.edu/~jab/GenJam.html

The genetic algorithm playground (a general purpose genetic algorithm toolkit where you can define and run your own optimisation problems) is available for download at:

http://www.aridolan.com/ofiles/ga/gaa/gaa.aspx#Download

Instructions are included.

Processes Within Genetic Algorithms

As already noted, genetic algorithms try to mimic evolution. To do this, they use three basic processes.

Reproduction

Production of new generations of code using parents with higher fitness ratings, that is having a higher probability of finding the answer to problems.

Crossover

Changing the code within two strings at a random place and creating two new strings of code by merging the 'split' strings. This process is used in nature where genes from parents combine to form a whole new chromosome.

Mutation

Changing one digit in the code on a random basis. For example, changing a 1 to a 0 without the processes of reproduction or crossover. This mimics random changes in genetic code and is especially useful where crossover does not provide an answer.

Use of Genetic Algorithms

Genetic algorithms are used to solve many large problems including:
- scheduling
- transportation
- layout and circuit design.

Two very detailed applications of genetic algorithms are available at:

A Genetic Algorithm Based University Timetabling System
http://www.asap.cs.nott.ac.uk/publications/pdf/crimea94.pdf
General Aviation Aircraft (GAA): Analysis of a Product Family Platform using Genetic Algorithm
http://www.personal.psu.edu/users/m/v/mvd119/doc/gapaper_1_.doc

Current Research in Genetic Algorithms

The following web addresses contain information on research in genetic algorithms at:

AIAI, the Artificial Intelligence Applications Institute at the University of Edinburgh
   http://www.aaai.org/AITopics/html/genalg.html
Indian Institute of Technology Kanpur Genetic Algorithms Laboratory
   http://www.iitk.ac.in/kangal/
Heuristics and Artificial Intelligence in Finance and Investment
   http://www.geocities.com/francorbusetti/
Papers on Genetic Algorithms can be found via Citeseer
   http://citeseer.ist.psu.edu/

Summary

This section has provided an introduction to genetic algorithms and shown how the process of applying them mimics the biological evolutionary process.

Self-Assessment Question

Question 1

Visit the website http://www.sambee.co.th/MazeSolver/mazega.html.

Write a brief explanation of how the system is working.

Question 2

Given the following problems to solve which of the following technologies would you use:

* an expert system
* a neural network
* a case-based reasoning system
* a genetic algorithm.

Problem 1

A brewery want a machine to smell beer to detect if any has gone off before it is canned. To help with this a robotic nose has been developed to smell the beer but which technology should they use for the decision-making component of the system?

Problem 2

A bank wants a system to decide if a loan applicant is likely to default on their loan payments, i.e., fail to pay back the loan. Which technology could be used for this?

Answer to Self-Assessment Question

Answer 1

You will notice that the solver is using the basic tools of genetic algorithms mentioned above. You should also see that the system gets better at solving the maze as more attempts are made. This happens because the better maze-solving routines are retained and the less effective ones eliminated from the system. Eventually, the algorithm is good enough to reach the end of the maze, although this can take a significant number of generations before this happens.

Answer 2

Problem 1

The obvious answer for this problem is a NN. Expert systems work from symbolic reasoning they are not good at dealing with sensory information. A NN, on the other hand, is very good at dealing with sensory data. A range of beers that smell bad would be required to train the network—or failing this a network could be trained on a range of normal smells and this could be used to detect unusual smells (though not necessarily bad beer).

If a program could be written to decode the sensory information, perhaps by turning it into a graph, a CBR system could also be developed. Such a system may start off empty, i.e., with no cases. However, as each batch of bad beer is detected by human staff this could be entered as a new case. The CBR system would then be able to identify any similar smells in the future.

Problem 2

If a human expert exists with sufficient knowledge to determine applicants who are likely to default on their loans then this expert's knowledge could be captured and turned into an expert system. Alternatively, a NN could be trained on past data (assuming bank records have been kept) to recognise the applicants who are unlikely to payback the loan.

SECTION 5: INTELLIGENT AGENTS

Introduction

This section provides you with an introduction to intelligent agents and their use within knowledge engineering.

Objectives

By the end of this section you will be able to:

- explain the characteristics of intelligent agents
- describe the architecture of intelligent agents
- understand some roles that intelligent agent can fulfil
- understand breath, depth and heuristic search strategies for planning tasks.

What Are Intelligent Agents?

Intelligent agents are entities, such as robots or computer programs that perform some useful functionality on your behalf and exhibit some fairly unique characteristics. To be classed as an intelligent agent the entity must be able to:

- perceive their environment in some way
- understand their purpose or goal
- interact with their environment
- react to changes in the environment
- exhibit aspects of intelligence, i.e., the ability to make decisions for themselves and potentially to learn as their experience grows
- make autonomous decisions, i.e., knowing their goal, be able to decide for themselves what actions they should perform next.

In some cases, e.g. when robots must move from one location to another, deciding on the next appropriate action to take will require planning (as discussed later in this section).

Some agents act as information gatherers and report the results of their search other agents perform actions that make direct changes to the world, e.g. a robot will move an object.

Figure 2.17 illustrates the general architecture of an intelligent agent.

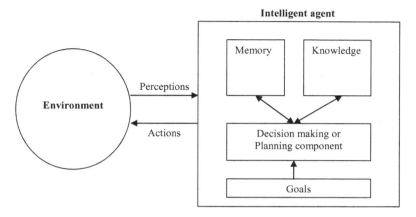

FIGURE 2.17. The general architecture of an intelligent agent.

Activity 20

Consider the task of designing a robot to perform general activities around the house such as cleaning, washing and ironing, etc. What advantages would there be in developing the robot as an intelligent agent?

Feedback 20

An ordinary robot would only perform actions when specifically instructed to and would therefore need constant supervision. However, by designing the robot as an intelligent agent it would decide for itself which action to perform next, e.g. when power was low it could decide for itself that recharging its batteries was more important than cleaning the house. Of course it may make some decisions of which you would not approve, such as cutting the grass at night, but you would then expect it to learn and modify its behaviour accordingly. Such a robot would also be able to respond to changes in its environment, such as a fire breaking out, and respond accordingly without waiting for specific instructions.

Consider an estate agent whom you have employed to find a house for you to buy. You may expect them to:

- understand your basic requirements and to decide for themselves which properties meet these requirements and which do not
- investigate new properties that become available in the market to see if these may meet your needs
- learn why you have rejected any properties they have shown you and update their knowledge of your requirements accordingly thus refining their future selection of houses

All of these behaviours demonstrate ability as an intelligent autonomous human and as such we take such behaviour for granted.

Activity 21

Consider the example above and imagine an intelligent software agent designed to search the web for current news regarding developments in science or technology. What behaviour would you expect of this agent to demonstrate?

Feedback 21

You may expect it to:

- identify news stories that are current and are on the subject of science or technology (even if these exact words are not used in the story)
- automatically search new websites or postings as they become available
- learn from your reaction to the stories which interest you the most, e.g. artificial intelligence\robotics, etc. and lookout for these in particular.

Multi-Agent systems

Activity 22

Consider separate agents that are developed to sell shares (at the maximum price) and buy shares (at the minimum price) on the stock market. What properties may such agents need that are not discussed above?

Feedback 22

With just the abilities discussed above these agents would be able to interact with their environment in order to buy and sell shares. However, it would be useful if these agents could interact directly with one another. If they could communicate directly then one agent would be able to buy the shares that the other agent wished to sell and thus both agents would benefit.

In the example above it would be very easy to develop mechanisms to enable the two agents to communicate directly. However, consider a more complex example. Imagine a game where characters, intelligent agents, are given the task of surviving and interacting in a simulated world. One character is entering a dangerous territory and meets another that is leaving. The character leaving that territory has information that the other may be willing to buy. The agents therefore need negotiation skills and complex communication skills.

In the real world the potential exists for developing software systems made up of intelligent agents cooperating to achieve a common goal and over the past few years some research has been done in this area. One obvious application for this technology would be the development of robotic soldiers where a sergeant would organise and manage a squad of privates. While the sergeant would issue instructions for the group, individual robots would still take autonomous decisions appropriate to their role within the group. Working as a group will require a common goal and the ability to interact and communicate.

Before cooperating multi-agent systems are developed, we should consider the complexity and potential cost verses the benefit that such systems would provide.

Activity 23
Follow the link below to AgentLand, or search other websites, and identify several agents that are available for download.

http://www.agentland.com/

Feedback 23
You may have found a range of agent software including:
• search agents
• web agents
• monitoring agents
• virtual assistants including virtual pets
• shop bots.

Searching and Planning

The topics of searching and planning have been important in the field of AI long before the idea of intelligent agents was first suggested. Every AI technique can be considered a method of searching for a solution and planning is important for many systems such as design and route finding systems. We will discuss these topics in the context of a robotic agent planning a path to a desired goal.

Consider the following map showing adjoining rooms.

A	B	C	D	E
	F	G	H	
	I		J	

Assume that a robot wants to travel from room B to room D. Also, assume that between each set of adjacent rooms is an unlocked door.

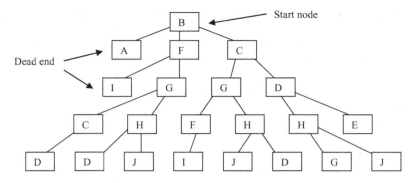

Layers below remain un-drawn

FIGURE 2.18. A search space.

Figure 2.18. shows every choice the robot could make assuming the robot does not double back on themselves and does not visit a room more than once.

This tree, if completely drawn, shows every possible route the robot could take starting from room B. We call this tree a *search space*. The robot's problem is to search this tree to find an efficient route to the desired room before taking its first step, i.e., to plan the journey in advance.

In the real world this problem could be more complex for two specific reasons:

- On many occasions the robot would not have a map and would need to develop one as they manually investigate their environment.
- The environment may not remain static and could change as the robot moves, e.g. unlocked doors could be locked, etc.

We will limit our discussion to the simplified case where these issues are not a problem.

There are three basic search strategies each with their own advantages and disadvantages . . .

- breadth first search
- depth first search
- heuristic, or knowledge-based search.

Breadth First Search

Using breadth first search the tree is considered one layer at a time as shown in Figure 2.19.

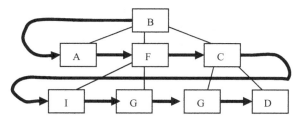

FIGURE 2.19. Breadth first search.

Firstly, the first layer is drawn and examined. As the desired room 'D' is not in the first layer, the next layer of the tree is drawn and searched. D is on this layer thus we have found a route, as denoted by the links, from B to C to D. The main advantage of breadth first search is that it will find the shortest route. However, breadth first search requires the entire tree to be drawn one layer at a time until the solution is found. While this is not difficult for the problem specified above, as it is unrealistically simple, for most realistic problems the search tree would be massive and the solution would not be found on the second layer thus keeping an entire search space in the memory of a robot would be unrealistic.

Depth First Search

Using the depth first search strategy the tree is considered one branch at a time as shown in Figure 2.20.

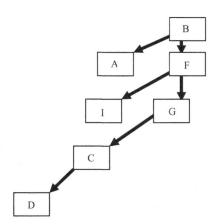

FIGURE 2.20. Depth first search.

Using depth first search the tree is explored one branch at a time. If a branch is unfruitful the search backtracks to examine the next possible branch and the previous branch is deleted. Thus in the example shown the nodes are examined in the following order: B, A (backtrack to B), F, I (backtrack to F), G, C, D (solution). The advantage of depth first search is that only one branch of the tree is examined at a time thus it requires far less memory than breadth first search. The obvious disadvantage is that the solution found is probably not the best. In this case the suggested route to room D is, B to F, F to G, G to C and C to D.

Heuristic Search

The final search strategy considered here is heuristic search. Heuristic search strategies rely upon knowledge to prune the search tree so that only a small part of the tree is considered. In most cases this makes sense and humans always use their knowledge of 'what makes sense' to guide their decision-making process and avoid wasting time with the multitude of options that are evidently poor choices. For example, when playing chess, most of the possible moves would place your pieces in danger—for no good reason. Even novice chess players learn quickly that they must consider which move to make carefully. Heuristic searches rely upon knowledge to guide the choices and are only as good as the knowledge that guides the search.

For the example problem above, let us assume that the robot knows that the room it is looking for is directly to the east of its current position (see Figure 2.21).

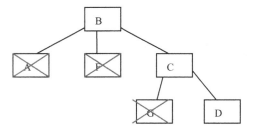

FIGURE 2.21. Heuristic search.

Given this knowledge, the robot knows that rooms A and F are not in the correct direction, thus these parts of the search tree are pruned and not drawn. Similarly, room G is not in the correct direction and this section of the tree is deleted. The remaining parts of the tree can be quickly searched to find the best solution (in the case there is only one solution remaining). For large problems, heuristic searches are the only realistic option; however, they do have one significant disadvantage. Depth and breath first searches are both guaranteed to find a solution, assuming a solution exists. However, using heuristic searches large parts of the search space are pruned and not explored thus a solution could be missed if the heuristics are poor.

Current Research in Intelligent Agents

The following web addresses contain information on research in intelligent agents:

FIPA The foundation for Physical Agents
  http://www.fipa.org/
Intelligent software agent lab
  http://www.cs.cmu.edu/~softagents/
Socially Intelligent Agents
  http://homepages.feis.herts.ac.uk/~com0qkd/aaai-social.html
Artificial Intelligence Group at the Jet Propulsion Laboratory
  http://www-aig.jpl.nasa.gov/
Artificial Intelligence Applications Institute
  http://www.aiai.ed.ac.uk/
Papers on Intelligent Agents can be found via Citeseer
  http://citeseer.ist.psu.edu/

Summary

In this section we have seen how intelligent agents differ from conventional software, we have discussed the characteristics and architecture of these systems and we have discussed the complexities of developing multi-agent systems. We have also compared three common search strategies and considered the application of these to agents that must plan their responses or actions.

Self-Assessment Question

Given the following map made up of towns (denoted by letters) and a road junction (J1) draw a complete search space starting from town A (assume no location is visited twice).

Identify the sequence of nodes visited when employing depth first and breadth first search strategies to find a route from A to D.

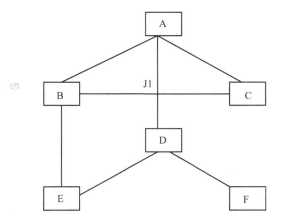

Answer to Self-Assessment Question

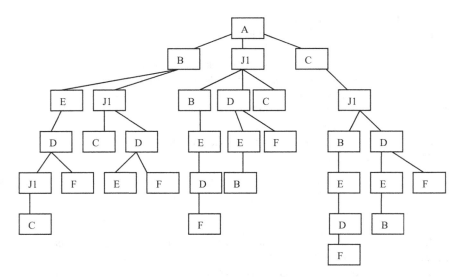

Finding a route from A to D using breadth first search the nodes visited would be A, B, J1, C, E, J1, B, D (the solution). Following the links would give us the route found, i.e., A, J1, D.

Using depth first search the nodes visited would be A, B, E, D (solution found) and the route would be A, B, E, D.

SECTION 6: DATA MINING

Introduction

This section provides you with an introduction to the task of data mining and explains how this is related to the subject of knowledge engineering.

Objectives

By the end of this section you will be able to:

- explain the goal of data mining
- describe some situations where data mining can be used
- understand the basics of how data mining works.

What Is Data Mining?

Data mining is essentially the *automated* extraction of *hidden predictive* information from collections of data.

Such collections of data would normally be large but these days may not necessarily reside in what would normally be considered to be databases. The data could, for example, be the contents of web server logs that record all accesses to all files on a company web server, though the earliest data mining relied on traditional (but large) databases.

Introduction

Data mining tools use data to predict future trends and behaviours. Many companies already collect and refine massive quantities of data. Data mining techniques can be implemented to increase the value of existing information assets. When implemented on high performance client/server arrangements, data mining tools can analyse massive databases to answer such questions as:

- Which of my customers are most likely to respond to a new promotional campaign, and why?
- Which customers who bought product A are also likely to buy product B?
- Which of my current customers am I likely to loose in the next year and which ones should I try hardest (and spend most money on in the form of offers and discounts etc.) to keep?

You may have seen film *Minority Report* in which the main character, played by Tom Cruise, walks through a shopping mall and is identified by the automated advertising devices and has specific products offered to him on the basis of his expected preferences.

If you have ever visited Amazon.com and set up an account, you will have encountered the intelligent way in which their system anticipates the type of products you might be interested in, either by recording what you have previously bought or even just by what you have previously viewed. This is data mining at work. It is this intelligence, this automated extraction of data without the need of human intervention, that allows us to consider data mining 'systems' as 'intelligent systems'.

Data mining is also sometimes referred to as *Knowledge Discovery* in databases (KDD) because knowledge is discovered in data. For example, stored data might indicate that I am between 50 and 55 years old, that I am married, own my own house and have a small family car of a particular model and age. Knowledge extracted from a database containing details of a range of products bought by some people in these precise set of circumstances, allows statistical predictions to be made about other products that might be desirable to other individuals in that same set of circumstances. The larger the original database—both in terms of how many people it contains and the range of information it contains about them, enables the predictions to be more and more precise and accurate.

This accumulation of knowledge, extracted automatically from data, justifies considering such systems as pseudo knowledge-based systems.

The Development of Data Mining

Data mining techniques are the result of a long process of research and product development. This evolution began when business data was first stored on computers, continued with improvements in data access, and more recently, generated technologies that allow users to navigate through their data in real time. Data mining takes this evolutionary process beyond retrospective data access and navigation to prospective and proactive information delivery.

Data mining is supported by three technologies:

- massive data collection
- multiprocessor computers
- data mining algorithms.

The most commonly used data analysis techniques in data mining are:

- neural networks
- decision trees
- genetic algorithms
- rule induction (the extraction of useful if-then rules from data based on statistical significance).

How Data Mining Works

Data mining works by modelling data. Modelling is simply the act of building a model in one situation where you know the answer and then applying it to another situation that you don't. Data mining software runs through the data and distils the characteristics of the data that needs to be in the model. Once the model is built it can then be used in similar situations to answer questions.

Mines of Data

Data that can be usefully mined need not necessarily be business data though perhaps this where most attention has been applied.

Activity 24
Suggest other types of data that exists in large quantities that could perhaps be mined to reveal useful knowledge.

Feedback 24
You might have been able to recognise that large quantities of data exist in the following domains and that applying data mining may reveal useful knowledge:
- Scientific data
- Medical and personal data: From government census to personnel and customer files
- Surveillance video and pictures
- Satellite sensing
- Digital media
- Text reports and memos
- The World Wide Web. Despite its unstructured and heterogeneous nature, the Web is the largest data collection that has ever existed.

Knowledge Discovery

The kinds of patterns that can be discovered depend upon the data mining tasks employed. Generally, there are two types of data mining tasks:

- *descriptive* tasks that describe the general properties of the existing data
- *predictive* tasks that attempt to make predictions based on inference.

Data mining functionalities and the variety of knowledge they discover include:

- *Data characterisation* summarises the general features of objects in a target class, and produces *characteristic rules*. The data relevant to a user-specified class can be retrieved by a database query and passed to a summarisation module to extract sets of characteristics of the data at different levels of abstraction.

- *Data discrimination* produces *discriminant rules* – the comparison of the general features of objects between a *target* class and a *contrasting* class. For example, it may be useful to compare the general characteristics of customers who rent more than 30 DVDs per year with those whose rent less than five.

- *Association analysis* – extracts association rules focusing on the frequency of items occurring together in transactional databases. Association analysis is commonly used for market basket analysis where it might be useful for example, to know what DVDs are often rented together or if there is a relationship between renting a certain genre of film on DVD and buying popcorn or chocolate.

- *Classification analysis* – organises data into given classes and uses given class labels. Classification approaches normally use a training set where all objects are already associated with known class labels. The classification algorithm learns from the training set and builds a model that can be used to classify new objects.

- *Prediction* has successfully been applied to forecasting consumer behaviour based on patterns discovered in past behaviour.

- *Clustering* – organises data into unknown classes. The clustering algorithm itself discovers appropriate labels for the classes.

- *Outlier analysis* identifies data elements that cannot be grouped in a given class or cluster. While in some domains they simply represent noise, in others they can reveal important knowledge.

- *Evolution analysis* models evolutionary trends in time related data.

- *Deviation analysis* – analyses differences between measured values and expected values and attempts to find the cause of the deviations (Zane, 1999).

Activity 25
Visit the Sevana IT Solutions and Services website at:
http://www.sevana.fi/context_data_analysis.php

There you will find a set of data entered and ready to be mined in the online data mining feature. Submit the example data to the mining process by pressing the Send button at the bottom of the page.

What type of output does this system generate?

Feedback 25
You will have discovered that the system outputs rules based on associations between simple items of data in the data set. For example, the following prediction is made:
According to your data we would predict that if one subscribes to *Information* then he would also like to subscribe to *Mobile audio*.

The Value of Mined Knowledge

Data mining allows the discovery of potentially 'useful' knowledge. Whether the knowledge is 'useful' or 'interesting' is subjective and depends on the user and the context in which they are working at the time. The measurement of the *interestingness* (a real technical term in this context) of the discovered knowledge can be based on quantifiable objective criteria or it may simply be that it confirms a hypothesis. Identifying and measuring the interestingness of patterns and rules discovered is essential for the evaluation of the mined knowledge and the data mining process as a whole. Finding ways to assess the interestingness of discovered knowledge is still an active area of research.

The following are representative of current work:
Hilderman, R. J. and Hamilton, H. J. (2001) Knowledge Discovery and Measures of Interest (The International Series in Engineering and Computer Science), Kluwer Academic Publishers.
http://crpit.com/confpapers/CRPITV60Nguyen.pdf.
http://www.cs.kent.ac.uk/people/staff/aaf/pub_papers.dir/PKDD-2005-Carvalho.pdf.

Classifying Data Mining Systems

Data mining systems can be categorised according to:

- the type of data source mined—such as spatial data, multimedia data, time-series data and text data, etc.
- the data model used—such as relational database, object-oriented database, data warehouse, etc.
- the kind of knowledge discovered—such as characterisation, discrimination, association, classification, clustering, etc.
- the mining techniques used—such as NNs, genetic algorithms, statistics, visualisation, etc.

A comprehensive system would provide a variety of data mining techniques to fit different situations.

Normally, it might be appropriate to distinguish between a *data* base, i.e., a store of data, and a *knowledge* base, i.e., a store of knowledge, but if a database contains knowledge *in potentia* can a database also a knowledge base?

Additional online data mining software demonstrations are available at:

Affymetrix Data Mining Tiool
http://www.affymetrix.com/support/technical/tutorial/dmt/start.html
Databeacon Open Client examples
http://www.affinite.co.uk/solutions_databeacon_open_examples.html

Current Research in Data Mining

The following web addresses contain information on research in data mining:
Microsoft Data Mining Research at:
   http://research.microsoft.com/dmx/ DataMining/
Bell Labs NJ: Statistics and Data Mining Research at: http://stat.bell-labs.com/
IBM Knowledge Discovery & Data Mining at: http://domino.research.ibm.com/
   comm/research.nsf/pages/r.kdd.html
Papers on Data Mining can be found via Citeseer at: http://citeseer.ist.psu.edu/

Summary

In this section we have seen how data mining techniques can be used to extract previously unknown knowledge from large data sources and how this knowledge can be used to gain a business advantage.

In this chapter we have now looked at a range of knowledge-based systems:

• expert systems
• neural networks
• case-based reasoning
• genetic algorithms
• intelligent agents
• data mining.

We have seen how these systems work and typical problems they are used to solve.

References

Zane, O. R. (1999). *CMPUT690 Principles of Knowledge Discovery in Databases* (http://
   www.cs.ualberta.ca/~zaiane/courses/cmput690/notes/Chapter1/ch1.pdf) accessed 12
   March 2006.

3

Knowledge Acquisition

Introduction

In this chapter we will be looking at knowledge acquisition, i.e., the process of obtaining the knowledge to be stored in a knowledge-based system.

Objectives

By the end of the chapter you will be able to:

- define knowledge acquisition
- explain how knowledge is acquired from a human expert
- explain the purpose and types of interviews in obtaining knowledge
- explain why it is necessary to record the results of interviews using techniques such as repertory grids.

What Is Knowledge Acquisition?

Knowledge acquisition (sometimes referred to as knowledge elicitation) is the process of acquiring knowledge from a human expert, or a group of experts, and using the knowledge to build knowledge-based systems.

An expert system must contain the knowledge of human experts; therefore the knowledge acquisition process primarily involves a discussion between the knowledge engineer and the human expert. Clearly, a knowledge acquisition session should not be like a visit to the dentist. The knowledge engineer should aim to be as friendly as possible.

In general, experts will be delighted to talk to anyone about their subject of interest, and will exhaust any knowledge engineer. This however, does not mean that the knowledge acquisition process is easy.

Interviews

During your study you may have developed some familiarity with the use of interviews in a systems development context.

These include:

- unstructured
- structured
- event recall
- thinking aloud.

A knowledge engineer can also use interviews as method of obtaining knowledge from human experts however they must also consider other sources of knowledge.

Activity 1

You are a knowledge engineer about to start on obtaining information for a new expert system. As part of this process, you are investigating the knowledge domain and have meetings arranged with a human expert. Besides talking to an expert, where else might a knowledge engineer look to find useful information?

Feedback 1

Sources of available knowledge include:
- procedure manuals
- records of past case studies
- standards documentation
- knowledge from other humans, less knowledgeable but more available then experts.

Clearly, we need a range of knowledge acquisition methods, including computer tools. We will also need to use a range of sources such as printed documentation and manuals.

Other Sources of Knowledge

Questionnaires are also valuable in many situations. There is clearly a considerable similarity between acquiring knowledge from experts in order to compile knowledge bases, and acquiring information from system users in order to develop a new or replacement information system.

Printed sources of knowledge can be very useful. In the specific context of knowledge engineering and acquiring knowledge of a particular domain, manuals, case studies and perhaps textbooks can also prove valuable.

It is particularly important that the knowledge engineer uses these sources. As well as detailed technical information, they can be used to familiarise the knowledge engineer with the subject matter. Thus when the knowledge engineer conducts the preliminary interviews with the expert, they are already familiar with the some of the terminology and have a basic grasp of the subject area. This prevents wasting of the expert's time by asking them to explain trivial information.

While various types of documentation provide useful background to a specific knowledge domain, there is no guarantee that the documentation is either complete or up-to-date. Therefore one of the main methods of obtaining knowledge is still to use human experts, as they are more likely to be aware of the current state of knowledge in their particular domain.

The skills required of a knowledge engineer have already been discussed in Chapter 1. Some specific skills will also be expected from the human experts from whom knowledge will be elicited. Characteristics expected from an expert include being:

- articulate
- motivated
- logical
- systematic.

Conducting Interviews

To conduct a successful interview the knowledge engineer will need to:

- plan
- use appropriate stage management techniques
- consider and use appropriate social skills
- maintain appropriate self-control during the interview.

Activity 2

Think about the planning required for an interview to obtain knowledge from an expert. The activities that must take place are similar to organising any meeting. So, consider what you must do to plan a meeting in an office about any subject—or plan a meeting of a student society, for example, to discuss an important issue.

Keeping this idea in mind, can you list the planning and stage management activities that need to take place before an interview?

Feedback 2

Planning

Ensure that the time and place of the interview are known.

Decide the purpose of the interview and based upon this what type of interview technique would be most appropriate.

Book the appropriate room for the interview to take place in; ensure appropriate refreshments are available.

Where appropriate plan the questions that need to be asked or collect appropriate materials to trigger the expert's memory.

Explain the nature and purpose of the interview with the expert. This will help the expert prepare for the interview.

Ensure that the expert understands what factors will hinder progress of the interview. In other words, check that the expert understands the outcome of the interview.

Ensure that appropriate recording devices are available, e.g. tape recorders, video and an assistant to take notes where necessary.

Stage management techniques

Consideration needs to be given to the location and the time of day of the interview. Experts may work unusual hours so what may normally be considered anti-social times may be appropriate for the interview.

Consider the room layout to minimise disturbance and maximise comfort.

Unlike a conversation the interview should not be assumed to be a natural form of interaction. They are a crucial process to knowledge acquisition, and the time should be used as effectively as possible. As noted above, the interview should be approached in an organised and professional manner – even when the interview itself is unstructured. Interviews have a particular advantage over other forms of knowledge acquisition procedures. The knowledge engineer can satisfy both themselves, and the expert, that they have grasped the points that the expert has been making.

There are various tips that can help during the interview process:

Firstly, avoid ambiguity. Comparative words like bigger; better and lighter are not always helpful, and certainly not precise. Bigger/better/lighter than what?

Secondly, bear in mind that the expert may miss out key parts of the reasoning process. Where parts of the process are potentially complex the expert may ignore some of these complexities in order to simplify the explanation so that the knowledge engineer will understand them. Similarly, when solving problems the expert may make what appear to be intuitive leaps. In reality these are probably cause and effect relationships that the expert has noticed from years of experience in the domain. However, because these steps are 'intuitive' rather than explicitly reasoned the expert may forget them during the interview process. For both of these reasons we need to consider how to ensure that the knowledge obtained is complete and accurate.

Questions useful to begin the interview process include:

- Can you give me an overview of the subject?
- Can you describe the last case you dealt with?
- What facts or hypotheses do you try to establish when thinking about a problem?
- What kinds of things do you like to know about when you begin to think about a problem?
- Leading on to find a little more detail; tell me more about how this is achieved?
- What do you do next?
- How does that relate to ...?
- How, why, when, do you do that?
- Can you describe what you mean by that?

Closing an interview by reviewing the information obtained, and perhaps by alerting the expert to the need for further interviews, is also important.

Activity 3
Suggest three questions or comments that would be appropriate in closing an interview.

Feedback 3
The following are good closing questions and comments:
- Is there anything else we've missed?
- Let me summarise that, and correct me if I'm wrong.
- What do you think we should cover in the next session?
- Have we covered everything we should have?
- Thank you for your help.

The next activity will give you a chance to consider the merits (and otherwise) of interviews as a method for knowledge acquisition.

Activity 4
Without making any comparison, evaluate the general advantages and disadvantages of interviews as a method of knowledge acquisition.

    Advantages   Disadvantages

Feedback 4

Advantages	Disadvantages
• Provide first hand information of the knowledge domain because the expert will be familiar with this domain.	• Time needed to transcribe and analyse the tapes. Conducting a 1-hour interview may result in 10 hours of work. Firstly, a transcript of the interview must be created (voice recognition software may help with this) then the transcript must be carefully analysed and relevant knowledge extracted. The knowledge extracted must be checked to ensure its accuracy and it must then be analysed to identify any gaps or areas of uncertainty. Subsequent knowledge acquisition sessions must be planned to resolve these issues.
• Knowledge engineer can satisfy both parties (engineer and expert) that the relevant points have been grasped. Additional questions or summaries can be asked at any time in the interview to check understanding of the points already covered.	• Possible discrepancies between the methods described and the methods used. The expert may not be able to explain some methods or processes particularly well, or the knowledge engineer may not fully understand the expert's comments due to lack of knowledge. This will lead to inaccuracies in the engineer's notes that will only be identified when those notes are being reviewed by the expert. Additional re-writing of the notes will therefore be required.
• Different interview types help to ensure that the knowledge domain is accurately recorded by placing a different emphasis on the method of collecting knowledge.	• Expert uses jargon that the knowledge engineer does not understand – this will be less problematic if the knowledge engineer does some preparatory knowledge acquisition, from books or other people, before talking to the expert.
	• The expert may have difficulty recalling information in an interview situation (although thinking aloud interviews should alleviate some of this problem).
	• The expert may not trust the knowledge engineer, or believe that the engineer has insufficient interviewing skills or knowledge of the domain to understand what the expert is explaining. This will tend to make information obtained in the interview incomplete as the expert becomes bored or sees the interview as a waste of time.

Having considered interviews in general we will now look at four very common types of interview:

- Unstructured
- Structured
- Event recall
- Think aloud interviews.

Unstructured Interviews

The unstructured interview is often the first interview to be conducted. The purpose of this interview is to enable the knowledge engineer to gain an understanding of the knowledge domain. The knowledge engineer invites the expert to talk about the knowledge domain in high-level terms. The expert is only interrupted to ask general questions or to retain focus on the specific knowledge domain.

It will rarely provide a complete or well-organised description of the knowledge and processes involved. However, it is fundamentally important to conduct unstructured interviews.

The interview does allow the expert to bring areas of subject matter that had not been considered to be important to the attention of the knowledge engineer. They can often result in the experts straying into topics of interest that may not have otherwise been discovered. However, unstructured interviews are time consuming and should be used with caution.

To summarise, here is a list of the main characteristics of unstructured interviews:

- used in the early stages of knowledge acquisition
- consist of free flowing dialogue, mainly from the expert
- include spontaneous questions from the knowledge engineer
- little prior planning carried out regarding the content of the interview
- interviews tend to take on a 'life of their own'
- rarely provide a complete or well-organised picture of the knowledge domain
- can introduce important topics that could otherwise be neglected in an interview that was too structured.

Structured Interviews

The structured interview is the second main type of interview. It is used to obtain in depth knowledge about the specific domain. The knowledge engineer will have some appreciation of the knowledge domain from the orientation interview, so this interview will focus on providing detail on the domain, involving many more

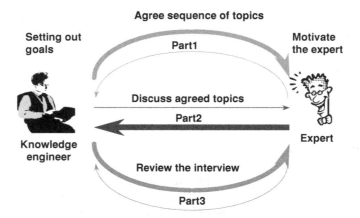

FIGURE 3.1. The sequence of structured interviews.

questions from the knowledge engineer. Some of the questions to the expert will focus on *why* a certain actions are taken, to obtain an understanding *how* the expert makes decisions.

Structured interviews are usually conducted after several unstructured interviews have taken place, and the knowledge that they contain has been analysed.

The interview normally consists of three parts (see Figure 3.1):

- Part 1 where an agreed sequence of topics is set out, and where the goals of the interview are described by the knowledge engineer. This can motivate the expert.
- Part 2 is where the discussion takes place, i.e., the questions are asked and the expert has a chance to answer.
- Part 3 is a fundamental part of the quality assurance process, and is a review of the interview, where the knowledge engineer can check that they have understood and obtained correct answers.

Here are the characteristics of structured interviews:

- focused on the specific area of knowledge
- relaxed to enable the expert to answer questions clearly and at an appropriate level of detail
- unhurried so as not to place the expert under time pressure
- interesting so both the knowledge engineer and expert can relate to the subject and increase retention of information for the knowledge engineer.

Event Recall Interviews

You may have previously encountered the fact gathering technique of *observation*. You will not be too surprised to learn that though observing the knowledge possessed by experts is not as simple as observing users of an information system, the knowledge engineer has something analogous available. This is the *event recall* interview.

Activity 5

Working from the analogy with observation as a fact gathering technique suggest what event recall might involve and what problems and advantages it might have as a tool for gathering knowledge from experts.

Feedback 5

You should have been able to recognise that a technique named 'event recall' would involve the experts describing how they dealt with a particular event – i.e., observing themselves in the past. Such recall should be in sufficient detail to allow the knowledge engineer to interpret each stage in the solution of the problem as applying a series of rules to particular aspects of the problem or stages in its solution.

You may also have been able to recognise that such a technique requires significant interpretative skills on the part of the knowledge engineer as well as articulation (and an accurate memory) on the part of the expert. The latter represents something of a disadvantage to the use of the technique.

Event recall interviews are very good at revealing the decision-making process itself; i.e., the sequence of thought processes. They are also very good for checking completeness of the knowledge acquisition sessions, though they have a tendency to degenerate into a general discussion, and this must be avoided.

In an event recall interview, a particular case study will be discussed effectively. The knowledge engineer may say to the doctor 'in the case of Mr. Smith, for example, talk me through the decision making process, "What questions did you ask and in what order?"'

Often it is not enough to know what questions an expert will ask. We must also learn the sequence in which those questions will be asked. Experts often develop the habit of focusing on critical questions first, and leave others until later if at all. The sequence of thought processes an expert goes through therefore, in making a decision, is often as important as the particular pieces of knowledge that may be applied to the problem at any particular point. Other knowledge acquisition procedures may not highlight this sequence of thought processes.

The *event recall* interview is often used when the validity of knowledge collected through other methods is in question or when the complexities inherent in the knowledge domain make it very difficult for the expert to articulate or even recognise how they apply rules to the solution of a problem.

Thinking Aloud Interviews

Thinking aloud interviews are similar to event recall interviews in that they attempt to capture the thinking behind a problem-solving process. In event recall, this process is in the past; in thinking aloud, it is in the present. In other words, thinking aloud interviews encourage the expert to explain how he or she is thinking through a specific situation. The aims of the interview are to fill any gaps in knowledge following the structured interview and to validate knowledge already obtained as well as obtain information about the sequence of steps taken by an expert in solving a problem. These interviews normally discuss actual cases, although for ethical reasons these cases may be simulated rather than real.

A yet further variation of this type of approach is sometimes referred to as introspective interviews. These involve asking the expert how they would solve a particular problem. The expert is encouraged to verbalise their thought processes. The knowledge engineer only intervenes to ask probing questions, such as how or why.

However, it should be noted that the process of verbalising their thoughts may distract the expert from solving the particular problem, and therefore can actually interfere with the normal thinking process.

Activity 6

As a knowledge engineer, you will need to use various methods to obtain knowledge from the human experts. Here are a number of situations where information is obtained from individuals.

Read the following situations and name a technique that can be used to obtain the information.
- A car manufacturer wishes to know what a few famous people think about their cars.
- A software manufacturer needs to obtain information on whether some software meets the detailed performance requirements expected of it.
- A novice chef wants to understand the process of planning a menu.
- Information on a certain soap powder is required from 5,000 different people in one country.
- Detail is needed on the actual steps involved to make a joint between two pieces of wood.

Feedback 6

- A car manufacturer wishes to know what a few famous people think about their cars.

Unstructured interviews are a good way of finding unspecified information on a particular topic. Structured questions, such as on a scale of 1–10 rate our cars road handling, will provide answers that are easier to analyse. However, by structuring the questions the interviewee will be unable to mention other issues that are of particular concern to them, e.g. the steering wheel is too small.

- A software manufacturer needs to obtain information on whether some software meets the detailed performance requirements expected of it.

As specific information is required on detailed performance requirements, specific questions can be created to obtain exactly the information required. Thus, structured interviews would be a good method here.

- A novice chef wants to understand the process of planning a menu.

Event recall interviews are specifically designed to obtain procedural information. Using this method the process of developing a previous menu, from start to finish, will be described. Questions that may distract the expert should be left until the entire process has been described. A think aloud interview could also be used if the expert had a current menu to plan.

- Information on a certain soap powder is required from 5,000 different people in one country.

Questionnaires are an efficient way of collecting information from a large number of people. Questions can be open or closed. Closed question with short yes/no style answers can be very easy to analyse but will clearly restrict the information obtained. Unlike an interview additional questions cannot be asked, it is therefore essential that the questionnaire is well designed. To help with this a pilot questionnaire with lots of open questions could be tested on a sample group. These replies will help in designing the final questionnaire.

- Detail is needed on the actual steps involved to make a joint between two pieces of wood.

As procedural information is required, an event recall interview could be used but perhaps a better method would be 'observation'. Using observation the actual process can be seen. The expert could verbalise the process they were undertaking, i.e., this would then be a think aloud interview. Subsequent questions can be asked to clarify any areas of uncertainty.

Other Knowledge Acquisition Techniques

Other knowledge acquisition techniques that can be used by the knowledge engineer include:

- Tutorial interviews
- Twenty question interviews
- Trigger interviews
- Teach back interviews
- Repertory grids.

Tutorial Interviews

The expert is asked to prepare a presentation on a subject area to help the knowledge engineer become familiar with the knowledge domain. Such interviews are often used at the start of the knowledge acquisition process to give the knowledge engineer a general overview of the subject.

Twenty Questions

An interview to gather important characteristics of a part of a domain. The person being interviewed can only answer 'yes' or 'no' to questions. Either the knowledge engineer asks questions to obtain basic concepts of the domain, or the expert asks questions to check the engineer's understanding.

A variation is where the knowledge engineer is supplied with a set of previously solved problems in the domain, and the expert poses the questions for the knowledge engineer.

Trigger Interviews

In these interviews, the knowledge engineer issues materials within the interview that are intended to trigger and stimulate the experts' responses, and to trigger particular memories. Triggers can include structured diagrams derived from earlier knowledge acquisition sessions, and this can be useful in presenting these to experts to check the quality of the knowledge they represent. Triggers can also include archive data from past instances of problem-solving activity.

Teach Back Interviews

These involve the knowledge engineer teaching back to the expert what they think they have learned from other knowledge acquisition processes. Such an approach highlights gaps or inaccuracies in the understanding of the knowledge engineer so these can be corrected.

Repertory Grids

The use of repertory grids is an additional knowledge acquisition technique that requires separate treatment. They were introduced as a method of recording an expert's view of a particular problem. The *elements* of the problem are recorded across the top of the grid; these are a list of people, objects or situations familiar to the expert. The rows in the grid contain the *constructs* relevant to the elements, which are obtained during the elicitation process. A construct represents a bipolar characteristic that each element in the grid has. For example, a person has a specific weight and eye colour. The aim of producing the grid is to show in what ways objects in the domain are alike (or differ) to help with the overall understanding of the domain.

Girds are prepared in the following way.

Stage 1: Define the Domain

Define the domain where the grid will be used. Examples of domains can include people, countries or different events and activities.

Stage 2: State the Elements

The elements are a representative sample taken from the domain. For example, the domain of people can include elements such as self, mother, father, son, doctor, etc.

The elements are then placed on a grid ready for further analysis as in the following grid, showing elements of the domain: Countries.

Britain	Chile	USA	Canada	Brazil	France	India

Stage 3: Define the Constructs

Constructs provide the means of differentiating between the different elements in the grid. Constructs can be set by the knowledge engineer, or provided by the expert. To obtain each construct elements are defined in terms of some factor that differentiates between the elements. Each factor, or construct, is then placed on the left of the table.

In the following example, the constructs include hot (vs. cold) and holiday destination and English speaking.

Crosses are placed inside the table to indicate which countries are hot, etc.

	Britain	Chile	USA	Canada	Brazil	France	India
Hot					X	X	X
Holiday destination			X	X		X	
English speaking	X		X	X			

When constructs are chosen by the knowledge engineer, care is needed to ensure that the constructs can explain differences between the elements in the domain. However, where the expert chooses constructs, there is a risk that they are not understood, or will not be particularly relevant to the system being built. The constructs are more likely to reflect the worldview of the expert, than provide insights into the domain. A joint discussion between the knowledge engineer and expert may help to overcome these problems.

Stage 4: Ranking the Elements

As an alternative to indicating which elements are/or are not members of each set the elements can be ranked in order, starting with one, with respect to the constructs identified. In other words, the constructs are used to order all of the elements.

	Britain	Chile	USA	Canada	Brazil	France	India
Hot	5	7	4	6	3	2	1
Holiday destination	4	5	1	2	6	3	7
English speaking	1	4	3	2	6	7	5

When ranking the elements it is easy to take on board the opinions of multiple experts and determine an average ranking.

Stage 5: Analysing the Grid

The constructs in the grid are now analysed to try to identify the differences and similarities between them. Various tools can be used to do this. Where similarities are discovered, then this information can be used to show how the different elements relate to each other in the specific domain.

Activity 7
This activity will take you through the process of using a repertory grid.
1. Visit the *WebGrid III* page at: http://tiger.cpsc.ucalgary.ca:1500/WebGrid/WebGrid.html.
2. Read the documentation at: http://tiger.cpsc.ucalgary.ca:1500/WGExisting.html – you will find it useful to print this document.
3. Close the window to take you back to the main WebGrid page.
4. Under the heading *Demonstrations of WebGrid III* is a section related to *Expert System Grids*.
5. Explore the demo grid about *Cendrowska contact lens decision*.

As well as considering the type of interview to be performed the knowledge engineer has other issues to consider including:

- how to document the knowledge acquisition process
- issues relating to the use of multiple experts.

Documenting the Knowledge Acquisition Process

Forms are used to broadly itemise the aims of the session, and can be given to an expert in advance of the session, to be used as an agenda. The forms can be completed during the interview as agreed by both parties.

Recording the results of knowledge acquisition process is important, as this allows the knowledge bases that are ultimately developed to be validated. If the correct paperwork is followed, it should be possible after a system has been developed to find details of the interview that was the source of an item of knowledge. Knowing this it will be possible to go back and question the relevant expert about the validity of that knowledge.

Dealing with Multiple Experts

In this situation, more than one expert is interviewed to obtain knowledge about a specific domain.

Knowledge acquisition involving multiple experts involves three distinct difficulties:

- the problems of dealing with experts individually, plus
- the problems of coordinating human interactions – especially if time is short
- the obstacles and risks of trying to integrate different knowledge and different methods of solving problems.

Clearly, using multiple experts can be difficult, and can involve obtaining conflicting knowledge. The experts may use different reasoning techniques and different processes to solve the problems, and these may not always be easily merged or linked together. If multiple experts are required and it is found that they use conflicting knowledge the feasibility of developing the expert system should be questioned unless the experts themselves can resolve their conflicting problem-solving approaches.

Despite the difficulties using multiple experts it is possible to iron out areas of uncertainty or conflicting knowledge, and to use one expert as a validation tool. This allows a higher quality knowledge base to be developed—potentially better than any one individual expert.

Repertory grids can be used as a simple method to represent the opinions of several experts. Each expert is asked to provide a ranked estimate and the values in each element are simply averaged.

Current Research

Knowledge acquisition tools have been developed to support the knowledge acquisition process. In some of these the domain expert works directly with the computerised tool.

The following websites have relevant information:

Automating Knowledge Acquisition

http://www.scism.sbu.ac.uk/inmandw/review/knowacq/review/rev12510.html

Flexible Knowledge Acquisition Through Explicit Representation of Knowledge Roles

http://www.isi.edu/expect/link/papers/swartout-gil-sss96.pdf

Easing Knowledge Acquisition for Case-Based Design

http://www.comp.rgu.ac.uk/staff/smc/kbs/kacbd/

Summary

In this chapter, we have seen that various types of interview are a crucial knowledge acquisition method. However, interviews:

• take time
• require planning
• require skill.

There is a range of interview types, and each should be used in appropriate contexts and at appropriate stages in the total process. It is usual to start with unstructured interviews, followed by structured interviews, and then careful use of event recall interviews; being particularly careful that they do not degenerate into unstructured interviews.

Other important knowledge acquisition techniques include documentation analysis, questionnaires, formal techniques and observation analysis.

Self-Assessment Questions

Question 1

You have obtained information concerning different methods of transport, and now need to construct an expert system to help people choose the most appropriate form of transport for their particular needs.

The modes of transport available are:

- walk
- cycle
- skateboard
- car
- train
- bus
- aeroplane
- tram
- taxi
- motor-bike.

Place these modes of travel in a repertory grid and choose three pairs of factors that will help to differentiate people's choices between the different modes.

Question 2

Investigate some of the repertory grid analysis tools by visiting the website below and following the links to the grids themselves.

http://www.psyctc.org/grids/grids.html

Question 3

In which type of interview (unstructured, structured and event recall) would you expect to find the following questions:

1. Starting from the first day of your last holiday, until the final day, please tell me everything that happened.
2. How do you play chess?
3. If the traffic light is on red should I start the car or stop it?

Question 4

For the following two problems identify which types of interview would be appropriate:

1. A knowledge engineer wishes to become familiar with a new subject area.
2. A knowledge engineer wishes to complete and check the knowledge obtained from earlier knowledge acquisition sessions.

Answer to Self-Assessment Questions

Answer 1

Suggestions for factors are given below; however, there are many possible factors that can be used.

	Walk	Cycle	Skateboard	Car	Train	Bus	Aeroplane	Tram	Taxi	Motor-bike
Short distance	1	2	3	8	9	5	10	7	6	4
Healthy	1	2	3	7	4	6	10	5	8	9
Limited budget	1	2	3	7	8	4	9	5	10	6

Answer 2

No specific solution.

Answer 3

1. This would be appropriate in an event recall interview that is used to obtain sequencing information and to check whether it matches knowledge collected previously via other interview techniques. We may need to consider the entire sequence activities starting at the very beginning and finishing at the very end of the event. In this example, for instance, it may be necessary to consider the actions leading up to the holiday from the first time that the holiday was suggested, to the choice of destination and the preparations that were made in order to go on the holiday. The post holiday sequence of actions may also be important—how you got home, unpacked, etc.
2. This sort of question would be appropriate in an unstructured interview. Questions in this type of interview are often short and the answers are often long. While this type of interview can often be time consuming, unstructured interviews are essential as they allow the expert to bring important issues to the attention of the knowledge engineer.
3. This sort of question is typical in a structured interview where the knowledge engineer is looking for specific information. The questions are often long and the answers relatively short. As the knowledge engineer is looking for specific information the questions need to be prepared in advance of the interview. Structured interviews are good for filling in the gaps left from earlier interviews.

Answer 4

1. The two most appropriate methods here are tutorial interviews and unstructured interviews. However, it is worth remembering that even before conducting these interviews the knowledge engineer should consider doing preliminary bookwork or talking to other people in order to learn some of the terminology.
2. This problem really has two parts: how to complete the knowledge acquisition process and how to check it.

Structured interviews can be used to plug any known gaps in the knowledge but what about unknown gaps? By conducting event recall interviews, particularly where difficult or unusual events are considered, issues will arise that were glossed over by the expert or missed by the knowledge engineer. If no such issues arise we can have some confidence that the knowledge obtained is complete.

Event recall interviews are also a useful method of checking the knowledge obtained. Does the procedure followed during a real event actually match the procedure as described in earlier knowledge acquisition sessions? The other interview technique that is most obviously useful for the task of checking the knowledge is the teach back interview—where the knowledge engineer prepares a presentation to the expert and the expert verifies they understand the subject correctly. There is one other very important method of checking the knowledge obtained. If a prototype expert system is created, incorporating the knowledge obtained, the quality of the knowledge in the expert system can be demonstrated by testing the reasoning powers of system developed.

4

Knowledge Representation and Reasoning

Introduction

In this chapter on knowledge representation, we will be looking at different knowledge representation schemes including rules, frames and semantic networks.

We will look at how to choose between them; the advantages and disadvantages of each and how to represent knowledge in a form suitable for knowledge-based systems (KBSs). We will also compare deep and shallow knowledge and consider the issues of brittleness and explanation facilities.

The chapter consists of five sections:

1. Using knowledge
2. Logic, rules and representation
3. Developing rule-based systems
4. Semantic networks
5. Frames.

Objectives

By the end of the chapter you will be able to:

- explain how knowledge can be represented in declarative programs
- describe and analyse the inference process
- explain the principles of backward and forward chaining
- analyse the type of chaining used by a specific expert system (ES)
- explain how semantic networks represent data
- identify the advantages and disadvantages of semantic networks
- explain how frames can be used to represent knowledge
- evaluate the risks associated with developing unintelligent explanation facilities
- explain the concept of brittleness.

SECTION 1: USING KNOWLEDGE

Introduction

This section introduces the subject of knowledge representation. It briefly looks at the use of rules and declarative programming. Rule-based approaches to knowledge representation are covered in depth in section 2 of this chapter.

Objectives

By the end of the section you will be able to:

- explain how knowledge can be represented in declarative programmes
- distinguish between shallow and deep knowledge in the context of ESs.

Different Types of Knowledge

Acquiring knowledge is one of the main objectives of humans. We have always sought to obtain knowledge, to apply that knowledge to solve everyday problems, and to expand on it to improve ourselves and our environment.

However, while some knowledge is easy to obtain and understand (e.g. what the sequence and meaning of traffic lights is), other knowledge may be difficult to obtain or interpret. For example, many of the problems being tackled by experts are poorly understood because the subject areas are very specialised and experts find it difficult to communication information on that knowledge area.

In many situations, experts do not have any formal basis for problem solving or communicating the results of that problem solving. So they tend to use 'rules of thumb' (heuristics) developed on the basis of their experience to help them make decisions in their particular field.

Heuristics implies that knowledge is acquired more by trial and error than by any definite decision-making process. This does not cast doubt on the value of heuristics: the rules established by experts through experience can often be valuable and this differentiates the 'expert' from less experienced people. An example of a heuristic is the statement that people with high blood pressure are more likely to have a heart attack. While not all people with high blood pressure have a heart attack it is still a useful rule of thumb and if a doctor advised you that it was critical to lower your blood pressure you would be unlikely to ignore this advice.

Deep and Shallow Knowledge

Expert systems, can have two types of knowledge: deep and shallow.

Shallow knowledge indicates that the system has been built with a working knowledge of the problem domain only and a system built on the basis of it will only be useful in some very specific situations. If the problem facing the ES is not covered by any of these basic relationships, then the system will not be able to provide a solution to that problem.

Deep knowledge is knowledge of the fundamental laws on which a system is based. This knowledge is not dependent on a specific situation and can thus be used to solve a range of problems. As with a human expert, the system will be able to 'understand' the causal links within the knowledge base. Including this type of knowledge within an ES is difficult, if not impossible, in many situations. Many systems are simply too complex to show all the causal relationships, and experts may sometimes make intuitive leaps to reach a conclusion, which the ES cannot mimic.

Shallow knowledge therefore tends to be:

• task dependent
• brittle
• additive
• but also provides effective reasoning.

On the other hand, deep knowledge tends to be

• task independent
• describes causal relations
• complete at a certain level of abstraction
• however reasoning with this knowledge can be difficult.

Activity 1
An ES has been produced to provide assistance in the diagnosis of faults in Brand X televisions.

Explain how the concepts of shallow and deep knowledge could be applied to this system.

Comment on how difficult deep knowledge is to apply in such a context.

Feedback 1
Shallow knowledge implies that the ES only has information concerning its domain—perhaps a database of common faults and probable causes and solutions for this particular brand of television. Using this knowledge the system will provide correct fault-finding diagnosis on most occasions.

However, this knowledge would not apply to fixing faults in TVs made by other manufacturers nor to other types of TV receivers such as plasma screen TVs if company X started to make these.

Deep knowledge could be built into the system, such as the relationship between voltage, resistance and current (Ohm's law) and other aspects of the physics of electricity. This additional knowledge might allow the ES to diagnose faults in other types of electrical equipment. However, such diagnosis would be working from first principles and reaching a diagnosis could be difficult and time consuming. Deep knowledge is therefore more difficult to apply because it is not based on specific knowledge of a particular piece of equipment that may be gained from experience.

Representing Rules in ESs

Most decision-making rules within ESs can be represented using the IF... THEN format, that is

IF ⟨situation⟩ THEN ⟨action⟩

Other clauses such as OR and ELSE can also be used within this construct to show alternative situations or different courses of action.

For example, a simple rule could be:

IF Christmas day falls on a Monday,
OR Christmas day falls on a Tuesday
THEN many factories will close for the whole of Christmas week.

Features of Rule-Based Systems

The main features of rule-based systems are:

- They represent practical human reasoning in the form of IF... THEN rules. Most humans use this type of statement (even if they don't realise it) so the syntax will be relatively easy to understand.
- The knowledge of the system grows as more rules are added. This implies that the accuracy of the predictions made by the system will increase as more rules become available.
- Where a conflict occurs between two or more rules, the rule-based system may be sophisticated enough to try to choose the best rule to use.
- Use an inference technique (either backward or forward chaining—explained later in this chapter) to manipulate expertise to solve a problem.

Procedural vs. Declarative Programming

Procedural Programming

A program written in C++ or Java consists of a set of procedures that must be performed *in a strict sequence* to accomplish a purpose. This is procedural programming.

Key features of procedural programming include:

- The programme is constructed as a sequence of step-by-step 'how to' instructions. However, explanations may be included to tell the user why certain activities are being carried out.
- The programming format implies automatic response to stimuli; there is little or no thinking about the response or course of action, these are included within the programme.

Declarative Programming

Rules in a KBS stand alone as statements of truth or fact and can be used by an inference engine to reach other true conclusions. This is declarative programming. The sequence of actions taken during processing is not defined. The inference engine will automatically select and apply rules as it sees fit.

Key features of declarative programming are listed below:

- It provides facts on a given knowledge domain, literally stating what things are.
- The statements within declarative programming provide information concerning the associations between different objects.
- Knowledge is normally shallow or surface-level, providing examples of associations that experts can visualise easily.

Activity 2

Explain what type of programming each of the following statements are examples of:

1. Smoking causes cancer.
2. Find the price of a new car. If the price is less than £10,000, then purchase the car, else leave money in the bank and check prices in another month.

Feedback 2

Statement 1 is an example of declarative knowledge because it provides a statement about knowledge within a domain.

Statement 2 is an example of procedural knowledge because it provides a list of instructions to carry out.

Before a KBS can be used to make decisions, the knowledge that the system will use must be encoded in some way and made available either as part of the ES itself or readily accessible to it. Three common methods of encoding knowledge are:

- rules
- semantic networks
- frames.

If knowledge is to be held in the system, then some formal method of holding that knowledge must be agreed to enable the user to encode the knowledge correctly. The inference engine must understand this knowledge representation scheme if it is to apply that knowledge to a particular problem and draw appropriate conclusions. Thus the inference engine dictates the knowledge representation scheme used. Some inference engines for example understand rules but not frames.

Activity 3

The main requirements for a knowledge representation language are given below. What do you think the 1st, 4th and 5th of these requirements means?
Representational adequacy

Inferential adequacy. New knowledge must be inferred from a basic set of facts.
Inferential efficiency. Any inferences that are made from the data should be made efficiently, so as not to waste user or processing time.
Clear syntax and semantics
Naturalness

Feedback 3

You should have been able to interpret the requirements approximately as follows:

Representational adequacy. The system must allow you to represent all the knowledge that you need to reason with.
Inferential adequacy. New knowledge must be inferred from a basic set of facts.
Inferential efficiency. Any inferences that are made from the knowledge should be made efficiently, so as not to waste user or processing time.
Clear syntax and semantics. The knowledge in the system must be in a format that can be understood and processed by a computer (i.e., inferenced).
Naturalness. The language needs to be easy to use. This means it must be in a format that is familiar to humans and can easily be used to represent the knowledge that is required in the ES.

Summary

This section has shown how knowledge can be stored in a KBS in the form of rules.

Self-Assessment Questions

Question 1

Does an Internet search engine use deep or shallow knowledge and declarative or procedural programming? Make a series of brief notes highlighting the main issues and considerations.

Question 2

You accidentally drop a plate and you instantly reach the conclusion that it will drop to the ground. As you are currently standing on a concrete floor you expect the plate to break on impact.

(a) Did you use deep or shallow knowledge to reach these conclusions?
(b) If a scientist wanted to calculate the trajectory of a rocket would they use deep or shallow knowledge?
(c) Would it be advantageous to apply the knowledge a scientist has to the problem of a plate dropping?

Answer to Self-Assessment Questions

Answer 1

Areas that you need to consider within your answer include:

An Internet search cannot, by its nature, include deep knowledge of any subject area. It is a general-purpose tool for finding matches for keywords, rather than looking for specific knowledge within a domain.

However, some element of deep knowledge may be noted in the system. The search engine must 'understand' how to parse the questions or statements given to it so that appropriate hits can be located for the user. For example, the question *'tell me about motor vehicles in the 1950's'* could be given to the search engine. The engine must be smart enough to realise that *tell me about* are not really part of the search, and that *1950s* is related to *motor vehicles*, otherwise a list of 1950s websites could be provided.

The type of programming used is likely to be procedural, particularly where questions need to be parsed in a specific way, or websites searched for specific keywords. The search engine is simply following a list of instructions to carry out these actions.

The use of declarative knowledge is limited, because most of the activities of the search engine can be carried out using a list of procedures, and the engine does not have to understand any of the knowledge domains being visited.

Answer 2

(a) You know from personal experience that if you drop an item it will fall and an item such as a plate will almost certainly break if it hits a hard surface. You did not need to understand the detail laws of physics to reach this conclusion.

(b) Understanding that items when dropped will fall will not enable a scientist to calculate the trajectory of a rocket. To calculate this you need to understand the laws of physics regarding gravity, momentum and motion. If you understand these laws you can apply them to a range of situations, e.g. determining the speed of a car rolling down a hill.

(c) You could determine what would happen to the plate based on the laws of physics but the calculations would be long and complex. In performing such calculation it would be possible to make a mistake. Why go through this long and complex process, taking the risk of making a mistake, when we know from years of personal experience what will happen?

From this example we can see that deep knowledge can be applied to a range of problems (and this can combat the issue of brittleness described elsewhere in this book) however it is not easy to obtain and can be difficult to apply. Thus for practical purposes shallow knowledge may be better. The appropriate use of deep or shallow knowledge is a decision that the knowledge engineer must make when considering each system to be developed.

SECTION 2: LOGIC, RULES AND REPRESENTATION

Introduction

This section explains the relationship between logic and rule statements. It then goes on to describe how rule-based systems are constructed.

Objectives

By the end of this section you will be able to:

• describe and analyse the inference process
• interpret propositional logic statements
• write propositional logic statements
• explain the principles of backward and forward chaining
• provide examples of the inference process using chaining.

Propositional Logic

Propositional logic is one method of representing knowledge within ESs. In this approach, symbols are used to show the relationship between different entities and values.

Specifically the symbols have the following meanings:

$\wedge$ and
$\vee$ or
$\neg$ not
$\rightarrow$ by implication
$\leftrightarrow$ is equivalent to
$\forall$ for all
$\exists$ there exists

Letters can be used to represent facts about the world. For example,

C = Barry drinks coffee
D = Barry eats cake

Using this narrative, statements such as the following can be made:

C $\wedge$ D Barry drinks coffee and Barry eats cake
C $\vee$ D Barry drinks coffee or Barry eats cake
$\neg$C Barry doesn't drink coffee
C $\rightarrow$ D If Barry drinks coffee then Barry eats cake
C $\leftrightarrow$ D If Barry drinks coffee then Barry eats cake and vice versa

If statements are related to each other, then inferences can be drawn regarding the information contained in the statements.

Activity 4
Use the two statements below to infer a possible third statement about a cloudy day.

Cloudy ∨ Sunny
¬ Sunny → Leave_sunglasses

Feedback 4
If the two states of the weather are cloudy or sunny, then if sunglasses are not needed when the weather is not sunny, then the following must be correct:

¬ Cloudy → Take_Sunglasses

In practice, more information would be required to make this a logical inference since it is possible to not wear sunglasses even though it is sunny. This might be a medical necessity for someone with severe problems with strong sunlight however.

The idea of inferring information from statements is important within ESs, and is discussed in more detail later in this section.

Propositional logic can include three different terms:

- constant symbols including names such as Barry
- variable symbols usually denoted by capital letters
- functional expressions containing a function followed by a number of arguments.

Statements in prepositional logic can be joined together using the symbols above to provide more complicated logical statements. For example, the following statement describes the food preferences of a snake called Slither:

Likes (Slither, carrots) ∧ Likes (Slither, cabbage)

In other words, Slither likes carrots and cabbage.

Finally, semantic statements can be expanded to include more general ideas. For example, the statement

∀X (likes (Slither, X) → eats (Slither, X))

implies that Slither eats everything that he likes. However, as Slither is a snake we may need to define X as a set of small mammals.

Activity 5
Explain the following statements in English.
- ∃X (grass_snake (X) → (¬eat (small_mammals, X)))
- ∀ X (clouds (black, X) → rain (clouds, X))

Feedback 5
- There exists in the set of grass snakes at least one snake that does not eat small mammals.
- From all clouds that are black, rain is possible.

Inference Rules and Propositional Logic

Inference rules can also work with propositional logic. The following activity allows you to infer something about Barry from a combination of propositional logic statements.

Activity 6
What can you conclude given the following two statements?

∀X (people (X) → breathe (X))
people (Barry)

Feedback 6
Because Barry is a member of the set of people, then Barry must breathe.
Breathe (Barry)

More complicated rules can be derived using the symbols already discussed above. For example,

∀X (grass_snake (X) → green (X))
Grass_snake (Slither)
Means that Slither is a grass snake and therefore he must be green.

Rule-Based Systems

Rule-based systems provide an approach to representing knowledge within an ES. As in the case of propositional systems rules can be used to describe what is true but they can also be used to describe what you can or cannot do in different situations.

The basic construction for rules follows the structure:

IF *something*, THEN *something else is true*. For example,
```
IF raining THEN you_should_carry_an_umbrella
```

Rule-based systems can be inferenced, i.e., processed by an inference engine, in one of two ways—namely *forward* or *backward chaining*.

Forward Chaining

In *forward chaining*, the inference engine starts with a set of facts, which are used to draw conclusions about the domain in which the system is working. Forward chaining starts from the data and works forward to the conclusions or goals of the system. The system is data-driven:

1. Enter new data.
2. Fire forward chaining rules.
3. Infer new data values from the rules fired.
4. Repeat Steps 2 and 3 until no new data can be inferred.
5. State the solution, or if there is no solution, then state that the rule base is insufficient.

Forward chaining works with data held in the volatile memory of the computer; this means that the data will be amended as the program is run. Data is amended as a result of rules firing.

Activity 7
This activity will help you understand forward chaining by asking you to apply the process to a small example.

Consider a system with three rules:
1. If someone is a third year student, then they need a job.
2. If someone is a third year student, then they live on campus.
3. If someone needs a job, they will look at job advoverts.

Suppose we put the following data into memory:

John is a third year student.

What will happen?

Feedback 7
You should have been able to recognise that in forward chaining, because the system is constantly alert for new data the system would have searched all the rules for any whose conditions weren't true before but are now. It then adds their conclusions into memory.

In this case, Rules 1 and 2 have conditions, which match this new fact (John is a third year student.). So the system will immediately create and add the two facts:

- John needs a job.
- John lives on campus.

These facts in turn can trigger rules. As each arrives, the system would look for yet more rules that are made true. In this case, the fact John needs a job would trigger Rule 3, resulting in the addition of another fact into memory:

- John will look at job adverts.

The fact that John lives on campus would not trigger anything else.

In some situations, it may appear that two or more rules should fire at the same time; in this case conflict resolution strategies will be required to determine which rule is to fire. The rule relating to data that has changed most recently will often take precedence. In other systems, rules are applied on a first come first served basis, i.e., as soon as an appropriate rule is found that can be applied, search for further applicable rules ends.

To summarise then, in a forward chaining system:

- Data is normally entered prior to the system commencing the inference process.
- Rules are normally checked individually.
- Relevant rules are grouped together to make the system easier to write and validate.
- Rules only fire when all the information concerning that rule is available.
- The inference engine is not programmed to ask questions and obtain new information while the program is running.
- Multiple conclusions can be reached.

While this inference process does work, it can be very time consuming and inefficient, especially where there are many hundreds or thousands of rules to be searched.

Backward Chaining

In *backward chaining*, the system starts with a hypothesis, then the truth or otherwise of the hypothesis is proved by checking the rules within the domain. In other words, the system is driven from the goals back to the data.

The basic steps involved in backward chaining are as follows:
1. State a specific goal.
2. Find rules that resolve the goal, i.e., answer the question.
3. When the program is running, the user answers questions to satisfy the antecedents of rules as required.
4. Obtain a result—which is that the goal can or cannot be achieved.

In backward chaining, the system does no work until required, i.e., goal is specified.

Activity 8

This activity will help you understand backward chaining by asking you to apply the process to a small example.

In the same three-rule knowledge base as we used in the previous activity we add the data:

```
John is a third year student.
```

What does the system do immediately?

What does the system do when we ask the following question:

```
Is there anyone who will look at job adverts?
```

Feedback 8

You should have been able to recognise that in backward chaining, because the system is goal driven, the system would do nothing at all until it was asked a question, i.e., provided with a goal to seek or a hypothesis to test.

When asked the question

```
Is there anyone who will look at job adverts?
```

the system would try to answer it. The first step would be to search either for a fact that gives the answer directly, or for a rule by which the answer could be inferred. To find such a rule, it searches the entire knowledge base for rules whose conclusions, if made true, will answer the question.

In this example, there are no facts directly giving the answer; there's one rule whose conclusion, if true, would supply an answer: Rule 3.

The system next checks the Rule 3's conditions. Is there anyone who needs a job? As with the original question, we look either for a fact that answers directly, or for a rule. There are no facts, but Rule 1 is relevant.

So we now check its conditions. Is there a third year student? This time, there is a fact that answers this: John is a third year student. So we've proved Rule 1, and by doing so also proved Rule 3, and that answers the original question.

But what if we did not know that John is a third year student. If no rule provides this as a conclusion and this is not currently known, then backward chaining systems will ask the user for an answer. Backward chaining systems will therefore engage in a dialogue with the user.

In the example above, backward chaining resolved the specific goal only—it did not determine that John lives on campus as this was not relevant. Forward chaining would find every possible conclusion.

Forward and backward chaining are inference methods, literally to try to infer from a set of rules what conclusion can be reached, or to infer whether or not a hypothesis is true given the rules available.

Activity 9

Forward chaining systems are said to be *data driven*, while backward chaining systems are said to be *goal driven*.

How else might this distinction be described?
Forward chaining systems
Backward chaining systems

Feedback 9

Forward chaining systems start with known data and then fire those rules in a specific order to infer new information.

Backward chaining systems start with a goal and then try and match given rules to that solution obtaining data as required.

So forward chaining systems work from the data given to them, while backward chaining systems work from the specified goal.

Activity 10

Below are some situations where forward chaining may be used within an ES. Suggest at least one example of each of these situations.

Suggest one situation in which forward chaining would not be used.

Obtain all the outputs that can be concluded about a set of data.
Many conclusions are possible from a single data item.
Situations where it is important to communicate new conclusions to a user in a
   timely manner.

Feedback 10

Possible examples of forward chaining are given below.

Obtain all the outputs that can be concluded about a set of data.
- Monitoring for mechanical problems on a production line. In this type of situation, there will be sensors or gauges that automatically collect such data without special arrangements having to be made. It is possible that more than one fault may appear at the same time.
- Scanning a new loan application for problem areas. Several different problems may appear in the same application.

Many conclusions are possible from a single data item.
- A fall in temperature can be caused by many different environmental factors including rain, nightfall, increase in cloud cover, etc. The data must be checked to find out which situation is correct.

Situations where it is important to communicate new conclusions to a user in a timely manner.
- Advice to shut down faulty machines—such as a nuclear power plant.
- Data entry errors.

Uses of Backward Chaining

The table below shows the circumstances under which you might use backward chaining.

Reason for backward chaining	Examples
There is a clear set of statements, which must be confirmed or denied.	Is machine one causing the quality control problem?
A large number of questions could be asked of the user, but typically only a few are necessary to resolve a situation.	When processing of a motor claim for vandalism; it is not necessary to know about personal injuries.
It is desirable to have interactive dialogue with the user.	Asking machine operator detailed questions about suspect machinery.
Rule execution depends on data gathering which may be expensive or difficult.	Real-time observations by the user.

Comparison of Forward and Backward Chaining

The following factors will help you consider the choice between a forward or backward chaining ES.

Factor	Reason
The logical reasoning process.	Some processes naturally use forward chaining logic, e.g. using errors in computer systems to determine the cause of the error.
What are the inputs and where do they come from?	Where there are few inputs but many outputs, then forward chaining will be more efficient.
What are the outputs and where to they go?	Where there are few outputs, then backward chaining is more appropriate.
Hypothesis driven.	Backward chaining is relatively efficient where hypotheses are involved.

Examples of Forward and Backward Chaining

The table below provides some examples of forward and backward chaining.

Use forward chaining	Use backward chaining
Sensor indicates machine failure; need to find out what happens next.	Defect observed in product; need to locate faulty machine.
User types erroneous input for insurance claim; need to alert user.	Suspect an overpayment on an insurance claim; need to check form for erroneous input.
Stock value suddenly drops; need to predict market responses.	FTSE industrials drop; need to know if a particular stock will be affected.

Note: FTSE: Financial Times Stock Exchange Index.

Now that you have learned about the techniques involved in the development of KBSs, it is worth being alerted to some of the main problems that can emerge in the actual building stage.

Self-Assessment Questions

Question 1

You are designing a KBS to diagnose faults in a nuclear power station. The plant operators wish to know everything possible about the state of the plant at any given time. Which of the following inference mechanisms would you use for this and why?

- Forward chaining
- Backward chaining.

Question 2

The citizens advice bureau want a KBS to advise clients whether or not they are entitled to housing benefit. Which of the following inference mechanisms would you use for this and why?

- Forward chaining
- Backward chaining.

Answer to Self-Assessment Questions

Answer 1

Due to the possibility of there being more than one problem, and that all possible problems need to be checked, forward chaining would have to be used. Clearly, this will require that all facts about the plant's current status are obtained in order that the system can give an overall diagnosis. However, this input is probably automatic so even though a lot of processing will have to be done by the computer it is not time consuming for the operators.

Answer 2

The system is trying to find out if a fact is true or not, i.e., is the client entitled to housing benefit 'yes' or 'no'.

If backward chaining were used the system would ask only the questions needed to determine the required answer. These facts can be gained while the system is running.

If forward chaining were used all the data would need to be collected up-front. This may require the client to answer many questions that are not relevant to the specified goal. For example, when considering other benefits the system may need to know about the client's disability status but this may not be relevant when considering the specified goal. Therefore the use of forward chaining could result in many facts being gathered which are never used. Processing an application would become a time consuming and inefficient process.

SECTION 3: DEVELOPING RULE-BASED SYSTEMS

Introduction

In this section you will learn about some of the difficulties of developing rule-based systems and how these can be avoided or overcome.

Objectives

By the end of the section you will be able to:

- identify the main problems in developing rule-based systems
- evaluate the role of explanation facilities in KBSs
- describe the process of evaluating KBSs
- describe the process of validating KBSs.

Main Problems in Building a KBS

Two of the main problems to avoid in building a KBS are:

- lack of explanation facilities
- brittleness.

Explanation Facilities

Explanation facilities are provided within an ES to explain to the user of that system how decisions have been made by the system, i.e., why particular rules have been applied. They are therefore a key part of any ES, with research showing (Wolverton, 1995) that users place significant reliance on explanation facilities.

The need for explanation facilities may appear to be obvious. Humans like to understand why they are being given advice by an expert so that they can see why certain courses of action have been recommended and they can see problems associated with other alternative actions. The output from ESs must therefore provide a similar level of explanation.

However, explanations provided by an ES may not be as detailed as those provided by a human expert. The latter has access to a significant amount of knowledge outside their area of expertise. The ES, on the other hand, only has knowledge in a very specific subject domain. Answers and explanations provided by the system may well be limited because those answers cannot be related to any wider context. Similarly, explanations will be limited where the knowledge base does not provide sufficient detail in the specific subject domain.

Rule Tracing

Rules within a knowledge base can be checked in two ways to ensure that the ES is providing the correct solutions to queries.

- A how trace enables the user to find out how an ES has arrived at a conclusion.
- A why trace helps the user understand why a particular question is being asked.

While both traces provide the user with some feedback on how the ES is working, they also suffer from the issue of simply providing a chain of reasoning. In other words, the traces simply link a problem and a solution—the ES can explain why a particular conclusion was reached but does not necessarily know why the appropriate rules were in the knowledge base in the first place. The system can state IF something THEN something else happens, but not why those events are linked— providing the 'why' sometimes calls for deeper knowledge and understanding.

Building Explanation Text into an ES

Explanation text can be built into the ES to help the user understand the outputs provided. For example, take the situation of a valve regulating water flow illustrated in Figure 4.1.

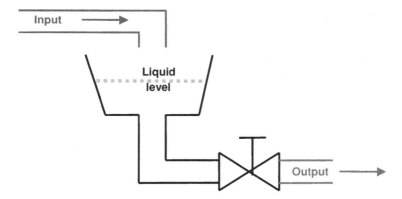

FIGURE 4.1. Valve regulating water flow.

When the valve is opened, then water will escape from the system.

A question and answer that can be built into the system could be:

Q. What happens to the water level when the value is opened a little more?
A. It will go down.

To check the logic in this statement, additional explanation can be added:

Q. Why?
A. Because the output flow will be larger than the input flow

Q. Why?

A. Because more water will be released through the output pipe

Q. Why will more water be released through the output pipe?

A. Because opening the valve widens the hole, letting more water through

Q. Why does this happen?...

Having placed these explanations into the system, questions can be asked such as:

How did you arrive at that answer?

The ES can then provide the rule explanations to show how the answer was derived.

For example:

User. What happens to the water level when the valve is opened?
ES. The water level will go down.
User. How do you know this?
ES. Because I applied Rule 46 which states when the valve opens, more water will be released. I then applied Rule 47 which states when more water is released then the water level will fall.

Activity 11

Here are four rules from an ES that is used to determine whether or not to turn on a heater.

R1: IF door_open AND dark THEN ADD cold
R2: IF breezy THEN ADD door_open
R3: IF cold THEN ADD start_heater AND close_door
R4: IF close_door THEN DELETE door_open

It is currently breezy and dark.

Write out a possible response from the ES in answer to the question.

Why did you apply Rule 2 first?

Feedback 11

The expert system, explaining why it applied Rule 2 first, would have given an explanation similar to the following:

'I was trying to determine whether or not a heater needs to be turned on. From the information available, I know that it is breezy, so I need to check whether or not a door is open as this is one of the reasons for cold'.

If the system was backward chaining, then it would apply Rule 3 first. If it was forward chaining, then it would apply Rule 2 first simply because it is the only applicable rule.

Dangers of Unintelligent Explanations

Many ES shells support IF.... THEN.... BECAUSE rules, e.g.

IF you are cold
THEN turn on a heater
BECAUSE this will warm you up

If an ES recommended turning on a heater and the user asked for a justification of this then the 'BECAUSE' part of the rule could be displayed to explain the recommendation. However, this is just some text that is regurgitated on demand. There s no 'intelligence' behind this justification. In particular there is no mechanism to ensure that this recommendation is appropriate to your individual circumstances. The system would still display the same justification if you were standing in a swimming costume at the North Pole! Clearly in such a situation better advice would be to put on warm clothing.

While explanation texts are useful, there are various dangers to be avoided in writing them.

- As systems grow in apparent intelligence they are given more responsibility. Care must be taken not to place too much trust in the ES; the user is still responsible for checking any ES answer for reasonableness.
- Adding poor quality or simplistic explanation facilities can inspire undue confidence in a system that does not warrant it. This may mislead the user into taking incorrect decisions.
- The apparent intelligence may vastly exceed the true level of understanding. It can be too easy for users to rely on the system believing that it is infallible. Of course, the ES is only as good as its rule base, and if this is incorrect, then solutions from the system will also be wrong. Poor quality explanation facilities may encourage the user to accept erroneous recommendations.

Brittleness

Brittleness is a property displayed by a KBS, where the *apparent* level of intelligence exceeds the *true* level of intelligence. The system may appear to be producing appropriate answers however when the problem to be solved requires knowledge not contained within the system it will not be able to solve the problem. Worse still the system may not recognise the limitations of its knowledge and will then propose a faulty solution. This situation can be made worse by the inclusion of an unintelligent explanation facility which will encourage the user to accept the faulty output.

Activity 12

This activity will help you apply your understanding of the concept of brittleness in a KBS to an actual example.

Consider a medical KBS in which brittleness is a characteristic of the knowledge base. What type of problems might emerge in relation to its responses to diagnosis questions?

What might a human doctor do when faced with a failure of their 'knowledge base'?

Feedback 12

You should have been able to recognise that the dangers associated with brittleness in a medical ES include:
- The system will fail to diagnose disorders that were unknown when its knowledge base was developed.
- It could reach the wrong diagnosis and try to justify it.

Hopefully, a human doctor will recognise the limits of their own knowledge and will seek help. In other words a human overcomes brittleness by:
- remembering previous situations
- reasoning from analogous situations
- using general knowledge
- learning more about the current problem.

It is relatively difficult to build all these features into an ES. Recent work on defining ontologies is helping to overcome the problem of brittleness. By defining an ontology the limits of knowledge contained within a system can be specified and thus it is possible that an ES could also recognise the limitations of its knowledge base (theoretically at least).

We should perhaps note that brittleness does not imply that a system was faulty when developed. An ES may have been able to diagnose every known ailment with 100% accuracy. However, as new ailments and treatments are discovered it is possible that the system will be used to diagnose patients with these disorders and it will then fail to do so as knowledge of these disorders is not included in the knowledge base.

The remainder of this section is devoted to the subject of evaluation and validation of KBSs. It must be stressed at the outset that you do not build a KBS *then* evaluate and validate it; these activities must be carried out as ongoing parts of the development process itself.

Evaluation of KBS

Evaluation of a KBS is an attempt to assess the overall value of the KBS. Evaluation of a KBS means checking, not only that the KBS has acceptable performance levels, but also that the system is useable, efficient and cost-effective.

The evaluation of a KBS involves two more terms, namely validation and verification.

- Validation measures the performance of the KBS. In effect, the output from the system is compared to the output that would be provided by an expert. A check is then made to ensure that the system is performing to an acceptable level of accuracy.
- Verification is checking that the KBS has been built correctly, i.e., that the rules are logical and consistent with the knowledge obtained via the knowledge acquisition process.

Evaluation is therefore part of the overall quality control procedures in building a KBS.

The Need for Evaluation

Evaluation of KBS is required in general terms to ensure that knowledge of the real world has been correctly entered into the knowledge base of the KBS.

Activity 13
In this activity you will explore the types of verification available in a number of knowledge engineering tools.

Search the Internet for reference to the tools below and make brief notes about the validation and checking function of any three:

Tool	Function
COMMET	
ONCOCIN RULE CHECKER	
KB-REDUCER	
COVADIS	

Feedback 13

COMMET ONCOCIN RULE CHECKER	Syntactic checking of the representation. detects the following issues on attribute-value rule bases: • conflict • redundancy • subsumption • missing rules. Rules are grouped by their concluding attribute, forming a table for each group. Verification issues are tested on each table by static comparison of rules. Inconsistencies and redundancies requiring more than two rules to occur cannot be detected. This problem is solved in KB-REDUCER and COVADIS.
KB-REDUCER	detects inconsistencies and redundancies in forward chaining and propositional rule bases.
COVADIS	detects inconsistencies in forward chaining and propositional rule bases.

There are three layers of distortion that can occur during this knowledge transfer procedure, as shown in Figure 4.2.

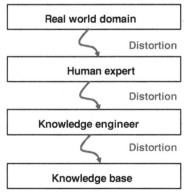

FIGURE 4.2. Distortion in the knowledge transfer process.

Activity 14

This activity draws on your previous knowledge of communication (human to human and computer network) and systems development to help you identify sources of distortion in the knowledge transfer process.

Complete the table below with suggestions of where distortion might appear at the various interfaces in the knowledge transfer process.

Interface	Cause of distortion
Real world domain—human expert	
Human expert—knowledge engineer	
Knowledge engineer—knowledge base	

Feedback 14

You should have been able to identify some of the following possible causes of distortion:

Interface	Cause of distortion
Real world domain—human expert	Distortion may occur between the real world domain and the human expert because the expert does not fully understand the real world context of their (possibly theoretical) knowledge. This can occur where the expert does not have the depth of *experience* in a particular domain, or where the knowledge in that domain changes frequently and the expert has difficulty keeping up to date.
Human expert—knowledge engineer	Further distortion occurs when the knowledge engineer attempts to elicit knowledge from the human expert. The engineer may not have sufficient knowledge of the domain, or the expert may not fully explain elements of the domain sufficiently well, resulting in an incomplete record of the domain.
Knowledge engineer—knowledge base	Finally, the knowledge engineer may incorrectly record the domain knowledge into the rule base of the KBS. The knowledge engineer may not realise this has happened, either because the elicited knowledge was incorrect in the first place, or due to lack of skill resulting in conflicting rules not being recognised.

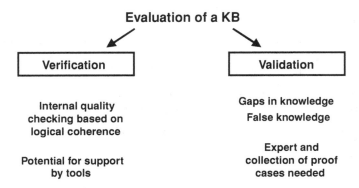

FIGURE 4.3. Evaluation of a knowledge base.

Validation and verification help to find these distortions in knowledge in various ways. Figure 4.3 shows some of the objectives of each method.

Activity 15
Consider how the distortion between the knowledge engineer and the knowledge base can be decreased or eliminated?

Feedback 15
There needs to be some method of checking that knowledge within the knowledge base is correct. The quickest method is to ask the human expert to check the knowledge in the knowledge base by asking the KBS questions and checking the responses. This process actually removes distortion caused by knowledge transfer from the expert down to the knowledge base itself.

Verification

Verification of a KBS is likely to involve checks for the following:

- Syntactic coherence—to check that all objects in the KB are correctly defined with respect to the inference engine.
- Logical coherence—to detect logical contradictions.
- Contextual coherence—to check that the KB is consistent with the model of the problem.

Examples of the type of errors that verification of the KBS is trying to identify are as follows.

Subsumed Rules

These occur when two rules have the same conclusion but one rule has additional conditions. For example,

Rule 1. IF A AND B AND C THEN X
Rule 2. IF A AND B THEN X

Rule 1 is subsumed within Rule 2 and could automatically be eliminated from the knowledge base without affecting its reasoning. However, the knowledge acquisition process should really be checked to confirm which of the two rules are correct.

Both rules cannot be logically correct; Rule 1 is incorrect if C is not necessary. If it is necessary, Rule 2 is incorrect.

Unnecessary IF Conditions

This situation occurs when the conclusions of two rules are the same and, except for one, the conditions of the rules are the same and this condition is reversed. For example,

Rule 1. IF the patient has pink spots AND has a fever THEN the patient has measles.
Rule 2. IF the patient has pink spots AND does not have a fever THEN the patient has measles.

These two rules could be combined to form one simpler rule....

Rule 3. IF the patient has pink spots THEN the patient has measles.

However, once again the source of the two rules should be checked and the appropriate rules amended or deleted.

Validation

In general terms, validation of a KBS involves ensuring that the work domain is correctly linked to and reflected in the knowledge domain. Checking this link means:

• defining the work domain (normally carried out at the beginning of the KBS project)
• defining the proof cases to use
• deciding how many proof cases to use.

Proof cases test the KBS by ensuring that the results from the KBS conform to the results already predicted by the human expert. The KBS will be validated where the proof cases match those of the human expert.

The number of proof cases required depends on variables such as the number of rules in the KBS and the accuracy required from the outputs. As the number of rules and the accuracy required increases, the number of proof cases also increases.

Validation may also involve checking the output from the KBS to some pre-defined measures such as:

- Accuracy—how well the system reflects reality
- Adequacy—how much of the required knowledge is included within the knowledge base
- Realism—whether the KBS provides realistic solutions
- Sensitivity—how changes in the knowledge base affect the quality of outputs
- Usefulness—how useful the outputs are for solving problems
- Validity—whether the outputs can be used to make accurate predictions.

The precise validation tests may vary according to the KBS being tested.

Standards in KBS Development

Using validation and verification controls will help to ensure that the finished KBS meets its objectives, and check that the knowledge base is providing correct answers to problems.

There are other factors which have contributed to the adoption of standards for the general software development process, i.e., including:

- The organisation producing the software needs to provide users with quality software that operates satisfactorily.
- The need to develop software within the constraints of time, money and available staff.
- The finished product must be at an acceptable level.
- The product must be easy to maintain, so documentation is an important area which must be addressed by any standards.

In 1991, only 13% of organisations claimed to use any formal or semi-formal method to validate their KBS. Methods being used were:

- Qualitative modelling
- Induction
- Customer satisfaction
- Regression testing
- Conventional testing
- In-house methods.

This was a relatively low percentage, although it probably related to the lack of experience in producing KBS at that time. Hopefully, the percentage of projects being validated has increased significantly since then, although there is a lack of empirical evidence to support this hope.

Another method of software validation is to use the International Standards Organisation standard 9003-3, which relates to software development generally (see Figure 4.4).

Quality system framework		Quality system lifecycle	.	Quality system support	
1 Management responsibility	5	Contract reviews	14	Configuration management	
2 Quality system	6	Purchaser requirements	15	Document control	
3 Internal quality audits	7	Development planning	16	Quality records	
4 Corrective action	8	Quality planning	17	Measurement	
	9	Design and implementation	18	Rules, practices and conventions	
	10	Testing and validation	19	Tools and techniques	
	11	Acceptance	20	Purchasing	
	12	Replication, delivery and installation	21	Included software product	
	13	Maintenance	22	Training	

FIGURE 4.4. The ISO9003-3 standard.

While this standard is not directed specifically at KBS, KBS and other application software share most of the development process. Application of the ISO 9000-3 will therefore help to provide quality KBSs.

The last area of quality to mention is the provision of appropriate documentation to allow the system to be used effectively. Documentation should be provided in three areas:

- The knowledge acquisition process should be adequately documented with transcripts of interviews, etc. If this is done then the source of individual items of knowledge contained within the ES can be identified and the knowledge can then be checked.
- User documentation so users understand how to use the KBS.
- Technical documentation so that the KBS can be amended by another software developer if required. The technical documentation is likely to be quite detailed and be much more extensive than the user documentation.

Summary

This section has explained how knowledge can be placed into ESs using rules. You also learned how chaining is used to determine results or prove a hypothesis from that knowledge. Finally, you learned about some of the problems associated with explanation and brittleness in KBSs as well as how KBSs can be evaluated and validated.

Self-Assessment Questions

Question 1

Using an ES

Try and find an ES on the Internet and then determine what sort of chaining is being used within that system. Explain your answer.

If you are not sure where to start looking for a system, you could try www.firstdirect.co.uk. This is an on-line banking site for the provision of various financial services such as mortgages, bank accounts, etc. There are some very simple ESs being used on this page, such as a mortgage calculator and application form to join the bank.

You might also try the ESTA system.

Other similar sites will also have this type of system available.

Question 2

A KBS is commissioned to diagnose spillages in a chemical factory. The system works for 2 years with 100% accuracy. During those 2 years the factory expands the range of chemicals it produces and starts to produce and store some extremely strong acids. At some stage an accident occurs, as they always do, and one of these acids is split. The cleaner follows the correct protocol and uses the KBS to diagnose the spillage before cleaning it up. The KBS is not aware of these new acids and incorrectly diagnoses the spillage. The cleaner follows the instructions given but as a consequence of the misdiagnosis is badly hurt.

Consider your answers to the following questions:

(a) Consider the following options and decide what caused this problem:

- The system wasn't validated
- The KBS was brittle
- The KBS was not verified.

(b) Is this a fault of the knowledge engineer who developed the system in the first place?
(c) What could have been done to prevent this problem?

Answers to Self-Assessment Questions

Answer 1

Most banking sites are trying to determine whether or not you are a good credit risk—that is, that you can manage your money correctly without going overdrawn. It is likely that both backward and forward chaining is being used.

There is a definite goal to the credit application—so backward chaining can be used to check from this goal to ensure that all necessary data has been obtained. In this situation, the data refers to a person's name, address, etc. Each item of data scores so many points, and a critical number of points will be needed to obtain specific services from the bank.

However, where the goal is not achieved, other evidence may be available to check the person's status—so forward chaining could be used to determine what information has already been obtained, and what additional information will be needed to meet the goal. For example, if a person has recently moved jobs or to a new address, then additional evidence (perhaps last address or detailed employment history) will be needed to 'top up' the points to reach the goal number.

Answer 2

(a) This is an example of a brittle system. The system worked perfectly when it was developed but when it was used to solve a problem outside of its knowledge the system failed.

(b) The knowledge engineer developed a system that was working with 100% accuracy when installed—it was only later that the system failed as the circumstances it was working in changed. Still in today's litigious society that may not prevent the knowledge engineer from being sued. So what could they have done to legally protect themselves? The best protection the knowledge engineer has is to demonstrate that they developed the system following a professional methodology and to a professional standard and that the process was documented. Thus, if the system was properly validated and this was documented the documentation would show that the system was working well when the system was installed. Further the knowledge within the system would also be documented and this would indicate which chemicals the system could correctly diagnose. Management at the chemical factory were then, one presumes, made aware that if new chemicals were stored on site the knowledge in the system would need to be updated to cover these.

(c) One way of preventing this accident would have been to develop an ontology within the KBS. If the system understood what chemicals it could diagnose then it could have checked the list of chemicals stored at the factory against this ontology. Knowing that new chemicals were stored at the factory the KBS could have refused to attempt a diagnosis as it would then know that its knowledge base was inadequate.

SECTION 4: SEMANTIC NETWORKS

Introduction

This section introduces semantic networks and their use within KBSs.

Objectives

By the end of this section you will be able to:

• explain how semantic networks represent data
• discuss the advantages and disadvantages of semantic networks.

Knowledge Representation in Semantic Networks

One of the oldest and easiest to understand knowledge representation schemes is the Semantic Net, which is a graphical representation of knowledge that shows objects and their relationships.

In these networks, objects are shown by nodes, and links between the nodes describe the relationship between two objects, for example,

• Mary is an instance of trainer, and trainer is a type of consultant.
• A trainer trains a programmer and a programmer is an employee.
• Joe is an instance of programmer.

From this we can clearly see the relationship that may exist between Mary and Joe.

Activity 16
This activity will help you begin to visualise a semantic network.

Draw a diagram representing the relationships between Mary and Joe, indicating, in the process, the relationship between a trainer, consultant, programmer and employee.

Feedback 16
Your diagram should be similar to this:

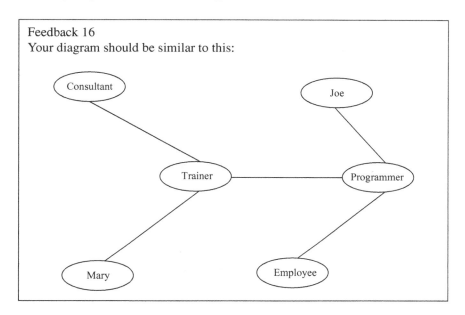

Such a diagram is the beginning of a semantic network but this can be improved by more closely defining the nature of the relationships.

Activity 17
This activity shows you how to describe the relationships in a semantic network.
1. Identify which lines on the diagram might be labelled 'is_a', i.e., to indicate that object A is an instance of object B.
2. Apply the labels to your diagram.
3. Decide on an appropriate label for the line that should not be labelled with this relationship.
4. Apply an arrowhead to the lines to indicate the direction of the 'is_a' relationship.

Feedback 17
Your diagram should now look like this:

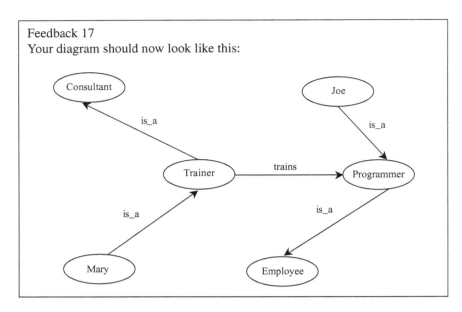

Semantic networks are a powerful and flexible graphical way of representing knowledge. They are often used as a communication tool between the knowledge engineer and the expert during the knowledge acquisition phase of a project.

Inheritance

Inheritance is concerned with how one object inherits the properties of another object.

Activity 18
This activity helps you grasp the concept of inheritance.

In the diagram you created in the previous activities, identify from which classes Mary and Joe inherit properties.

Feedback 18
You should have been able to recognise that Mary, in being a trainer, inherits the properties of the consultant class and that Joe, in being a programmer, inherits the properties of the employee class.

It is possible to describe this graphical representation of knowledge simply and precisely and this will help to achieve the objectives of the semantic network as a

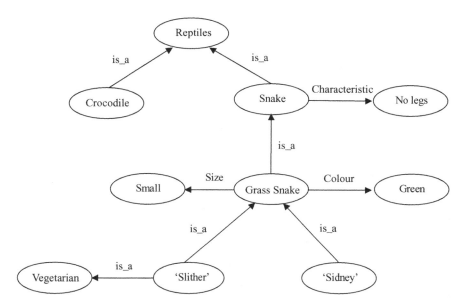

FIGURE 4.5. A graphical representation of a semantic network.

store of knowledge for use by a KBS. The hierarchical nature of the diagram helps explain the elements of the network. For example, in Figure 4.5., Grass Snakes are a sub-class of the total class of reptiles—so all grass snakes must be reptiles. Similarly, both Slither and Sidney are grass snakes. As the class of grass snakes also has properties of Small and Green, then Sidney and Slither must be small and green as they belong to this class. However, Slither is a vegetarian, so this attribute applies to Slither only (grass snakes are normally carnivores).

However, the very simplicity of the semantic network means that it can actually be too flexible, i.e., there are too many ways to represent something. This can lead to extreme complexity when representing exceptional cases, e.g. if Sidney was not green due to some illness.

Activity 19
Look at the following diagram.

What conclusions might you draw about what slither eats?

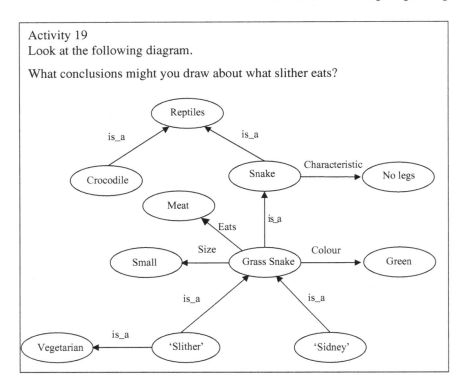

Feedback 19
You should have been able to recognise that from this semantic network it would be possible to conclude that the grass snake Slither is a vegetarian *and* Slither eats meat. Clearly, these conclusions are contradictory. Which conclusion we reach *depends where in the network we start and which links we follow*. This process is unreliable.

Thus, to perform inference using a semantic network you must understand the meaning of the links and follow the correct links. As the links can be many, and varied, performing inference using a semantic network is complex and unreliable.

Representing Exception Data

When exception data (e.g. Slither is yellow) is stored on a semantic network it can quickly become large, cluttered and difficult to read.

Reasoning with Semantic Networks

Semantic networks can be very difficult to reason from, as an inference engine must understand what type of link exists between nodes within the semantic network, and there are no constraints on allowable links.

To understand the semantic network that describes Slither, you need to understand the links, i.e., the words 'is_a', 'eats', 'vegetarian', etc. If an inference engine were to reason with this network, then it must have some understanding of these words and this is difficult to build in.

Semantic networks are particularly good at representing knowledge in the form of hierarchies. They can also represent complex causal relationships—though the diagrams can become large and complex. Their explicit links and visual diagrams can make knowledge quite clear. Much of the reasoning with semantic networks is in the form of deducing *indirect* links between concepts based on *direct* links explicitly stated. This is difficult for an inference engine to achieve in practice however, because it needs to understand the links and the conclusions depend on successfully searching the network. For this reason, semantic networks are often used only as a communication tool between the knowledge engineer and the domain expert and after the knowledge has been obtained it is then converted into another format that is easier to process.

Advantages of Semantic Networks

The advantages of semantic networks to represent knowledge include:

• They tend to be a powerful and adaptable method of representing knowledge because many different types of object can be included in the network.
• The network is graphical and therefore relatively easy to understand.
• Can be used as a common communication tool between the knowledge engineer and the human expert during the knowledge acquisition phase of designing an ES.

Disadvantages of Semantic Networks

The disadvantages of using semantic networks to represent knowledge include:

• It can be difficult to show all the different inference situations using a network.
• They are less reliable than other knowledge representation techniques because inferring becomes a process of searching across the diagram.
• Diagrams can become very complex.
• The wide range of possible kinds of links and the ways they might combine to form indirect linkages, plus the large number of concepts usually included in a

semantic network make this form of representation susceptible to a combinatorial explosion.

- Semantic networks have difficulty associating procedural knowledge with the facts represented by the network and, since they lack any means of bundling-related facts into associated clusters, usually result in a proliferation of many different concepts and linkages producing a complex representation that may require extensive search operations to reach conclusions.

Limitations of Semantic Networks

Semantic networks as a representation of knowledge have been in use in Artificial Intelligence for many years. Some of the earliest uses of a nodes-and-links approach were in the work of Quillian (1968) and Winston (1975), where semantic networks were used as models of associative memory. Quillian (1968) focused on how natural language is understood and the capturing of meaning by a machine. Winston (1975) focused on machine learning and structural descriptions of an environment.

Creations and uses of semantic networks have led to a number of epistemological problems, which numerous researchers have attempted to address these problems. Barr and Feigenbaum state that:

In semantic network representations, there is no formal semantics, no agreed-upon notion of what a given representational structure means, as there is in logic, for instance.

Semantic networks do tend to rely upon the procedures that manipulate them.

The system is limited by the user's understanding of the meanings of the links in a semantic network. Links between nodes are not all alike in function or form. We therefore need to differentiate between links that assert some relationship and links that are structural in nature.

Summary

In this section you have learned about the role of semantic networks in knowledge representation. In the process, you discovered the limitations of such an approach and why semantic networks can be used as a communication tool between the knowledge engineer and the domain expert.

Current Research Links

Semantic Research

http://www.semanticresearch.com/

Concept Maps as Hypermedia Components

http://ksi.cpsc.ucalgary.ca/articles/ConceptMaps/CM.html#Abstract

Plumb Design Visual Thesaurus

http://www.plumbdesign.com/products/thinkmap

The Combination of Hypertext and Semantic Networks for the Representation of Knowledge

http://www.datafoundry.com/semantic.htm

Scientific American: The Semantic Web

http://www.sciam.com/article.cfm?articleID=00048144-10D2-1C70-84A9809EC588EF21

Semantic Networks, Concept Maps, Knowledge, Knowledge Representation

http://www.ipli.com/semantic.htm

Using Semantic Networks as a Mindtool

http://www.conroe.isd.tenet.edu/educ/pub_htm/Pub_htm/DOCS/MINDTOOL/SEMANTIC.HTM

Semantic and Real Networks: Does Browsing Make Sense?

http://perso.wanadoo.fr/universimmedia/nohi/enohip2.htm

Self-Assessment Question

Read the article in Scientific American about 'The Semantic Web' at: http://www.sciam.com/article.cfm?articleID=00048144-10D2-1C70-84A9809EC588EF21.

Comment, with examples, on the accuracy of the sentence in the first paragraph under the heading knowledge representation that reads:

Knowledge representation, as this technology is often called, is currently in a state comparable to that of hypertext before the advent of the Web: it is clearly a good idea, and some very nice demonstrations exist, but it has not yet changed the world. It contains the seeds of important applications, but to realise its full potential it must be linked to a single global system.

Quote freely from the article in your answer if appropriate.

Answer to Self-Assessment Question

You may have referred to such characteristics of current knowledge representation technology as:

- the limiting of the questions that can be asked in order to allow the computer to answer reliably, or at all
- the centralisation involving the requirement to share exactly the same definition.

On the other hand, you may have noted the potential improvements claimed for approaches incorporating XML, RDF, URIs, etc.

SECTION 5: FRAMES

Introduction

This section provides an introduction to how knowledge can be represented in ESs using frames.

Objectives

By the end of the section you will be able to:

- explain how frames can be used to represent knowledge
- describe how ontologies can be used to represent knowledge.

Frames

Frames are a simplified version of a semantic network where only 'is_a' relationships apply.

Frames provide a method of storing knowledge, collecting specific information about one object in an ES. In essence they allow both data and procedures to be included within one structure.

An example frame for a coffee mug object can be drawn as follows:

Coffee mug FRAME	
IS_A	Mug
COLOUR	
CAN_HOLD_LIQUID	True
NUMBER_OF-HANDLES	Default = 1
SIZE	Range: Small, Medium, Large
PURPOSE	Value : drinking coffee
COST	Demon (£ needed)
MATERIAL	Default = pottery

Within that structure, slots (i.e., rows) can:

- store details of each data object
- provide links to other frames

- contain procedural code, linking to other applications to obtain data or write data
- indicate whether or not certain properties of each object are needed within that frame.

In practice, three different types of slots are used:

1. Named slots having a standard filler value of certain data items. For example, the slot for number_of_wheels in a car frame will have a default value of four. This can be overwritten where the specific type of car being described (such as a three-wheel car) does not meet this default value. Range values can also be specified, e.g. the size must be small, medium or large.
2. Slots showing relationships using the term IS_A. For example, a car is a motor vehicle. The IS_A motor vehicle slot will therefore link the frame for car with a frame describing the basic features of a motor vehicle.
3. Slots contain procedural code. For example, the number of miles that a car can travel, i.e., its range, is determined by the current petrol stored in its tank and by the engine size. The slot for range can therefore store procedural code to calculate the range (if needed) based on the slots for current_petrol and engine_size. This procedural code is called a demon (in this case an if_needed demon) and is activated automatically if a value for range is needed.

Activity 20

Complete the following frame for a car based on the information provided above. Remember that cars are available in a range of sizes and that they are part of the overall set of motor vehicles.

Car FRAME

IS_A
MANUFACTURER
CAN_TRAVEL_ON_ROADS
NUMBER_OF-WHEELS
SIZE
PETROL_TANK_CAPACITY
CURRENT_FUEL
ENGINE_SIZE
RANGE

```
Feedback 20
                              Car FRAME
IS_A                          Motor_vehicle
MANUFACTURER
CAN_TRAVEL_ON_ROADS           True
NUMBER_OF-WHEELS              Default = 4
SIZE                          Range: Small, medium, large
PETROL_TANK_CAPACITY
CURENT_FUEL
ENGINE_SIZE
RANGE                         If_needed:  Calculate  from  current_
                              fuel and engine_size
```

Levels Within Frames

The levels of information within frames are:
- The highest level in a frame is literally FRAME, which stores the name of the specific frame.
- Below this there are SLOTS, with each slot providing information on one of the attributes of that frame.
- Within the slot, the FACET provides detail on each attribute. This detail may include a value, ranges that can be applied to the attribute, default values or calculated values including demons.
- Finally, the DATA provides specific information about each *attribute*, such as the NUMBER_OF_WHEELS being 4 in a frame describing a motor vehicle.

Inheritance

One of the main advantages of using frames is the principle of inheritance. This means that frames can inherit the attributes of other frames, in a hierarchical structure. For example, a frame for a cup can provide some basic attributes in a number of slots about that object. These attributes can be given to other objects that share those attributes.

Figure 4.6 shows the attributes of a mug being applied to two other drinking receptacles, namely a tea mug and a coffee mug.

FIGURE 4.6. Mug frames.

The Mug FRAME provides some detail on mugs. These slots can then be used in the Coffee mug and Tea mug frames.

Using the idea of inheritance, the objects lower in the hierarchy automatically inherit the contents of the corresponding slots, unless this data is overwritten, e.g. tea mugs store tea (not just an unspecified liquid). The default value for number of handles is inherited and not over written as most Tea mugs have one handle. This may over written lower down the hierarchy of frames when we define a frame for Fred's mug. Initially in this frame the slot for NUMBER_OF_HANDLES would contain an inherited default value, and therefore we may assume that Fred's mug has one handle. However, as the ES runs we may find out that this specific mug is very large and has two handles—at this point the appropriate slot in this frame would have a specific value stored in it over riding the inherited default value.

Activity 21
Use the Motor Vehicles frame (below) and the information specified to complete a three-wheeled Car frame.

Three-wheeled cars are manufactured by 'Smith's'. They have 1.1 litres engines and have a maximum speed of 100 kilometres per hour.

	Motor Vehicle FRAME
CAN_TRAVEL_ON_ROADS	True
NUMBER_OF-WHEELS	Default = 4

> Feedback 21
>
> Three-wheeled Car FRAME
>
> | | |
> |---|---|
> | IS_A | Motor Vehicle |
> | MANUFACTURER | Smith's |
> | CAN_TRAVEL_ON_ROADS | True (inherited from car frame) |
> | NUMBER_OF-WHEELS | 3 |
> | ENGINE_SIZE | 1.1 litres |
> | Maximum Speed | 100 kilometres per hour |
>
> Remember that the NUMBER_OF_WHEELS slot does not take on the default value in this situation but is overwritten with the new value of 3.

Advantages of Using Frames

The advantages of using frames are that they can:

- be represented in the form of a table, making the information easy to read and assimilate.
- store default values. So where a frame has an IS_A slot, that frame is linked to another frame containing generic information for a particular group of frames. The generic information is used to fill slots in the frame, rather than having to enter all of these manually.
- use default values in the reasoning process. If later, the default value is found to be incorrect, then the system can overwrite the default value and then run through its reasoning again to see if this changes any conclusions it reached earlier. In this way, frames can be used to mimic default reasoning, which humans often use.
- be structured hierarchically and thus allow easy classification of knowledge.
- reduce complexity by allowing a hierarchy of frames to be built up.
- clearly document information using common formats and syntax.
- combine procedural and declarative knowledge using one knowledge representation scheme.
- constrain allowed values, or allow values to be entered within a specific range.
- enable demons to be specified that when triggered perform some automatic procedure (often used to ensure slot values are consistent).

Disadvantages of Using Frames

The disadvantages of using frames are that they:

- can be inefficient at runtime because they do not provide the most efficient method to store data for a computer.
- can lead to 'procedural fever', that is the apparent requirement to focus on making appropriate procedures rather than checking the overall structure and content of the frames.
- require care in the design stage to ensure that suitable taxonomies, i.e., agreed structures for the terminology are created for the system.

Before closing this chapter, we need to look at an additional approach to storing knowledge in a KBS, one that is of current and increasing interest and quite closely related to frames.

Ontologies

In philosophy, the term 'ontology' refers to 'a particular theory about the nature of being or the kinds of existence'.

From a knowledge engineering perspective, the term ontology is often used as a synonym for the terminology in some domain.

Activity 22
A number of researchers in the knowledge engineering field have suggested the following knowledge engineering-specific definitions of ontology. Suggest what implications these definitions have for knowledge representation.

An ontology is an explicit specification of a conceptualization (Gruber, 1994).
An (AI-) ontology is a theory of what entities can exist in the mind of a knowledgeable agent (Wielinga and Schreiber, 1993).

An ontology for a body of knowledge concerning a particular task or domain, describes a taxonomy of concepts for that task or domain that define the semantic interpretation of the knowledge (Alberts, 1993).

Feedback 22
You may have been able to suggest the following implications for knowledge engineering of the term ontology defined above:

Gruber's definition, though not explicitly stated, suggests that an ontology is a meta-level description of a knowledge representation.

Wielinga and Schreiber's definition emphasises that we want to apply the notion of ontology to all knowledgeable agents, including humans. Since different knowledgeable agents will often have different symbol-level representations, it is convenient to formulate ontologies at the knowledge level. Ontologies can therefore be used as mediators between knowledge as it is understood by a domain expert and knowledge as it is represented in a KBS.

Alberts's definition emphasises that it is not the terminology itself that constitutes the ontology but the *semantic interpretation of the terms*. Another important aspect of this definition is that ontologies can be specific for tasks or for domains. That is, both the domain and the task at hand may affect the ontology.

Combining the above definitions results in the following definition:

Ontologies can be classified according to the *amount and type of structure* of the conceptualisation and the *subject* of the conceptualisation. In relation to the former, it is possible to distinguish three categories:

- Terminological ontologies, such as lexicons, specify the terms that are used to represent knowledge in the domain.
- Information ontologies which specify the record structure of databases.
- *Knowledge modelling ontologies* specify conceptualisations of the knowledge and usually have a richer internal structure than information ontologies. They are often customised for a particular use of the knowledge they describe.

Within the context of KBS development, knowledge modelling ontologies are the most useful. A detailed description of the use of this type of ontology applied to electronic medical records is available at: http://www.cs.man.ac.uk/mig/ftp/pub/papers/alr-foundations.pdf.

By creating an ontology within an ES we can define the limitations of the knowledge stored and thus hope to combat brittleness.

Other Knowledge Representation Issues

When selecting a suitable knowledge representation scheme the most natural form of representation should be aimed for. This may involve using a combination of different techniques to provide advantages of each without the disadvantages of any. It is possible, for example, to use within one KBS, a mixture of the rules and frames, if both of these representation schemes are supported by the development tool.

It is also important to work to the strengths of that knowledge representation scheme, and understand the tools used.

Both the cost and complexity of using a combination of knowledge representation schemes must be considered and measured against the gains in flexibility.

It is often necessary to break the problem into parts. Complexity tends to increase with the problem size, and decomposition techniques can produce efficient KBSs. A 2000 rule KBS will be too much for many computers to cope with. However, a KBS which consists of 20 rule sets, each one having 100 rules can be processed efficiently.

Appropriate planning for the knowledge representation scheme used must take place involving the definition of the appropriate types of knowledge representation scheme that will be used when organising the knowledge.

Tools that best support the different representations need to be identified. If none of the available tools provide exactly what is required, then the next best possible choices must be evaluated. This includes identifying their strengths so that these can be applied to the task.

A knowledge-based structure should take maximum advantage of the knowledge representation scheme. The problem should not be conceptualised in procedural terms as this can result in inefficient code.

No single knowledge representation method is ideally suited for all problems. As a knowledge engineer you may be well advised to sacrifice the goal of uniformity and explore the possible benefits of multiple knowledge representation schemes.

Current Research Links

Using Explicit Ontologies in KBS Development

htp://ksi.cpsc.ucalgary.ca/IJHCS/VH/VH1.html

Natural Language & Knowledge Representation Research Group

http://tigger.cs.uwm.edu/~nlkrrg/

KR, Inc.

Principles of Knowledge Representation and Reasoning, Incorporated

http://www.kr.org/

Knowledge Representation Laboratory

http://kr.cs.ait.ac.th/

Self-Assessment Questions

Question 1

Represent the following facts as a set of frames, using the notation described earlier:

'The aorta is a particular kind of artery that has a diameter of 2.5 cm. An artery is a kind of blood vessel. An artery always has a muscular wall, and generally has a diameter of 0.4 cm. A vein is a kind of blood vessel, but has a fibrous wall. Blood vessels all have tubular form and contain blood'. (With thanks to Alison Cawsey [1998] for permission to use this question.)

Question 2

A knowledge base is required to categorise pets and store details of appropriate foods, environmental needs, etc. The system will then diagnose medical problems and offer advice on the appropriate care. Which of the following three knowledge representation methods would you use for this problem and why?

- Rules
- Frames
- Semantic networks.

Answer to Self-Assessment Questions

Answer 1

You should have four frames as follows:

BLOOD VESSEL FRAME	
IS_A	Blood Vessel
DIAMETER	2.5 cm
FORM	Tubular
CONTAINS_B LOOD	True

ARTERY FRAME	
IS_A	Blood Vessel
DIAMETER	default: 0.4 cm
WALL	Muscular

VEIN FRAME	
IS_A	Blood Vessel
WALL	Fibrous

AORTA FRAME	
IS_A	Artery
DIAMETER	2.5 cm

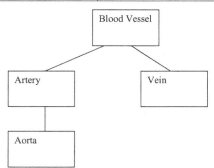

Note that the FORM and CONTAINS_BLOOD slots can be inherited from the BLOOD VESSEL frame and therefore do not need to be repeated in the VEIN and ARTERY frames.

Answer 2

Semantic networks could be used for this problem but inference, i.e., the diagnosis, would be complex. Therefore, it may be better to restrict the use of semantic networks to the knowledge acquisition phase of the project, i.e., use them as a communication tool between the knowledge engineer and expert. After this stage the knowledge would be converted into another format.

Frames are much simpler being restricted to is_a style relationships. Frames would provide a good method of storing the data about the pets and it would be easy to categorise them into suitable hierarchies, e.g. small mammals, reptiles, etc. Similar pets could inherit data and characteristics from frames higher up in the hierarchy, thus simplifying the data stored (food etc.). Data on pet ailments could be stored as procedural code (demons) associated to particular slots, e.g. a cat frame could have a slot called eating disorders and another called infections. However, encoding this knowledge as procedural code could get messy so let us consider rules as an alternative to frames.

With rules storing details of the pets could be complex and difficult to visualise however defining rules to describe pet problems and the associated symptoms would be quite easy. Thus, using rules storing details of the actual pets would be complex but invoking inference to diagnose problems would be easy.

Perhaps the best solution would therefore be to use a combination of rules and frames for this problem.

References

Inference, Forward and Backward Chaining
Cawsey, A. (1998). *The Essence of Artificial Intelligence*. Prentice-Hall: London, England.
Wolverton, M. (1995). Presenting significant information in expert system explanation. In *Seventh Portugese Conference on Artificial Intelligence* (EPIA95), Portugal, October 1995.
Semantic Networks
Quillian, M. (1968). Semantic memory. In Minsky, M. (editor), *Semantic Information Processing*. MIT Press: Cambridge, MA, pp. 216–270.
Alberts, L. K. (May, 1993). YMIR: An Ontology for Engineering Design. Thesis, University of Twente, Enschede, The Netherlands.
Winston, P. W. (1975). Learning Structural Descriptions from Examples, in The Psychology of Computer Vision, Winston P. (ed.), McGraw Hill, New York, 157–209.

5

Expert System Shells, Environments and Languages

Introduction

This chapter extends your knowledge of knowledge-based systems by providing the opportunity for you to familiarise yourself with the tools for their development.

The chapter consists of three sections:

1. Expert system (ES) shells
2. Expert system development environments
3. Use of artificial intelligence (AI) languages.

Objectives

By the end of the chapter you will be able to:

- define and explain what an ES shell is
- explain the main elements of an ES shell and how they work
- evaluate the advantages and limitations of ES shells
- evaluate the advantages and limitations of ES development environments
- evaluate the advantages and limitations of programming languages.

SECTION 1: EXPERT SYSTEM SHELLS

Introduction

This section provides a brief introduction to the use of ES shells. It begins with an overview of the different software tools available to produce ESs, followed by a more detailed look at ES shells.

Objectives

By the end of the section you will be able to:

• evaluate some of the commonly used ES shells.

Tools Available to Produce ESs

There are three main tools available to help with the development of ESs:

• Programming languages
• Expert system shells
• Expert system development environments.

Expert system shells provide a framework to produce an ES, so the knowledge base and rules are simply added to this framework. Expert system shells are examined in this section.

Expert system development environments provide a more powerful and flexible framework within which an ES can be written. They generally allow multiple knowledge representation schemes to be used and allow knowledge bases to be segmented. These tools are covered in Section 2 of this chapter.

Programming languages include conventional computer languages, such as C++ and Java, as well as languages specifically designed for AI applications, these include LISP and PROLOG. More detail on the use of languages is provided in Section 3 of this chapter.

What Are ES Shells?

Expert system shells are the main choice for building small ESs due primarily to their ease of use. The shell is really a ready-made ES without a knowledge base. All the programming components are there, waiting for rules to be entered into

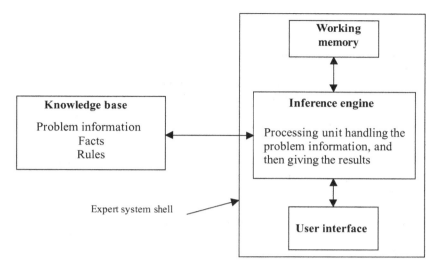

FIGURE 5.1. Expert system shell.

the system. Expert system shells therefore provide a quick way to develop an ES without having to build the entire system from scratch.

The basic structure of an ES shell and its relationship to a knowledge base is illustrated in Figure 5.1.

Activity 58
Based on your experience of using an ES shell suggest two possible benefits of using such tools. What are their weaknesses? Suggest two.

Feedback 58
You should have been able to suggest some of the following. The benefits of using an ES shell are that:
- Programming time is decreased because the basic shell of the ES has already been produced.
- Expert system development can focus on entering knowledge into the knowledge base.
- Non-programming experts can acquire a knowledge of how the shell works without having to understand in detail how to program an ES.
- Knowledge may be entered into the system by non-programming experts, especially where the system provides a user-friendly interface.

The weaknesses of ES shells are that:
- Shells can normally only support one knowledge base and one knowledge representation scheme. A system with a large knowledge base can be very

inefficient to run and difficult to maintain. In much the same way as a large program is split into functions and procedures, it is desirable to split a large knowledge base into several smaller knowledge bases. Shells cannot usually support this.

- Shells usually have limited flexibility when inferencing (e.g. backward chaining only) and it may be that for part of a problem forward chaining would be ideal while for another part of the same problem backward chaining would be ideal.
- Shells tend to be inflexible or at least difficult to modify. This means that knowledge may not always be entered in exactly the correct format in the ES.
- The knowledge domain may be simplified within the system because the shell cannot represent the full complexity of the domain.
- It is easy to let the shell dictate the format of the system, rather than choose the ideal format and then find a tool that supports this format.

Domain-Specific Shells

Domain-specific shells are simply ES shells that have been written to represent knowledge within a specific domain. For example, shells are available to assist with the help desk, scheduling and configuration of systems. The shells provide a specific user-interface to assist with the trapping of knowledge, but tend to be more expensive than more general ES shells. Case-based reasoning (CBR) Express is one example of a domain-specific shell.

Examples of ES Shells

Expert system shells include:

- Crystal
- JESS.

Crystal is an old ES shell that has the following facilities:

- a relatively simple inference engine that supports a knowledge base of rules
- facilities for creating a graphical user-interface
- a backward chaining inference engine
- automatic, but basic, explanation features
- can interface with text files, databases, spreadsheets and C code.

While Crystal is not a modern tool it was used in a variety of real world applications. This included an ES created by a bank to assess mortgage applications.

JESS by comparison is a modern ES shell written in Java. Unlike Crystal it was not designed for the creation of standalone ESs but is instead designed to support the development of hybrid intelligent information systems, i.e., systems containing both procedural and declarative components (see Chapter 6 for more details of hybrid intelligent information systems).

JESS was written entirely in Java and was designed in such a way that components created by JESS can be integrated directly with procedural components, assuming that they are also written in Java. To facilitate this JESS has the following features:

* tools for extending Eclipse, an Integrated Development Environment often used for developing Java programs
* an inference engine that supports both forward chaining and backward chaining
* the ability to perform reasoning upon other Java objects.

JESS does not provide graphical user-interface facilities directly. However, Java programmers already have facilities to create these and JESS programmers have access to all of the Java API.

As systems created with JESS are written in Java this provides and easy method of developing web-based ESs.

More details of JESS and the JESS software itself can be found on the Internet at: http//www.herzberg.ca.sandia.gov/jess/.

Summary

This section has examined the use of ES shells as tools used in the development of ESs.

Self-Assessment Question

Question 1

Find two ES shells on the web and contrast them.
Identify their main features.
Identify any major differences in usability between each shell.

Answers to Self-Assessment Question

Answer 1

Your answer will be very dependent upon the specific shells you find and compare.

Much of your evaluation will represent your personal experience of the software and you may have developed preferences for the different ways in which the two programs approach the same task.

Generally speaking, most shells are relatively simple tools that support one knowledge base using one knowledge representation scheme. Many shells also offer additional features such as automatic explanation facilities, graphical interface development tools and some support for integrating the system with other programs and/or databases.

SECTION 2: EXPERT SYSTEM DEVELOPMENT ENVIRONMENTS

Introduction

This section provides a brief introduction to the use of ES development environments. It considers the main limitations with ES shells and looks how one industry standard tool overcomes these limitations.

Objectives

By the end of the section you will be able to:

• evaluate the advantages and limitations of ES development environments.

Activity 59
Search the WWW and read some of the documentation for Aion BRE, a system produced by Computer Associates. Identify the characteristics of the system that make it an improvement over ES shells.

Feedback 59
You may have been able to recognise the following main advantages:
• supports multiple segmented knowledge bases
• allows inference engines to be tailored to each knowledge base
• supports multiple knowledge representation schemes, rules (with forward and backward chaining)
• supports object-oriented knowledge representation (similar to frames but more flexible)
• appropriate for the development of large systems but also much more expensive, complex and more difficult to learn
• separates control and domain knowledge thus supporting knowledge base reuse (discussed in Chapter 6).

Expert system development environments are in many ways similar to ES shells. However, as we have seen, while still specifically designed to support the development of ESs, they are much more flexible than ES shells.

In particular, they allow larger ESs to be developed in a structured way and they offer much more flexibility in the way knowledge is represented.

They also allow the separation of control and domain knowledge. This is an important issue that enables knowledge reuse.

The advantages that ES development environments offer when compared with ES shells will become much more apparent when you work your way through Chapter 6. This explains current thinking with regard to life cycles and methodologies used when developing ESs. You will see that segmented knowledge bases and the separation of control and domain knowledge are important concepts that are supported by modern ES development environments such as Aion BRE.

In Chapter 6, you will see how Aion BRE has facilities required by current methodologies and can be used to develop a larger well-structured application.

Expert system development environments do however have one particular disadvantage when compared with ES shells. As they are more flexible, they are also larger, more costly and more complex to learn. Therefore when choosing a tool to develop an ES a sensible rule would be to 'use a shell where you can and an environment where you should'.

Summary

This section has provided an introduction to the use of ES development environments and you have had the opportunity to review one modern industry standard tool.

Self-Assessment Question

Question 1

You have been asked to develop a small web-based ES to advise prospective students of appropriate courses at a university.

Consider each of the following types of tool and select the most appropriate for this problem:

- An ES shell
- A knowledge-based system (KBS) development environment (e.g. Aion BRE)
- A conventional programming language (e.g. C++ or Java).

Answers to Self-Assessment Question

Answer 1

This problem is quite small and this would indicate the use of a shell (e.g. Crystal). However, this can significantly restrict the knowledge representation scheme allowed and if the shell does not support the knowledge representation method most suitable for this problem (e.g. frames) we may be forced to consider a more flexible tool such as KBS environment (e.g. Aion BRE). Furthermore, not all shells would allow the system to be integrated with the WWW (though JESS will).

If a more flexible knowledge base were required we may need to consider the use of an AI language (e.g. PROLOG) see next section. However, nothing in the problem suggests that such flexibility is required.

The use of a conventional programming language would be most costly of all as it has no inbuilt inference capabilities and thus the inference engine would need to be programmed from scratch. This is the most flexible of all options but should only be considered if all other options are deemed inappropriate. The use of a procedural programming language would at least allow the system to be very easily integrated on to the web.

SECTION 3: USE OF AI LANGUAGES

Introduction

This introduces PROLOG, a programming language not specifically designed for the development of ESs but one designed for the creation of many AI applications.

Objectives

By the end of this section you will be able to:

• evaluate the advantages and limitations of programming languages for the development of ESs.

Expert System Languages

There are two main classes of languages, procedural and declarative.

Procedural languages include C++ and Java. These are relatively general-purpose languages that can be used in many different programming situations, e.g. expert systems, Microsoft Windows programs and company-specific applications. They are organised as a set of procedures, very similar to the way that a chapter in a book is divided into a series of paragraphs. While they offer no specific support for the development of ESs they do offer the ultimate in flexibility. As such languages such as these can be used to develop systems where other tools may be inadequate. For example, the development of a hybrid expert/neural network system may require this level of flexibility. However, this choice of tool should be a last resort as they offer no specific support for the development of ESs.

On the other hand, the declarative programming language PROLOG is specifically designed for programming AI systems from scratch and can be used to develop ESs. When developing ESs, PROLOG offers even more flexibility than an ES development environment. However, it has limited inbuilt facilities, i.e., less specific support for the development of ESs. Thus developing an ES using PROLOG will take considerably longer than if shell or environment was used as required features need to be programmed. Thus there is a trade off between flexibility of tool and lack of specific support.

The following tools are placed in increasing order of flexibility. They are also in order of increasing complexity and hence development time:

• Shells
• Development environments
• AI languages
• Procedural languages.

When choosing between these options you should use a shell where you can and an environment where you should and a language only if you must.

An Introduction to PROLOG

This chapter now introduces you to the PROLOG programming language.

Programs written in declarative languages include a set of declarations about a specific field of knowledge. Using this declaration, the ES can determine the truth of a statement as well as work out solutions to problems.

Most ES languages, including PROLOG, give knowledge to an ES in the form of facts.

PROLOG programs are made from *terms*, which can be either:

- A *constant* is a single entity (like zebra, 'John') or a non-negative integer (like 24)
- A *variable* is a series of letters that begins with a capital letter (like John). *Note*: constants cannot begin with a capital letter unless they are enclosed in quotes.
- A *structure* is a predicate with zero or more arguments, written in functional notation. For example,

```
animal(zebra).
speaks(boris, russian).
```

A *fact* is a term followed by a period (.). A *rule* is a term followed by :- and a series of terms (term1, term2, . . . , termN) separated by commas and ended by a period (.). That is, rules have the following form:

```
term :- term1, term2, ..., termN.
```

A PROLOG program is a series of facts and rules:

```
speaks(boris, russian).
speaks(john, english).
speaks(mary, russian).
speaks(mary, english).

understands(Person1, Person2) :-
    speaks(Person1, L), speaks(Person2, L).
```

This program can be translated into the following English facts:
- Boris speaks Russian.
- John speaks English.
- Mary speaks Russian.
- Mary speaks English.

and the following rule ...

- Two people can understand each other if they both speak the same language.

A fact in English may be written as:

The expert system monitors the ventilator.

This fact contains two important components:

- a relationship or *predicate* in the PROLOG language. In this example, the predicate is *monitor.*
- objects or *arguments* in PROLOG (objects are normally people, things or other items being acted on by the predicates). In this example, the objects are *expert system* and *ventilator.*

In PROLOG, the fact would be expressed (all in lower case) as:

```
monitors(expert_system,ventilator).
```

In other words, the activity is placed at the beginning of the fact. The people or objects affected by the activity appear inside the brackets, normally with the person first, followed by any collective noun (e.g. class of pupils) or names of objects. Note also that the syntax demands full stops at the end.

PROLOG uses various symbols.

Symbol	Meaning
,	And
;	Or
:-	If

Activity 60
Express the following facts in PROLOG
1. A person travels on a train.
2. The teacher instructs the class.
3. John drives a car.

Feedback 60
1. `travels(person,train).`
2. `instructs(teacher,class).`
3. `drives(john,car).`

Note that in all situations the activity is placed before the brackets, which contain the objects/arguments affected by the activity/predicate.

While the order of arguments within the brackets have no significance within PROLOG, the order must be used consistently. For example, writing 'the doctor treats the patient' should always be written as:

`treats(doctor,patient).`

Rather than sometimes as:

`treats(doctor,patient).`

and at other times as:

`treats(patient,doctor).`

Expressing Facts in ESs

Facts can be expressed in ESs using the same format as the action statements above. For example, the fact *my surname is Smith can* be expressed as

`surname(smith)`

Activity 61
Explain the meaning of these statements in PROLOG
1. age(fred, 56).
2. value(pH,7.27).

Feedback 61

PROLOG statement	Meaning
`age(fred,56).`	Fred is 56.
`value(pH,7.27).`	The pH value is 7.27.

Using Facts in ESs

Given a set of facts, an ES can review those facts to determine if any apply in a given situation. For example, a system can be provided with the following set of facts.

Fact	PROLOG statement
Fred is male	`male(fred).`
Tina is female	`Female(tina).`
Susan is female	`Female(susan).`
Fred is on a ventilator	`ventilator(fred).`
Susan is on a ventilator	`ventilator(susan).`

Queries can be given to PROLOG in the format:

```
? - ventilator(fred).
```

In other words, please find out if Fred is on a ventilator. The ES then searches the knowledge base to see if this fact is known and a suitable response is provided.

Notice that these statements are different from those statements indicating a relationship between different objectives. In this situation, the statements simply express facts. Also, where there is more than one object within a class, such as female in this situation, then the overall class name appears outside of the brackets, with the class example (the name) inside of the bracket. Using this format means that a search can be made for a specific object name, such as female, and then all items matching that search will be quickly identified.

Figure 5.2 shows the ES answering the queries:

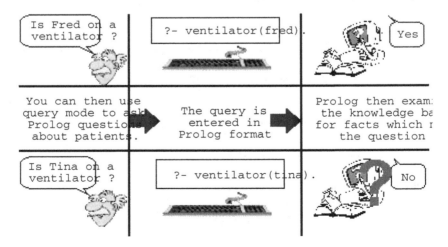

FIGURE 5.2. Querying an expert system.

```
? - ventilator(fred).
```

and

```
? - ventilator(tina).
```

Activity 62

Produce PROLOG statements for the facts listed below.

Remember that the person owning an object will normally appear inside of the brackets, with the object being owned appearing outside the brackets.

Fact   PROLOG statement
Bill is male
Linda is female
Peter is male
Bill has a single ticket
Linda has a return ticket

What PROLOG query would you use to determine whether Bill has a return ticket?

Feedback 62

Fact   PROLOG statement
Bill is male   male(bill).
Linda is female   female(linda).
Peter is male   male(peter).
Bill has a single ticket   single_ticket(bill).
Linda has a return ticket   return_ticket(linda).

You should also have been able to construct the following to query whether Bill has a return ticket:

```
? - return_ticket(bill).
```

Extracting a Set of Records from an ES

The question structure within PROLOG can be used to identify and extract a set of related facts from the total of all facts given to PROLOG. A variable is placed where a query is to be made about the facts, PROLOG then searches through the facts and returns any matches.

For example, we may need to find out which patients are female from the set of facts concerning patients used above. The PROLOG statement will be written as:

```
? - female(Patient).
```

The initial capital letter in 'Patient' indicates that it is a variable; all variables must begin with an uppercase letter.

Activity 63

Using the information concerning train tickets from the last exercise, write a PROLOG query that will find people holding a return ticket.

Feedback 63

```
? - return_ticket(Customer).
```

You may use a different noun to Customer. This is fine, as long as it describes the person travelling on the train (and uses a capital letter). Other possible examples could be Traveller, Commuter, etc.

Combining Queries

In some situations, it will be necessary to extract records from two sets of different facts using PROLOG.

For example, names of some males and respiratory conditions are stored in the following facts.

```
male(tim).
male(marc).
male(simon).
resp(tim,acute).
resp(marc,medium).
resp(simon,acute).
```

A match will be generated from this set of facts to the query male(X) where X is an instance of male. A match will also be generated from this set of facts to the query resp(X,Y) if the patient X has a respiratory condition of the state Y.

However, a reasonable question to ask the ES is:

'Do any male patients have an acute respiratory condition?'

Or in PROLOG format:

```
? - male(X),resp(X,acute)
```

Literally, is there an X who is male and has a respiratory condition that is acute?

Given the facts above, a solution cannot be found directly because the gender male is not linked to the respiratory condition facts. Therefore, PROLOG will have to check the two sub-goals and match the results from these before the query can be answered.

Activity 64

Given the PROLOG facts below, write a query that asks PROLOG to search for any female who has a return ticket.

Facts one	Facts two
male(fred).	single_ticket(bill).
female(linda).	return_ticket(peter).
male(peter).	return_ticket(linda).
male(nigel).	single_ticket(john).
female(jayne).	single_ticket(nigel).

Feedback 64

Your query should be as follows:

```
? - female(X),return_ticket(X).
```

Inferences

The principle of inference has already been discussed. PROLOG can perform backward-chaining inference from facts provided to it. For example, the following clause can be used to determine whether or not two people can marry.

```
can_marry (X, Y) :-
   male (X),
   female (Y),
   not_married (X),
   not_married (Y).
```

From this information PROLOG can determine that two people can marry if X is male and Y is female, and if neither person is already married.

Activity 65

Examine the PROLOG program listing below, and the following goals:

```
suspect(X).              Who is a suspect?
find_motive(X,M).        Who had a motive?
killer(X).               Who was the killer?
```

By working through the logic on paper try to list the suspects, those with a motive and finally find the killer.

PROLOG Program

```
/* Adapted from a program created by the Prolog Develop-
ment Center the makers of Visual Prolog */

  person(bert,55,m,carpenter).
  person(allan,25,m,football_player).
  person(allan,25,m,butcher).
  person(john,25,m,pickpocket).
  person(barbara,39,f,doctor).

  had_affair(barbara,john).
  had_affair(barbara,allan).
  had_affair(susan,john).
  had_affair(susan,bert).

  killed_with(susan,club).
  killed(susan).

  smeared_in(bert, blood).
  smeared_in(susan, blood).
  smeared_in(allan, mud).
  smeared_in(john, chocolate).
  smeared_in(barbara, blood).

  owns(bert,wooden_leg).
  owns(john,pistol).

/* Background knowledge */
  operates_identically(wooden_leg, club).
  operates_identically(bar, club).
  operates_identically(pair_of_scissors, knife).
  operates_identically(football_boot, club).

  owns_probably(X,football_boot):-
    person(X,_,_,football_player).
  owns_probably(X,pair_of_scissors):-
    person(X,_,_,hairdresser).
  owns_probably(X,Object):-
    owns(X,Object).

/* Suspect all those who owned a weapon with which Susan
could have been killed * /
suspect(X):-
  killed_with (susan,Weapon),
  operates_ identically(Object,Weapon),
  owns_probably(X,Object).
```

```
/* Men who have had an affair with Susan have a motive
'jealousy'. */
  find_motive(X,jealousy):-
    person(X,_,m,_),
    had_affair(susan,X).

/* Females who have had an affair with someone that Susan
knew also have a motive. */
find_motive(X,jealousy):-
  person(X,_,f,_),
  had_affair(X,Man),
  had_affair(susan,Man).

/* Pickpockets have a motive 'money'.*/
find_motive(X,money):-
  person(X,_,_,pickpocket).

/* How to work out the killer */
killer(Killer):-
  person(Killer,_,_,_),
  killed(Killed),
  not(Killed= Killer), /* i.e., Not suicide */
  suspect(Killer),
  find_motive(Killer,_),
  smeared_in(Killer,Goo),
  smeared_in(Killed,Goo).
```

Feedback 65

This is an exercise in backtracking, not a test of your ability to solve murder mysteries.

The suspects are Bert and Allan.

The following people had a motive:
• Bert (jealousy)
• John (jealousy)
• Barbara (jealousy)
• John (jealousy).

Bert is guilty because he is a suspect, has a motive and is smeared in the same stuff as the victim.

Working with Lists

PROLOG provides a mechanism for working with lists – its main mechanism for handling large quantities of data.

A list can be broken down into two parts: Its head, i.e., the first element and its tail, i.e., the rest of the list after the first element has been removed (this may be empty).

For example, in the list [fred, albert, jim], the head is the element 'fred' and the tail is the list [albert,jim].

Activity 66
Identify the head and tail of the following lists:
[alice,tim,bert]
[alice,tim]
[alan]
[ ]

Feedback 66

List	Head	Tail	Explanation
[alice,tim,bert]	Alice	[tim,bert]	
[alice,tim]	Alice	[tim]	*Note*: here the head is a single item but the tail is a list. It only has one element in it but is nonetheless a list.
[alan]	Alan	[ ]	Here the tail is an empty list.
[ ]	Fail		This will fail because the PROLOG cannot assign a value to the head.

When a list is matched to notation in the form [X|Y], X is instantiated to (given the value of) the head and Y is instantiated to the tail.

Activity 67
Assuming the following, very short, program is entered ...

letters([a,b,c,d]).

What would be the result of the following goal?

letters([H|T]).

Feedback 67
The result of the above will be true (or Yes) when H is 'a' and T is [b,c,d].

The program in the next activity displays each element of a list. It takes the first element from the front of a list, prints out this element and then calls the function print (i.e., itself) to display the rest of the list.

In other words

- to print the list [a,b,c] means print 'a' and then print the list [b,c].
- to print the list [b,c] means print 'b' and then print the list [c].
- to print the list [c] means print 'c' and then print the list [].

Thus a function call to print the list [a,b,c] will cause 'a' to be printed and then 'b' and finally 'c'.

When a function uses itself, as the print function does in Program 3, then this is called recursive programming. It is unusual, complex for beginners but nonetheless a powerful mechanism.

Activity 68
Read through the following program carefully. Try to follow its logic.

```
print([X|Y]) :-
    write(X), /* write is a function to print out a value*/
    nl, /* nl prints a new line */
    print(Y).
```

What would this program do with the following goal?

```
print ([a,b,c,d,e]).
```

Feedback 68
The program will print out the following

```
a
b
c
d
e
f
```

A More Complex PROLOG Program

Imagine a member function, which has two parameters, an element (an item we are looking for) and a list (in which we are looking for it).

Given such a function an example goal might be:

```
member(sunderland,[newcastle,durham,sunderland,middlesbrough-
h]).
```

This member function could be written as follows:

```
member(X,[X|_]).
member(X,[_|Y]) :- member(X,Y).
```

The first line of the member function splits the list into two parts and says that if the element has the same value as the head of the list then, irrespective of the rest of the list, that element is a member of the list.

In other words given the element 'fred' and the list '[fred,bert,jim]' fred is a member of the list.

The second line of the member function says that, after failing the first test of membership, the list should be split into two parts and we must now check to see if the element is a member of the remaining section of the list. The head is of no concern because we have already determined that the element is not the same as the head of the list.

For example, given the element 'fred' and the list '[bert,jim,fred]' as fred is not the first element in the list we must check the rest of the list, i.e., [jim,fred]. If 'fred' is a member of this shorter list then it must also be a member of the original list.

Summary

This section has provided an overview of how the PROLOG programming language uses rules to make decisions and uses lists as a method of storing data.

Self-Assessment Questions

Question 1

Given the following PROLOG facts, write a query to search for any male who has a single ticket.

Facts one	Facts two
male(fred)	ticket(bill,single)
female(linda)	ticket(peter,return)
male(peter)	ticket(linda,return)
male(nigel)	ticket(john,single)
female(jayne)	ticket(nigel,single)

Question 2

You have been asked to develop an online university admission system that offers intelligent advice and makes automatic course offers. The system will have a web front end and contain an ES to advise prospective students of appropriate courses at a university. The system will make actual course offers (subject to confirmation of results) to prospective students. The web-based KBS system is to be integrated with a University admissions database system so that prospective overseas applicants gain advice and where appropriate make an automatic application. It has also been decided that the system should contain an ES integrated with a CBR system. The system will only make offers if both the ES and the CBR agree that an offer should be made.

Consider each of the following types of tool and select the most appropriate for this problem:

- An ES shell
- A KBS development environment (e.g. Aion BRE)
- An AI language (e.g. PROLOG)
- A conventional programming language (e.g. C++ or Java).

Answer to Self-Assessment Questions

Answer 1

Your query should be as follows:

```
? - male(X),ticket(X,single)
```

Answer 2

The system specified is very complex containing an ES integrated with a web-based information system, a CBR system and a conventional information system. If this entire system were to be developed using one tool then it requires a flexible solution, certainly most shells would not be appropriate nor would PROLOG.

PROLOG does not have the facilities to develop the web front end or the CBR system though it could be used to develop the knowledge-based component and this could be integrated with components created with other software. The use of

PROLOG would allow more flexibility for developing the ES component. However, nothing in the problem suggests that such flexibility is required.

A conventional programming language could be used to develop the entire system but would not contain any tools to support the ES component, thus everything would need to be developed from scratch and this would be costly and take time.

Aion BRE would support the ES component and, as it is a full OO (Object Oriented) programming development tool, it could also be used to develop the other components. Thus if one tool had to be chosen this would be the best choice. However, in the real world an application such as this would be developed in separate components using a range of tools. Thus Aion BRE could be used to develop the ES component, a visual programming environment could be used to develop the web-based front end, a CBR tool could be used to develop the CBR component and a procedural programming tool could be used to develop the database/information system. These separate components would then be integrated to form one complete system.

6

Life Cycles and Methodologies

Introduction

In this chapter we will be looking at life cycles and methodologies designed to support the development of knowledge-based systems (KBSs). We will be revisiting prototyping, which you have probably encountered before.

There are also three specific methodologies designed to overcome some of the problems associated with designing KBSs:

- Blackboard architectures, a method for structuring large-scale KBSs.
- Problem-solving methods (PSMs)—of which KADS (knowledge-acquisition design system) is an important example.
- The Hybrid methodology (HyM) designed to support the development of hybrid information systems, i.e., the integration of KBSs with traditional information systems.

The chapter consists of six sections:

1. Need for methodologies
2. Blackboard architectures
3. Problem Solving Methods (PSMs)
4. Knowledge Acquisition Design System (KADS)
5. The Hybrid Methodology (HyM)
6. Building a well-structured application using Aion BRE.

Objectives

By the end of the chapter you will be able to:

- explain the advantages and disadvantages of using conventional methodologies
- evaluate the place of blackboard architectures in knowledge engineering

- evaluate the use of control and domain knowledge within expert systems (ESs)
- evaluate the advantages and limitations of using PSMs
- describe the KADS
- evaluate the place of HyM in knowledge engineering
- describe how a well-structured application can be implemented using an industry standard tool
- describe the current areas of methodology research.

SECTION 1: THE NEED FOR METHODOLOGIES

Introduction

This section provides an overview of the common aspects of the different methodologies discussed in the later sections.

Objectives

By the end of the section you will be able to:

• Explain the advantages and disadvantages with using conventional methodologies.

Problems with Conventional Life Cycles

Traditional information systems usually perform some clearly definable processing tasks, and may have requirements that are relatively clear—though this does not preclude the possible need to developing throwaway prototypes as part of the requirement analysis phase in order to determine these requirements.

Such systems are often created using the classic waterfall approach to software development. This follows a six-stage life cycle of:

1. analysis
2. design
3. implementation
4. validation
5. installation
6. maintenance.

While these steps provide a useful structure for a traditional software development project, they can be problematic—particularly when applied to the development of a KBS. These issues are discussed in more detail below. Prior to this discussion, attempt Activity 1.

Activity 1

Given the stages in traditional information system design noted above, what might be the principle activities carried out within each stage of a specifically KBS development?

Stage	System	Principal activities
1	Feasibility study	
2	Knowledge acquisition	
3	Design	
4	Implementation	
5	Validation	
6	Maintenance	

Feedback 1

Stage	System	Principal activities
1	Feasibility study	Checking whether or not it is feasible to write and implement an ES. Feasibility may mean looking at whether or not the ES will be accepted socially as well as whether sufficient resources are available to develop the system in the first place. Economic feasibility will require that the knowledge to be built into the system is relatively scarce and also relatively stable.
2	Knowledge acquisition	The knowledge to be input into the ES is collected from human experts.
3	Design	The ES is designed. The initial design will show the logical structure of the system; this structure will then be used to write an appropriate ES using rules or frames or both.
4	Implementation	Writing the system is completed and it is implemented, normally on a test basis.
5	Validation	The logic within the system is tested, possibly by providing the system with a series of problems where the output is known in advance. A check is made to ensure that the system provides the same or better outputs than those devised by human experts.
6	Maintenance	The system is maintained by expanding the rule or frames as new knowledge becomes available or old rules become out-of-date or are updated by new information.

The waterfall model of software development provides a well-structured life cycle that has on occasion worked well for the development of procedural information systems however it has one very significant weakness. For the waterfall model to work a clear and detailed set of user requirements must be obtainable during the analysis stage.

Problems with Project Specification

In the development of KBSs, unlike other types of information systems, the end goals are often not clearly defined. In particular, it is difficult to specify the knowledge that the ES must contain. For this reason the waterfall model is inappropriate for the development of KBSs.

Use of Prototyping

One of the main problems with designing ESs is the lack of any firm goals. Expert systems are primarily concerned with the capturing and processing of abstract knowledge. The knowledge domain as well as the activities involved in knowledge acquisition and processing will not be clearly defined, so the actual outputs from the system will be difficult to determine. In a conventional system, outputs can be stated precisely because inputs and processing activities can be clearly explained.

Even when the outcomes can be defined it is difficult to specify both the knowledge that is to be included within an expert system and the quality of the reasoning processes it requires. If these cannot be defined, then it is impossible to define specifications that the design and implementation can be assessed against. For this reason, the waterfall life cycle is problematic when developing any expert system. Prototyping, on the other hand, has an iterative life cycle that allows specifications to be clarified as throughout the lifetime of the project.

Capturing knowledge for KBSs can also be difficult, because detail of the knowledge to be encoded into the system may have to be checked with the human expert a number of times. This does not represent a weakness in system design, but simply shows that additional care is needed in checking the accuracy of any KBS design compared to a conventional system. In KBS terms, this checking of the logical system design is most often done by prototyping.

The prototype is therefore used to check user requirements by providing a mock-up of the knowledge within the system (see Figure 6.1).

This iterative approach has four key stages, which are repeated as necessary:
- preliminary requirements are identified
- a design phase is performed
- a prototype is implemented
- the prototype is evaluated.

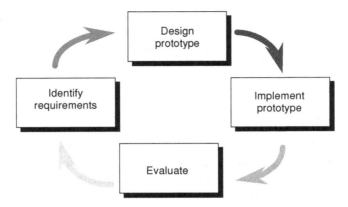

FIGURE 6.1. An incremental prototyping approach for large or complex systems.

This leads to the design and development of a larger system.

Having obtained requirements from the users and performed some knowledge acquisition the rules are implemented in a prototype. The accuracy of the prototype is checked or evaluated by users, and a new prototype produced based on the expert's opinions and suggestions. This process continues until the prototype accurately represents user requirements. The initial prototype therefore evolves into the final system.

This life cycle is particularly suited to KBSs. Knowledge-based systems can be very difficult to define even if the task they are required to perform is clear. It is difficult to define when the knowledge they contain is complete, and when the reasoning is up to the required standard. The availability of a cyclical iterative process is therefore extremely useful as it allows the quality of the reasoning process to be inspected and approved even when it was not possible to specify.

Activity 2
On the basis of your previous knowledge of prototyping, suggest what the advantages of this approach would be for the development of KBSs specifically in relation to:
• the accuracy of the knowledge base
• the quality of the reasoning applied to rule construction
• the involvement of users.

Feedback 2

You should have been able to suggest the following advantages:

- Allows the accuracy of the knowledge base to be demonstrated during iterations of the life cycle. Any errors or inaccuracies within the knowledge base should be identified as the prototype shows the use and relationship between different rules.
- The quality of the reasoning is open to inspection. The detail of the knowledge base can be checked prior to detailed programming; again, any errors or inaccuracies should be identified.
- It provides an easy mechanism to involve the users, management and experts. All parties involved with the design and development of the ES can be involved in the checking of the system.
- Involvement of management, experts and users is an important part of convincing sceptics and gaining acceptance for the system.

Such an approach also allows the project to be signed off as complete. When the prototype is complete, then this should represent the final version of the rule or case base within the system, hence later signoff will be more of a formality than a detailed check.

Limitations of Iterative Processing

The main limitations of iterative prototyping include:

- The ability to develop small projects does not always mean that it is possible to develop and maintain large real-world versions.
- The difficulty in defining the costs and timetables. The number of iterations of the prototype will not be clear. This may result in high costs and development taking longer than expected as additional iterations are carried out.

Clearly, we need to overcome some of these problems.

Problems with Project Management (Users/Timescale)

As the development of a KBS is based on knowledge and human reasoning rather performing numerical calculations, management and users may be sceptical of the system. Prototyping provides a mechanism for involving such people in the project and overcoming their doubts; however, the iterative nature of the life cycle can itself cause additional problems as the number of required iterations, and thus the final cost/timescale, cannot be defined.

Need for Segmented Knowledge Bases and Control over Inference Process

Within a simple ES or KBS, the inference engine is separated from the knowledge base. The reason for doing this is to allow the inference engine to be reused for new problems.

However, this approach has limitations.

- Control knowledge is implicitly mixed with domain knowledge; this issue is discussed in more detail later.
- The representation of the knowledge is limited by what one inference engine understands.
- Large KBSs can be difficult to maintain. Normally, a problem can often be broken down into smaller problems, and these smaller problems may require a range of knowledge representation schemes. This will not be possible with one particular inference engine.
- Finally, large KBSs can be very inefficient when searching for the knowledge to be applied to a current problem, and thus the knowledge base needs to be segmented.

To overcome these problems we need methods that provide structure to a knowledge base, and to allow a range of knowledge representation schemes to be applied to different stages of a problem. Methods of providing this structure, including the use of blackboard architectures, are described in this chapter.

Self-Assessment Questions

Question 1

Consider the limitations of the waterfall and prototyping life cycles and justify the need for a methodology when developing large-scale KBSs.

Question 2

Consider any other software development methodologies you are familiar with and evaluate whether or not these can be used to develop ESs.

Answer to Self-Assessment Questions

Answer 1

The waterfall model of software development provides a well-structured life cycle; however, this model is inappropriate for the development of large KBS and the use of prototyping is required in order to identify the knowledge required within the system. However, prototyping does not solve all of the issues. In particular:

- the final cost/timescale, cannot be defined
- large KBSs can be difficult to maintain
- large KBSs can be very inefficient.

To overcome these problems we need methodologies that support the development of structured and segmented knowledge bases.

Answer 2

Other system development methodologies that can be used to develop commercial systems include:

- Structured systems analysis and design methodology (SSADM)
- The spiral model
- The 'b' model.

Information about these systems can be found in many different analysis texts.

Structured systems analysis and design methodology is less suited to ES development than conventional information systems because, for example, it does not recognise the additional difficulties in relation to defining user requirements faced by knowledge engineers when building an ES.

Both the spiral and 'b' models could incorporate knowledge engineering. The 'b' model may be particularly suitable, with the emphasis on testing and evaluation at the end of the model.

Details of these methodologies can be found in various places including the www.

SECTION 2: BLACKBOARD ARCHITECTURES

Introduction

This section provides an introduction to the use of blackboard architectures in knowledge engineering.

Objectives

By the end of the section you will be able to:

• evaluate the place of blackboard architectures in knowledge engineering
• recognise appropriate contexts for the application of the blackboard architecture.

Introduction to Methodologies

Three different methodologies are explained in this chapter. These are:

• Blackboard architectures
• KADS
• HyM.

All three methodologies use a similar structure or set of techniques to build an ES. They are, therefore, related to each other at the structural (macro) level, although there are differences in approach at the detailed (micro) level.

The Blackboard Metaphor

Blackboard architectures provide a problem-solving model for organising knowledge. They operate in a similar manner to a group of people working together to solve a problem, where the results of their discussion are placed upon the blackboard for all of them to see.

The basic structure of a blackboard system is shown in Figure 6.2.

Example of Real Blackboard System in Use

Expert systems generally work best in small, narrowly defined domains of expertise. What if several such ESs were arranged to work cooperatively (just as

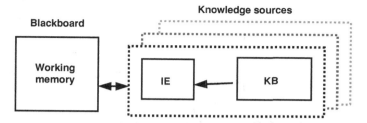

FIGURE 6.2. Blackboard system architecture.

human experts from different specialisms do) so that they could solve problems in a combination of these areas? This is the idea behind blackboard architectures.

In the HEARSAY project an early blackboard system—a computer was connected to a library catalogue in order to be able to answer spoken enquires about the library's stock such as:

- What has John Smith written since 1974?
- Which of his reports are on computing?
- List these reports.

It is not easy to program a machine to understand such spoken queries because language is very complex and might be considered to consist of the following 'layers':

- Phonetic—turning sound waves into word components, e.g. boy, s.
- Morphemic—connecting word components together to form other words, e.g. boy + s = boys.
- Syntactic—ordering the words according to the grammar of a particular language. For example, 'Fast ran the athlete.' is an inappropriate ordering of 'The athlete ran fast'.
- Semantic—the meaning from the words, e.g. 'Blue dreams eat noisily.' has words in the right order but the sentence is meaningless.
- Textual—structure: connecting sentences to make paragraphs and whole texts.

It would be extremely difficult to write a single ES that coped with all of these problems. The designers of HEARSAY in fact wrote five separate ESs—one for each separate 'layer' of language and got them to cooperate via a blackboard.

The actual input to the system is the spectrogram showing the variation of energy in different frequency bands of the spoken input as it varies over time. HEARSAY replaces the speech stream at the lowest level of its blackboard (multi-level database, indexed by time flowing from left to right) with a set of time-located hypotheses as to what phonemes might be present, with confidence levels associated with the evidence for such phonemes in the spectrogram. This relation between fragments of

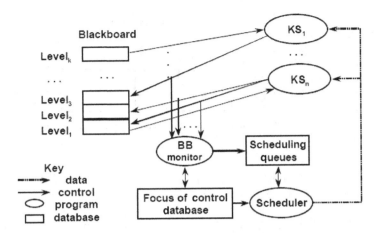

FIGURE 6.3. The HEARSAY blackboard system.

the spectrogram and possible phonemes is mediated by a processor called a *knowledge source* (KS) which consists of a small KB with its own inference engine. A second KS hypothesises words consistent with phoneme sequences and computes their confidence values in turn. A third KS applies syntactic knowledge to group such words into phrases. In addition to these bottom-up processes, KSs may also act top-down, e.g. by trying to complete a phrase in which a verb has been recognised as plural by seeking evidence for a missing 's' at the end of a noun which precedes it. As the result of such processing, an overall interpretation of the utterance— both of the words that constitute it and their syntactical relationship—may emerge with a confidence level significantly higher than that of other interpretations (see Figure 6.3).

Activity 3
This activity will help you understand the processes associated with a blackboard system.

Imagine the following:
• A group of human experts are seated in a semicircle around a blackboard (the more old-fashioned version of 'whiteboards', i.e., large surfaces on which writing and drawing can be displayed for lecture purposes).
• Each expert is a specialist in an area relevant to the problem.
• When an expert thinks they have a contribution to make, they add their ideas, calculations and suggestions, etc. to the board.
• The new information, result, conclusion may enable another expert to make a contribution.
• The process continues until the problem is solved.

Suggest one main reason why there might be problems managing the process.

> Feedback 3
> You should have been able to suggest that managing such a process would require:
> - a protocol for scheduling which expert can contribute if two attempt to do so at the same time
> - an agreement about terminology, language, modelling frameworks, etc.

HEARSAY also provides scheduling whereby the activity of processes and their interaction through the blackboard database is controlled. Each process (KS) is viewed as an agent that embodies some area of knowledge, and can take action based on that knowledge. Some KSs are grouped as computational entities called modules in the final version of the HEARSAY-II system. The KSs within a module share working storage and computational routines which are common to the procedural computations of the grouped KSs. HEARSAY is based on the 'hypothesize-and-test' paradigm which views solution-finding as an iterative process, with each iteration involving the creation of a hypothesis about some aspect of the problem and a test of the plausibility of the hypothesis. Each step rests on a priori knowledge of the problem, as well as on previously generated hypotheses. The process terminates when the best consistent hypothesis is generated satisfying the requirements of an overall solution.

Though the KSs cooperate via the blackboard in an iterative formation of hypotheses, no KS 'knows' what or how many other KSs exist. This ignorance is maintained to achieve a completely modular KS structure that enhances the ability to test various representations of a KS as well as possible interactions of different combinations of KSs.

At any one time the blackboard contains all current hypotheses. Each hypothesis has an associated set of attributes, some optional, others required. Several of the required attributes are:

- the name of the hypothesis and its level
- an estimate of its time interval relative to the time span of the entire utterance
- information about its structural relationships with other hypotheses
- validity ratings.

The task of the system is therefore essentially a search problem where the search space is the set of all possible networks of hypotheses that sufficiently span the time interval of the utterance, connecting *hypotheses directly derived from the acoustic input* to those that *describe the semantic content of the utterance*. No KS can single-handedly generate an entire network to provide the element of the search space. Instead, the KSs cooperate to provide hypotheses for the network that provides an *acceptable interpretation* of the acoustic data. Each KS may read data, add, delete, or modify hypotheses, and attribute values of hypotheses on the blackboard. It may also establish or modify explicit structural relations among hypotheses. The generation and modification of hypotheses on the blackboard is the exclusive means of communication between KSs.

Each KS includes both a precondition and a procedure. When the precondition detects a configuration of hypotheses to which the KSs knowledge can be applied, it invokes the KS procedure, that is, it schedules a blackboard-modifying operation by the KS. The scheduling does not imply that the KS will be activated at that time, or that the KS will indeed be activated with this particular triggering precondition, because HEARSAY uses a 'focus of attention' mechanism to stop the KSs from forming an unworkably large number of hypotheses. The blackboard modifications may trigger further KS activity—acting on hypotheses both at different levels and at different times.

Changes in validity ratings reflecting creation and modification of hypotheses are propagated automatically throughout the blackboard by a rating policy module called RPOL. As mentioned earlier, the actual activation of the KSs occurs under control of an external scheduler that constrains KS activation by functionally assessing the current state of the blackboard with respect to the solution space and the set of KS invocations that have been triggered by KS preconditions. The KS most highly rated by the scheduler is the one that is next activated.

The Purpose of Blackboard Architectures

Blackboard architectures—as is beginning to emerge from what we have seen so far:

- provide a problem-solving model for organising knowledge
- provide a potential strategy for applying the knowledge
- allow a range of knowledge representation methods to be applied to a given situation.

Blackboard systems allow the knowledge base to be segmented, making it more maintainable, and making the implementation more efficient. This also allows a range of knowledge representation methods to be applied.

When applying a blackboard architecture, the knowledge base is segmented into modules, each with its own inference engine; each module is called a KS. The reasons for using segmentation include:

- It allows each module to use its own knowledge representation method.
- By segmenting one large knowledge base into several smaller KSs the system becomes more efficient and maintainable.

However, each module must provide information in an agreed format, so that other modules can use it. To facilitate this working memory is sub-divided into regions and structured appropriately, this is called the blackboard.

Communication between modules will then take place only via the blackboard with each KS contributing to the solution whenever the data it requires is available on the blackboard.

Application of Blackboard Architectures

Knowledge-based systems and blackboard architectures can be used in a variety of situations. The following example is based on building a house.

A large KBS to design an entire house would be difficult to build and inefficient to run. Therefore, to solve this problem, several smaller KBSs can be developed. Each smaller KBS can have its own inference engine and these can use different knowledge representation schemes if required.

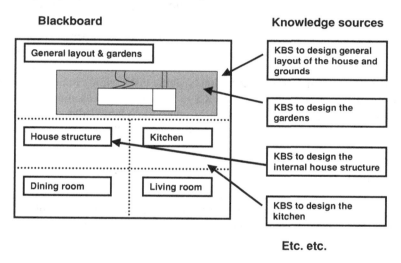

FIGURE 6.4. Blackboard architecture for house building system.

Initially, the KBS is used to design the general layout of the house and the surrounding grounds and paths.

Other KBSs will then be used to provide more detailed designs of the gardens, the internal structure of the house, and even the precise layout of the kitchen. However, the design must proceed from the high level first, so that the KBS dealing with the more detailed designs have the parameters within which to operate. For example, the kitchen KBS needs to know the size of the kitchen and location of doors, windows and plumbing, etc. to be able to place sinks, washers and worktops in the correct location.

So, to start at the beginning, imagine also a blackboard designed to communicate these designs. Pictorially, we see areas of the blackboard segmented off, one area showing the general layout of the gardens, one area which will display the house structure, one area that will display the design for the kitchen and dining room, etc.

Each KS communicates and writes results, or draws their designs on the blackboard. Initially, the blackboard will be empty although all of the KSs will be allowed access to it. Initial requirements of the house and garden (including the dimensions and positioning of windows, etc.) will be added to the blackboard. When this is complete, the KBS for the garden design, and the KBS to design the internal structure, will both be able to start their work.

Thus one large KBs is segmented into several smaller KS's.

Advantages and Limitations of Blackboard Architectures

As indicated earlier, when you wish to link several sources of expertise, in problems that naturally have 'layers', then the blackboard architecture is a good approach.

The overall problem is broken down into specific tasks, aiding maintenance, improving efficiency and allowing each KS to use whatever reasoning mechanism is most appropriate to it. Thus, the most appropriate knowledge representation scheme may be used by each KS and overall a range of schemes may be used. This aids flexibility.

Summary

In this section you have been introduced to the nature and potential application of blackboard systems and have seen how a real system was used.

SECTION 3: PROBLEM-SOLVING METHODS

Introduction

This section explains the use of general Problem Solving Methods (PSMs) and some of the generic issues affecting the use of all PSMs.

Objectives

By the end of the section you will be able to:

• evaluate the use of control and domain knowledge within ESs
• discuss the advantages and limitations of using PSMs.

Problem-Solving Methods

Problem-solving methods, in common usage, specify the sequence of tasks that are needed to solve a problem, and the knowledge required by the method.

Knowledge acquisition was traditionally seen as an exercise in acquiring domain knowledge from the expert. How that was processed was the responsibility of the inference engine.

In practice, for efficiency reasons the knowledge was structured so that the fundamental questions were asked first, and the inference proceeded to a solution following the same reasoning process as the expert used. This reasoning process is called *control knowledge* and is quite different from subject (or domain) knowledge.

More recently knowledge acquisition has come to be viewed as a modelling exercise where the reasoning processes, the domain knowledge and even the behaviour of the organisation can all be modelled separately. By modelling the problem-solving behaviour of experts, we can develop PSMs for generic tasks such as design, diagnosis and scheduling.

PSMs and Tasks

Among the requirements of an intelligent system is a certain degree of robustness: the system should be able to support some changes to its task specification. One way of providing such an ability is to allow the user to modify the system in order to control how tasks are performed and to specify new tasks within the general capabilities of the system itself. Those modifications are modifications of the system knowledge base that concern a certain subset of the knowledge: the control or problem-solving knowledge.

One way of achieving such robustness is to couple an ES with a knowledge-acquisition tool where some domain-independent theory of the problem-solving process is explicitly represented.

Activity 4
This activity helps you recognise the advantages of separating domain-independent PSMs from domain knowledge.

Look at the following problem that was presented to students in an examination: Air (Cp = 0.24 Btu/lb°F) enters a preheater at 80°F and leaves at 300°F; flue gases (Cp = 0.24 Btu/lb°F) enter at 600°F. A total of 180,000 lb of air per hour are heated by 188,000 lb of gas per hour. The coefficient of heat transfer, U, is 125 Btu per hour per sq ft per deg °F. Calculate the surface area of the tubes if the heater is arranged in parallel flow.

If we suggested that the 'problem solving method' involved:
• stating the problem
• listing symbols and their meaning
• listing assumptions
• identifying equations
• calculating
• stating the answer.
What advantages might there be in separating PSMs from the knowledge that might need to be applied?

Feedback 4
You should have been able to recognise that:
• The PSM is open to inspection, and can be improved without necessarily affecting the domain knowledge.
• By separating the PSM from the domain knowledge we enable reuse of either.
• Two or more PSMs for solving the same generic task can be compared, and we can use whichever is more suited to a particular task.

Examples of PSMs

Problem-solving methods generally fall into two categories:

• Classification—where solutions are selected from a pre-enumerated set
• Construction—where solutions are created during problem solving.

Actual examples of PSMs include:

- propose and revise (P&R), e.g. for an elevator configuration
- acquire and present, e.g. for a report
- extrapolate from a similar case, e.g. for sizing requirements for a computer system.

We will look at the first of these in some detail.

Propose and Revise

Propose and revise is a PSM to accomplish a configuration task. Propose and revise works by proposing a value for each parameter of a system at a time and checking to see whether each parameter satisfies all constraints on it.

In particular, within constructive problems, a configuration design task can be solved by the P&R problem solving method (Marcus and McDermott, 1989). This method belongs to a family of similar methods for configuration problems (propose critique-and-modify, propose-and-exchange, etc.) and simulates how a human being proposes the components of a design in a step-by-step manner meanwhile analysing whether it violates some constraints. If so, a remedy is applied based on heuristic knowledge in order to modify the original proposal. This process is repeated until, if possible, a satisfactory configuration is found.

The abstract structure of this method assumes the existence of three kinds of knowledge to be represented with three knowledge bases:

- derivative knowledge
- compatibility knowledge
- remedy knowledge.

Activity 5
This activity will help you understand the nature of the P&R PSM.

Below are descriptions of the three kinds of knowledge mentioned above. Indicate on the left-hand which kind of knowledge the description relates to. Hint words in the descriptions have been removed to make this more challenging.

This knowledge is used to verify a proposed design and includes a set of criteria to identify _____ cases. This knowledge can be formulated as a set of constraints where each constraint expresses the set of _____ conditions.

This is knowledge to propose a design that includes specific criteria to deduce a complete design from initial specifications. This knowledge can be formulated as direct relations between initial data, intermediate parameters and final parameters (numerical or qualitative) that describe how each parameter obtains its value from the values of other parameters. One important requirement of this knowledge is that these relations do not have to include loops to avoid circular calculation.

This knowledge includes a set of criteria to solve a violation detected in the design. This knowledge can be represented as rules that define types of _____ actions (fixes) to solve each type of violation. Together with this knowledge, there are a set of preference criteria based on priorities to select fixes when different fixes can be used for the same violation.

Feedback 5	
Compatibility knowledge	This knowledge is used to verify a proposed design and includes a set of criteria to identify *incompatible* cases. This knowledge can be formulated as a set of constraints where each constraint expresses the set of *incompatible* conditions.
Derivative knowledge	This is knowledge to propose a design that includes specific criteria to deduce a complete design from initial specifications. This knowledge can be formulated as direct relations between initial data, intermediate parameters and final parameters (numerical or qualitative) that describe how each parameter obtains its value from the values of other parameters. One important requirement of this knowledge is that these relations do not have to include loops to avoid circular calculation.
Remedy knowledge	This knowledge includes a set of criteria to solve a violation detected in the design. This knowledge can be represented as rules that define types of *remedy* actions (fixes) to solve each type of violation. Together with this knowledge, there are a set of preference criteria based on priorities to select fixes when different fixes can be used for the same violation.

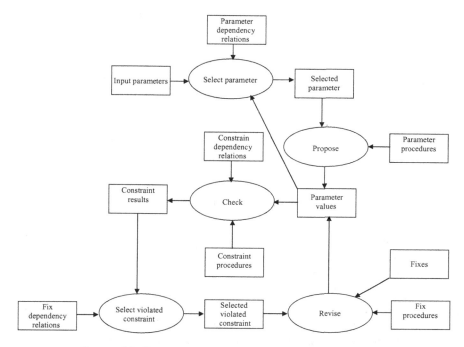

FIGURE 6.5. Example of propose and revise inference structure.

Propose and revise was originally implemented by SALT, a knowledge acquisition tool that generates P&R systems (Marcus, 1988). Propose and revise has been modelled for the VT (vertical transportation) task, based on the description made by Yost (1994). The VT task defines the design problem in which the goal is to configure an elevator.

Figure 6.5 illustrates the inference structure for P&R abstracted from the VT domain.

In Figure 6.5, the SELECT PARAMETER inference chooses one parameter to have its value computed. The inference uses the *Input Parameters*, the *Parameter Values* already computed and the *Parameter Dependency Relations* to obtain a *Selected Parameter*.

The PROPOSE inference computes the value of the selected parameter. The inference uses the Selected Parameter and the *Parameter Procedures* to compute new Parameter Values.

The CHECK inference verifies the constraints after computing parameter values. The inference uses the new Parameter Values computed, the *Constraint*

Procedures, and the *Constraint Dependency Relations* to compute the Constraint Results.

The SELECT VIOLATED CONSTRAINT chooses one violated constraint to be revised. The inference uses the *Constraint Results* and the *Fix Dependency Relations* to generate one *Selected Violated Constraint*.

The REVISE inference remedies a violated constraint. The inference uses the Selected Violated Constraint, *Fixes* and *Fix Procedures* to repair the constraint violation, and to propose new Parameter Values (Coelho and Lapalme, 1996).

As implemented in the SALT software (SALT—a knowledge-acquisition tool for propose-and-revise using a role-limiting approach) there are three types of knowledge roles:

- procedures to assign a value to a parameter, which would result in a design extension
- constraints that could be violated in a design extension
- fixes for a constraint violation.

The user can enter one of the three types of knowledge: PROCEDURE, CONSTRAINT and FIX. For each type of knowledge, a fixed menu (or schema) is presented to the user (in SALT's case a domain expert) to be filled out.

An example of the information provided by a user for a constraint is as follows (from [Marcus and McDermott, 1989]):

1	Constrained value	CAR-JAMB-RETURN
2	Constraint type	MAXIMUM
3	Constraint name	MAXIMUM-CAR-JAMB-RETURN
4	Precondition	DOOR-OPENING = SIDE
5	Procedure	CALCULATION
6	Formula	PANEL-WIDTH * STRINGER-QUANTITY
7	Justification	THIS PROCEDURE IS TAKEN FROM INSTALLATION MANUAL I, P. 12b.

Reusing PSMs and Reusing Domain Knowledge

Problem-solving methods can be reused on other similar problems in different domains. For example, the general process of designing a car may be very similar to the general process employed when designing a house. Thus the PSM may be reused for other design tasks.

Furthermore, different PSMs for different problems can potentially use some of the same domain knowledge. For example, a knowledge of electronics and electrical components within TVs can be used by a PSM to fix faults in current TVs. This domain knowledge can be used by another PSM to design new TVs. Thus domain knowledge can be reused for different applications.

Activity 6

This activity will help you extend your understanding of the concept of reuse in relation to PSMs.

Visit the Internet Reasoning Service at: http://kmi.open.ac.uk/projects/irs/

Produce a set of brief notes on the types of reuse described there.

Feedback 6

Your notes should clearly distinguish:
- direct reuse
- parameterised reuse
- generic plug and play.

Genericity or Ease of Use?

To enable reuse we need to develop a library of PSMs. However, these are often difficult to classify, as we need to specify the:

- genericity, i.e., the task independence
- formality
- granularity, i.e., the scale of the PSMs contained within the library.

Furthermore, there is a usability/reusability trade off to consider.

Activity 7

Consider the following scenario. You have at your disposal two very successful professional designers.

Person A has successfully designed a wide range of things: houses, bridges, gardens and even a railway station but they have never designed any electrical device.

Person B has successfully designed: HiFi, MP3 payers, digital cameras and computers but all they have ever designed is electrical equipment.

Which person would you choose to design a new plasma screen TV?

Which person would you choose to design a museum?

Feedback 7

When it comes to choosing the best person for the job you have to consider which one has the most appropriate knowledge.

- For the task of designing the plasma screen TV you presumably choose person B. Even though they have never designed a TV before they clearly have a detailed knowledge of electrical systems, having already designed a range of electrical devices.
- For the task of designing a museum you presumably choose person A. Person B is a very successful designer however they have never designed anything except electrical equipment. Person A has had a very varied design career. Even if they know nothing about museums they can draw on a wide range of experience. Presumably before designing the museum they will need to find out about museums and they may need to expand their design knowledge slightly. For example, they may need to learn how to design crowd control spaces.

This scenario demonstrates an important concept: the issue of generic knowledge verses ease of reuse. Person A has a generic design knowledge that can be reused in a wide range of situations, however before it is reused it may need adapting/updating. Person B can easily reuse their knowledge, without the need for adaptation, however this knowledge is more focused, i.e., less generic, and therefore can only be reused in a limited range of situations.

Task-independent PSMs will require refinement and adaptation before they can be used but can be reused in a wide range of situations.

Task-dependent PSM may require little or no adaptation but can only be reused in some circumstances.

A very generic design PSM, i.e., a task-independent PSM, may be used to design houses, cars and clothes. However, because it is a very generic PSM, it may need to be refined for each task before use. In contrast, a task-dependent PSM created specifically for designing electrical equipment may be used to design TVs, DVDs or computers without any adaptation but would not be appropriate for other design tasks such as designing houses or gardens.

The use of PSMs has one significant advantage over the use of blackboard architectures, namely they promote reuse. By separating control knowledge from domain knowledge reuse of both is enabled.

Activity 8

Consider the following scenario. A KBS is created for a car mechanic to diagnose faults in a range of cars. This system is created with the control and domain knowledge as separate components. Thus we have:

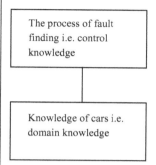

Identify other situations in which we can reuse the control knowledge.

Identify other situations in which we can reuse the domain knowledge.

Feedback 8

By plugging in knowledge of other equipment such as mobile phones or computers the control knowledge can be reused to make other fault-finding KBS. These could be used by other technicians.

By creating a control method to describe the process of designing equipment the domain knowledge of cars can be reused to create a KBS that designs cars.

Limitations of PSMs

The limitations of PSMs include:

- To enable reuse we need to develop a library of PSMs. However, PSMs are difficult to classify. We need to specify the genericity (task independence) and granularity (size).
- There are reusability—usability trade offs to consider. Task-independent PSMs will require refinement and adaptation before they can be used. They can however be reused in a range of situations. Task-dependent PSMs require little adaptation before use, but they are less easily used elsewhere.

Summary

This section has provided an introduction to how KBSs can be supported with separate libraries of PSMs.

Web Links
Generic Task Toolset
http://www.cis.ohio-state.edu/lair/Projects/GTToolset/toolset.html
IBROW
http://swi.psy.uva.nl/projects/IBROW3/home.html
KEML
ftp://swi.psy.uva.nl/pub/keml/keml.html
Protege
http://smi-web.stanford.edu/projects/protege/
Sisyphus III
http://www.psyc.nott.ac.uk/research/ai/sisyphus/
VITAL
http://kmi.open.ac.uk/~john/vital/vital.html

Self-Assessment Questions

Question 1

Contrast the reusability of task-dependent and task-independent PSMs.

Question 2

Describe the role of the following three inferences in the P&R PSM:

- propose
- check
- revise.

How does the select parameter inference function?

Suggested Solutions

Answer 1

Task-independent PSMs require refinement and adaptation before they can be used
but they can be reused in a range of situations.
Task-dependent PSMs require little adaptation before use but they are less easily
reused elsewhere.

Answer 2

The PROPOSE inference computes the value of the selected parameter.
The CHECK inference verifies the constraints after computing parameter values.
The REVISE inference remedies a violated constraint.

The SELECT PARAMETER inference chooses one parameter to have its value
computed and uses the Input Parameters, the Parameter Values already computed
and the Parameter Dependency Relations to obtain a Selected Parameter.

SECTION 4: KNOWLEDGE ACQUISITION DESIGN SYSTEM (KADS)

Introduction

This section provides an explanation of the KADS methodology.

Objectives

By the end of the section you will be able to:

• describe KADS.
• Understand how KADS is an example of a PSM.

Purpose of KADS

In general information systems development, there are many methodologies that can be used to provide an overall control of that development.

Within KBS development however, there was no overall design strategy for a considerable time.

Activity 9
This activity will draw on your knowledge of information systems development to help you anticipate the need for something significantly different in relation to methodologies for KBS development.

Considering the process of developing an information system, what factors might make it difficult to directly apply such methodologies to the development of KBSs?

Feedback 9

You should have been able to recognise that most information systems are concerned with data and KBSs are concerned with knowledge. Data is generally much more accessible—being stored in databases of one kind or another, whereas knowledge is stored in the minds of experts.

Knowledge-based systems also tend to be more complex. Information systems often perform numerical calculations which have a correct answer, e.g. a worker who works for 10 hours for £10 per hour should get paid £100. £99.99p while very close would be an incorrect answer. A KBS on the other hand simulates a human being making decisions. While decisions can be good decisions or bad decisions they cannot usually be clearly categorised as right or wrong. For example, when choosing a university course, clearly some courses are in a subject that will interest the student more than others and some will lead to qualifications that will enable a graduate to find work more easily than others. Taking these factors into account you may choose to do a degree in computing. If you are not reasonably able in mathematics doing an engineering degree may be a poor choice for you—but this decision could not be clearly categorised as a wrong decision. Thus checking the quality of the outputs from a KBS is much more difficult than checking the outputs from an information system.

The KADS is an attempt to overcome this difficulty by providing a system for knowledge engineers and ES developers to follow.

Knowledge acquisition design system aims to solve two specific problems in KBS development:

• Firstly, large-scale problems could not easily be solved by one knowledge base—especially if it was restricted to one knowledge representation scheme—and which was very inefficient to run and difficult to maintain. This was overcome by the development of blackboard architectures and the same principle of segmented knowledge bases is supported by KADS.
• Secondly, the benefits of explicitly separating control and the domain knowledge became clear as the modelling approach was adopted, and thus the KADS methodology was developed as a problem-solving methodology (see previous section).

Knowledge acquisition design system, and its more recent variant, CommonKADS, is the most commonly used methodology within Europe for the development of KBSs. KADS is the most prominent example of a PSM-based methodology, thus discussions in the previous section apply to KADS.

Knowledge Acquisition in KADS

The KADS approach includes the following knowledge acquisition activities:

- Elicitation—eliciting the knowledge
- Analysis—interpreting the knowledge
- Formalisation—formalising the knowledge so that it can be used in a computer.

Before KADS, there was an approach to knowledge acquisition that consisted simply in:

- acquiring domain knowledge
- transferring knowledge (somehow) to a KBS.

In this approach the experts reasoning process was not modelled—it was left to the inference engine to determine if/when to apply the knowledge.

The KADS approach treats the knowledge-acquisition process as a modelling activity, i.e., the expert's problem-solving knowledge is modelled, among other models, this leads to the efficient application of domain knowledge and allows reuse of control and domain knowledge.

Multiple Models in KADS

Based on the ideas of modelling the PSMs, KADS supports the development of various models. These include:

Process or organisation model, where the processes within the organisation are modelled in order to assess the role and impact of the KBS. This reduces the friction that may occur when trying to implement the KBS within the organisation.

Expertise model, models the problem solving or expert behaviour required of the system. Knowledge acquisition design system libraries of reusable PSMs have been created to support prediction, assessment, design, planning and schedule tasks.

Activity 10
This activity involves you in discovering the characteristics of some of the other models used in KADS.

Other models that may be used in the KADS approach include:
- Application model—defines the functions of the system with respect to users
- Task model—defines the tasks that the KBS must perform
- Cooperation model
- Conceptual model
- Design model.
  1. Search the Internet for documents relating to the last three of these models.
  2. Make brief notes on their purpose.

Feedback 10
You should have been able to locate documents describing the models as follows:

Cooperation model—specifies how subtasks in the task model should be done if
cooperation is necessary. This model would need to be applied if, for example,
the solution of a problem by the system required information from the user.

Conceptual model—this is essentially a combination of the models of expertise
and cooperation as these together specify the overall behaviour of the system.
Such a model would be based on abstract descriptions of the objects and operations that the system needs to know about.

Design model—specifies how to implement the system in the form of descriptions of computational and representational techniques as well as hardware and
software requirements.

Theses models essentially represent steps in defining the goals of the KBS development.

Some of the advantages of this multiple model approach in KADS are that those
involved in the development of the KBS can more easily identify, describe and
select characteristics of the targeted system as well as focus on specific aspects
while ignoring—at least for the moment—other components.

Activity 11
This activity will help you visualise the relationship between the various models
used in the KADS methodology.

Complete the following diagram that illustrates the relationship between the
various models.

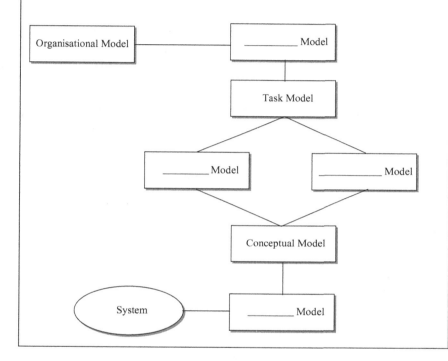

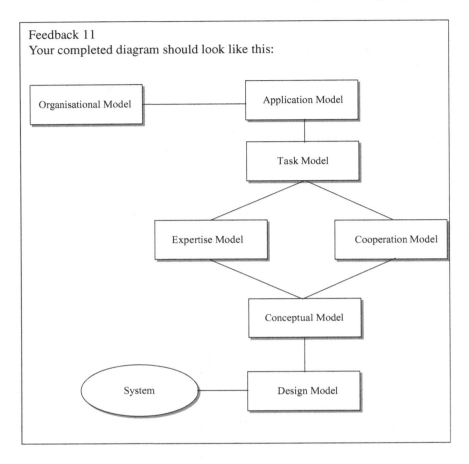

Feedback 11
Your completed diagram should look like this:

The KADS Four-Layer Model

As well as using modelling as a technique for describing the components of a KBS during the process of its development, KADS views a completed KBS using a model with four layers. This four-layer model provides a method of representing knowledge within an ES (see Figure 6.6).

Domain Layer

The domain is the static knowledge in the KBS. The basic knowledge and some relationships are recorded by the knowledge engineer using the linguistic level of the conceptual model.

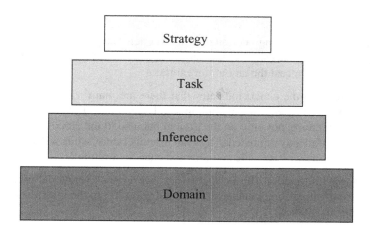

FIGURE 6.6. The four-layer KADS model.

The Inference Layer

Knowledge is grouped into related units, or meta-classes and a useful classification system is devised. Relationships between knowledge may be identified and recorded in frames or semantic networks. In this layer, knowledge is being transformed from the linguistic level to the conceptual level.

Task Layer

This layer describes how the domain knowledge and inferences from that knowledge can be used to solve a specific task. It uses the conceptual links in the knowledge and then attempts to add the epistemological relationships.

Strategy Layer

This layer deals with the overall approach and planning involved in solving a problem. The aim is to identify problems in the knowledge-building process (e.g. inconsistent rules) at an early stage in the system design process. It therefore attempts to place a formal structure on knowledge, moving from the epistemological level to the logical level prior to implementation.

Activity 12
You are a knowledge engineer attempting to elicit knowledge to build a new ES. The knowledge domain is weather prediction. You are currently working on a module to forecast the amount of rainfall.

Knowledge from the expert indicates that there are many variables affecting accurate weather forecasting including wind speed and direction as well as overall temperature, not only on the ground but also in the clouds. The expert notes that rainfall may be preceded by a fall in temperature, while winds blowing off the sea to the west provide an increased chance of rainfall.

As far as the information allows, start to produce a four-layer model for a KBS by outlining which components of the model will refer to the information and knowledge available.

Feedback 12
You should have been able to produce an outline similar to the following:
Domain layer
Data concepts include: temperature, wind speed, wind direction, amount of cloud cover, etc.

Inference layer
Inferences from the data concepts will include:

Falling temperature indicates increased probability of rain.
A westerly wind from the sea normally provides increased chance rain.

Task layer
The basic task or reasoning technique is chosen, with a decision being made concerning task-driven or goal-driven structures (or alternatively a choice will be made between backward or forward chaining).

Strategy layer
The formal structure of the knowledge is identified (this is a forecasting model) and the appropriate data structures designed.

Strengths and Weaknesses of KADS

A major advantage of the KADS approach is in the idea of generic task models (GTMs), also known as interpretation models. These can be thought of as skeleton models for typical tasks or task fragments, such as 'classification' or 'system diagnosis' stored in generic *task libraries*. Knowledge engineers can use suitably chosen GTMs to guide the knowledge-acquisition process in a new domain, refining and combining GTMs to produce a fully specified model.

KADS does have weaknesses, for example:

- It is difficult to translate between or connect the different layers.
- All the layers are rarely used; most people tend to use the diagrams, but these are not expressive enough for all requirements.
- KADS systems typically end up with large amounts of documentation for relatively modest systems and are hard to change.
- KADS does not itself specify the representation types to be used in describing its various models.

The last point is important, since we must decide what our needs are for representations. Suitable representations must have a two-sided functionality, i.e., they must be able to:

- express the language of the testing techniques
- describe systems in such a way that they are recognisable to those who must contribute to the development of evaluation models.

Summary

In this section you have seen how the KADS methodology can be used to construct a variety of models to bridge the gap between required behaviour and system behaviour for a KBS.

Web Links

CommonKADS

http://www.commonkads.uva.nl/frameset-commonkads.html

SECTION 5: THE HYBRID METHODOLOGY (HyM)

Introduction

This section provides an introduction to HyM and its use within the design of hybrid intelligent information systems (HIISs).

Objectives

By the end of the section you will be able to:

- evaluate the place of HyM in knowledge engineering.

Hybrid Methodology (HyM): An Introduction

HyM is a more recent ES development methodology—developed, in fact, at the University of Sunderland—aimed at supporting the creation of HIISs. It aims to provide an enhanced software development life cycle that supports project development both incrementally and in one go. The methodology recognises that many information needs in society can be satisfied by the development of conventional information systems. However, additional use could be made from these systems by integrating intelligent or KBSs with them.

Activity 13
This activity will help you understand the concept of HIISs by asking you to integrate what you know of conventional information systems with the knowledge of KBSs you have gained so far from this book.

Compare and contrast the main features of conventional information systems and KBSs.

Feedback 13
You should have been able to highlight the differences between conventional and KBSs approximately as follows:

Conventional information systems
Conventional information systems are designed to provide *specific functions over a collection of shared data* in some *information repository*. The data being used is generally well structured and therefore susceptible to traditional processing.

KBS
Intelligent systems or KBSs or intelligent systems are designed to *manage and handle* **knowledge** *and deduce other information from that knowledge.* The system uses *declarative knowledge and some reasoning mechanism* to help reach appropriate decisions. Many KBSs are *tailor-made to the specific knowledge domain* that they are working in.

The HyM methodology supports the development of systems that integrate procedural information processing and declarative knowledge-based processing. These two types of processing are modelled and integrated in systems created with the methodology.

An overview of the HyM life cycle is shown in Figure 6.7.

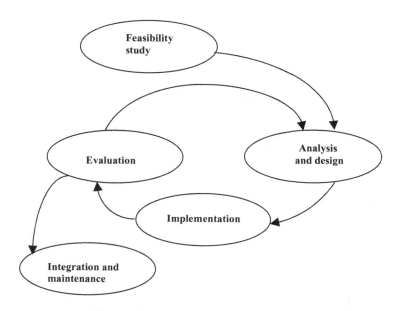

FIGURE 6.7. The HyM life cycle—overview.

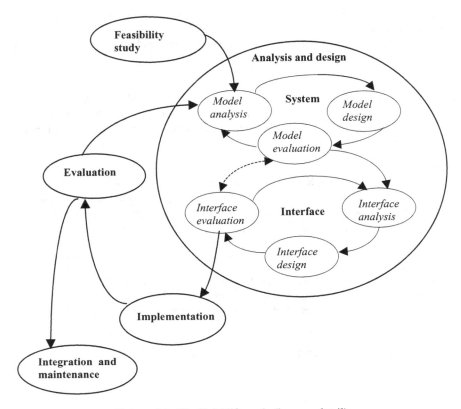

FIGURE 6.8. The HyM life cycle (in more detail).

HyM Development Life Cycle

The HyM development life cycle in more detail looks like Figure 6.8.

As already suggested, the development follows the standard life cycle approach with all systems going through the phases of:

- Feasibility study
- Analysis and design
- Implementation
- Evaluation
- Integration and maintenance.

The life cycle also includes some iteration, within the combined analysis and design stage which can be completed using incremental prototyping.

Looking at the analysis and design stage of the HyM life cycle in even more detail (see Figure 6.9), we can see that provision has been for the development of user

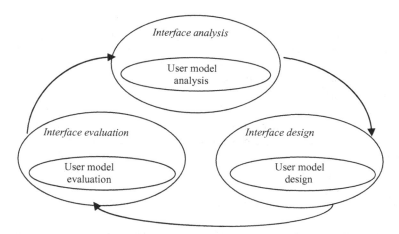

FIGURE 6.9. Integrating user modelling into HyM.

models. By explicitly promoting the creation of user models the HyM methodology is recognising that different system users have different needs, this is particularly true for the users of HIIS, and by modelling these needs a system can be developed to take into consideration the individual needs of the user when responding with advice or recommendations.

The HyM life cycle bears some similarities to both the Waterfall model and the evolutionary prototyping approach to software development.

The HyM Life Cycle and the Waterfall Model Compared

The classic Waterfall life cycle is simple to understand but as a tool to control a software-engineering project, fundamentally flawed. It implies a strongly sequential process through the steps of systems analysis, design, coding, testing and maintenance. It presumes that at the end of the analysis stage all of the details and functionality of the required system can be determined. However, as many projects have shown, it is not always possible to obtain a perfect set of requirements and this has caused many projects to overrun in terms of development cost and time.

Even when adapted to allow previous stages of the life cycle to be revisited, the Waterfall model is still flawed. While previous stages can be revisited, it still strongly implies moving forward through the life cycle and that by revisiting previous stages a backward step is being taken. Furthermore it implies that at the testing stage it is permitted, presumably sometimes even necessary, to go back as far as the analysis stage. This has specific implications for the cost of any software-engineering project. To find out during the design phase, that more analysis is required has quite different cost/time implications than finding out during the testing phase.

In particular, when developing KBSs there is a particular difficulty to be addressed—this is specifying the knowledge to be contained with the system. It is very difficult when developing a KBS to define exactly what knowledge is required. For example, if a KBS is advising a university applicant about suitable courses it should presumably offer advice based upon the subject and career interests of the applicant but should it also assess the applicant's academic suitability and personality traits? When assessing academic suitability should it assess intellectual skills only or other skills such as creative, group work, communication and social skills? This problem is aided by the use of a prototyping life cycle where the knowledge base can be iteratively evaluated and gaps in the reasoning process identified and corrected. Finally, it will be shown by demonstration that the reasoning capabilities of the knowledge bases are adequate even when it was impossible to initially define what knowledge was required.

Thus by comparison with the Waterfall model, HyM has an integrated analysis and design phase with a highly iterative loop. Preliminary analysis is followed by preliminary design and then by an evaluation stage. These three steps are repeated until evaluation shows that the analysis has fully captured the requirements of the knowledge base components and that the design adequately reflects those requirements.

Throwaway prototypes are used as part of the analysis stage.

Activity 14
This activity helps to interpret the advantages the HyM life cycle has over the Waterfall model.

Drawing on your knowledge of the Waterfall model gained in previous modules, suggest what advantages are available with the HyM life cycle.

Feedback 14
You should have been able to suggest some of the following:
- There is no implication that analysis should be finished prior to the design starting with implied failure when this is not the case.
- Contrary to this there is a strong implication that more analysis will be required after preliminary design has taken place. In doing the preliminary design a better understanding of the problem can evolve and this knowledge can help guide the further analysis that will be required for complex projects.
- Emphasis is placed on evaluation. This is essential to ensure that the finished analysis fully captures the requirements for the system and that the design of the system is also satisfactory. Thus, when the analysis is finished we can have confidence in the final product.

The HyM Life Cycle and the Spiral Model Compared

When developing knowledge based, or hybrid components, specific quality issues need to be addressed by the evaluation. These include ensuring the completeness and depth of knowledge and ensuring the quality of the reasoning processes encapsulated within the system. As part of this evaluation process it will be necessary to test the quality and completeness of the knowledge and reasoning processes designed by developing throwaway prototypes (implemented using a shell or convenient tool).

However, there are several fundamental differences between this approach and the spiral model:

- Unlike the spiral model this is not an incremental development phase. The loop within the analysis and design stage has one purpose only, to ensure the quality of the design for the part of the final system currently under development. This iteration will occur whether or not the decision was made to develop the entire system in one phase or incrementally. These incremental iterations are the outer loop of the HyM life cycle, not the inner loop within the analysis and design phase (see Figure 6.8).
- By separating these two loops the incremental loop will be less frequent and more definable. This will facilitate better planning for large projects and help generate foreseeable project end dates.
- Finally, unlike the spiral model, the inner loop does not encompass the development phase. Thus software is not constantly evolving into the finished product. Any prototypes developed during the analysis and design phase are throwaway prototypes used as analysis, design and evaluation tools. From the designs generated 'clean' products (i.e., with entirely fresh code) are developed during the implementation stage.

The HyM life cycle thus addresses the weakness of the spiral model, namely its lack of scalability and its weakness as a management tool.

User Centred Design (UCD) and the Role of Intelligent Interface Technology

In the early stages of the analysis and design phase emphasis is placed firmly on management of stable data and knowledge so as to ensure validity of systems. However, considering the needs of the users become increasingly important as the functionality of the system becomes clearer. In other methodologies user involvement varies from participation only at evaluation stages, to right through the entire life cycle. In the HyM methodology UCD is promoted implying that system users are made a central issue throughout the design process.

Two distinguishable user tasks are advocated, as a member of the design team responsible in core system development and a wider role in interface design.

A particular issue to be considered is the behaviour KBS or hybrid components within the system. As discussed in a previous chapter we expect human experts to be able to explain their reasoning and thus we would like a KBS to have this facility also. One issue to be considered is the format of these explanations.

Activity 15

Consider the following two statements and identify which statement is intended for a patient and which is intended for a nurse.

Statement 1. 'Metatarsal ligament stretched, prognosis is good, immobilise and elevate'.

Statement 2. 'The patient has strained a ligament in the foot. The foot will be OK within a week or two but it needs to be strapped up for support and rested with the foot raised'.

Feedback 15

These two statements have the same meaning however you should have been able to recognise that the first statement was issued by a doctor for a nurse the second was the doctor's explanation for a patient.

By appreciating that patients and nurses have different levels of understanding a doctor can tailor their messages appropriately.

A HIIS must make its messages appropriate to the needs of the user. This requires a level of intelligence on behalf of the interface. A user model is an essential part of intelligent interface technology as it is this that allows the system to understand the needs of the user and respond accordingly. In HyM the development of a user model is an integral part of the interface cycle. In the case of HIIS, the user model's role is clear: to model users for the purpose of tailoring system responses.

Strengths of HyM

The HyM life cycle has the following advantages when developing HIISs:

- Separate loops to allow incremental development, at the discretion of the project manager, and for quality control. This will improve project management and aid the estimation of final dates for the deployment of the finished system.
- A highly iterative, combined analysis and design phase that will guide the analysis required for large complex projects and facilitates an evaluation of the analysis undertaken and the corresponding system design. This is essential to ensure the completeness and quality of the reasoning contained within the system.
- Separation of stable functional requirements from volatile user considerations to facilitate the development of reusable repositories and components.

- The seamless integration of information system technologies and knowledge-based technologies, either tightly or loosely coupled depending upon the requirements of the system.
- Support for the development of intelligent interfaces allows system messages to be tailored to the needs of the user.

Hybrid Intelligent Information Systems (HIISs)

Many applications are developed with no integration between conventional and intelligent systems. However, the increased amount of data being made available to businesses means that more complex systems are required to access and retrieve that data; in other words there is a need for hybrid systems. Development of these systems will mean that large stores of data will be managed more efficiently providing some benefit to organisations and society as a whole.

Format of a HIIS System

Hybrid intelligent information systems include two types of knowledge:

- algorithmic
- expert's reasoning.

Algorithmic knowledge refers to the format of the computer software, where object-orientated programming will be used to produce and control the knowledge base and handle problems.

Expert's reasoning is captured by means of rules and frames in the standard elicitation process. The rules and frames are converted to objects within the HIIS system.

Structured analysis methods are used to analyse system-structured procedural functions. Information management methods are used for the data analysis and a knowledge analysis method (e.g. KADS) is selected to perform the knowledge analysis.

An intelligent integrated hospital patient system, as described below would be one example of a HIIS (see Figure 6.10).

Imagine an intelligent integrated hospital patient system made up of the following three component systems:

- A patient administration system
- A patient diagnostic system
- An intelligent appointment system.

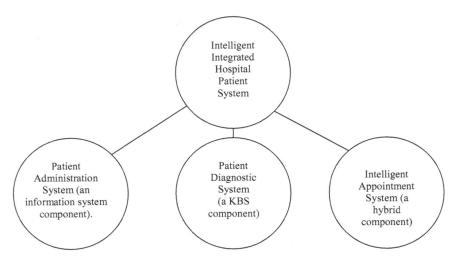

FIGURE 6.10. A hybrid intelligent information system.

The patient administration system would be a conventional procedural record keeping system, i.e., a database system used to manage patient records, details of drugs prescribed, a doctor's records and test results.

The patient diagnostic system would be a KBS used by doctors to aid diagnosis in certain complex situations. As this is integrated into the same system as the patient administration system it would be able to share access to the same databases and thus automatically have access to patient data stored elsewhere in the system. Similarly, a diagnosis made by this component could be recorded and accessed by the patient administration system.

These two components integrated together would thus form a HIIS and enjoy the benefits offered by seamlessly sharing data.

The intelligent appointment system would in itself represent a highly coupled HIIS and demonstrates the power of integrating these two diverse technologies. Imagine a conventional patient appointment system with added diagnostic knowledge. Instead of appointments being offered to patients on a first come first served basis, the knowledge component could grade the appointment as 'Life threatening', 'Urgent' or 'Non-urgent' and appointments could then be offered on this basis. Thus, patients with life-threatening conditions would gain priority access over others.

The architecture of a HIIS system is shown in Figure 6.11. This consists of 3 levels:

• Repositories Level,
• Components Level, and
• HISS Level.

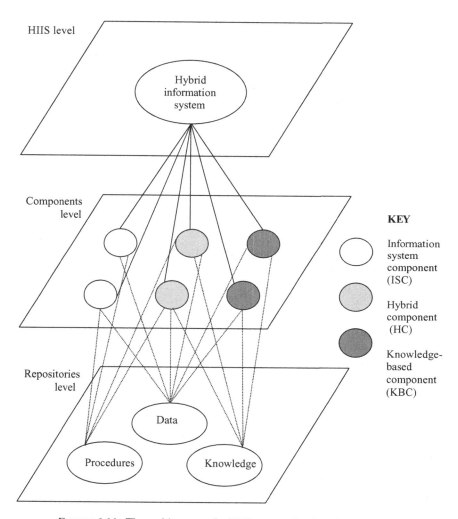

FIGURE 6.11. The architecture of a HIIS system developed using HyM.

Repositories Level

This contains the knowledge, procedures and databases to be used within the system. While each of these can be designed separately, care must be taken to ensure that they contain detail relevant to the domain being modelled.

Components Level

This level contains the three different types of software used in a HISS system—conventional information system components, KBS components and hybrid components. The KBS components can be ESs, neural networks, case-based reasoning components or any other type of knowledge component. Thus within one system it is possible to integrate conventional information system components and KBS components. Integrating information system components with KBSs allows the development of large software systems where elements of those systems exhibit intelligent characteristics.

Hybrid Intelligent Information System Level

At this level the software is viewed as a complete unified system.

Summary

In this section you have learned how the HyM methodology provides an appropriate approach for the development of systems integrating the components of conventional and intelligent systems.

Self-Assessment Question

Question 1A

A large KBS is required to diagnose equipment faults on a North Sea Oil Extraction Platform (a very large and complex piece of equipment).

Which of the following methodologies would be appropriate method for this problem?

• Blackboard architectures
• KADS
• HyM.

Question 1B

For the application above it has now been decided to develop the KBS in such a way that some of the knowledge contained within the system will describe problems that are common to other Oil Extraction platforms and this knowledge may be reused when developing future systems. Briefly assess the support each of the following methodologies give to a knowledge engineer who wishes to develop reusable knowledge components.

• Blackboard architectures
• KADS
• HyM.

Question 2

The University of Sunderland is the main participant in current research into HyM. Obtain a list of current published papers and try and identify any practical applications of HyM from this list.

Answer to Self-Assessment Question

Answer 1A

When choosing an appropriate methodology (blackboard architectures, KADS and HyM) we need to consider

- the scale of the problem
- the need to separate control and domain knowledge
- the limitations imposed by one inference engine
- the maintenance of large KBSs
- and the ability to integrate procedural and declarative reasoning.

The problem as described is clearly huge and therefore for efficiency and maintenance reasons it is essential to segment the knowledge base. One knowledge base implies one inference engine. Segmenting the knowledge base allows the use of multiple inference engines and hence flexibility in the choice of knowledge representation schemes. It is not certain if multiple knowledge representation (KR) schemes are required here but the scale of the problem would indicate this is a possibility. For all these reasons it is necessary to segment the knowledge base and thus the use of a methodology such as blackboard architectures is essential.

However do we need to consider the use of KADS or HyM?

KADS has various advantages over blackboard architectures but the most important are the separation of control and domain knowledge (enabling reuse) and advanced modelling features, e.g. modelling the impact of the KBS on the organisation. It is not clear that either of these features is required for the application specified.

When considering HyM we need to consider if a hybrid intelligent information system is required. The specification above suggests only a KBS is required. In some applications it is easy to see the benefits of integrating a KBS with a conventional information system (e.g. a KBS to recommend suitable courses could be integrated with an online application form) but until such an advantage is suggested HyM would not be the most appropriate methodology.

Having considered the alternatives it would appear that blackboard architectures is the most appropriate methodology to apply.

Answer 1B

Knowledge reuse has now been specified; this eliminates blackboard architectures as a candidate methodology as using this methodology no attempt is made to separate control and domain knowledge.

Problem-solving methodologies (of which KADS is an example) are very good at promoting reuse, as specified in the problem. However, there are still complex issues to be resolved. There is of course the usability/reusability trade off to consider, the development of PSM libraries and the difficulty in specifying task genericity/granularity.

There is still no indication that a hybrid system is required thus HyM is not the most appropriate methodology.

Despite the issues, KADS is the clear choice here.

Answer 2

A list of current research papers (from 2000 to 2003) is provided below and following on from this is a short description of one system developed following the HyM methodology.

S. L. Kendal, K. Ashton and X. Chen, 'A Brief Overview of HyM: A Methodology for the Development of Hybrid Intelligent Information Systems', *Proc. of the 15th Int. Conf. on Software Engineering and Knowledge Engineering*, San Francisco, California, USA, July 2003; ISBN 1-891706-12-8

K. Ashton and S. L. Kendal, 'Introducing User Centred Design into a Hybrid Intelligent Information System Methodology', *Proc. International Conference on Computing and Information Technologies*, Montclair, New Jersey, USA, October 2001

S. Kendal and X. Chen, 'Towards Hybrid Knowledge and Software Engineering', *Proc. International Conference on Computing and Information Technologies*, Montclair, New Jersey, USA, October 2001

K. Ashton, S. L. Kendal and M. R. Hawthorne, 'HyM: A Hybrid Methodology for the Integration of Conventional and Knowledge Based Information Systems', *Proc. 4th International Conference Neural Networks and Expert Systems in Medicine and Healthcare*, Greece, June 2001

U. Rashad, P. Arullendran, M. Hawthorne and S. Kendal, 'A Hybrid Medical Information System for the Diagnosis of Dizziness', *Proc. 4th International Conference Neural Networks and Expert Systems in Medicine and Healthcare*, Greece, June 2001

S. Kendal, X. Chen and A. Masters 'HyM: A Hybrid Methodology for the Development of Integrated Hybrid Intelligent Information Systems', *Proceedings of Fusion 2000—3rd International Conference on Information Fusion*, Paris, July 2000.

A Hybrid Medical Information System for Dizziness

The main area where this methodology has so far been used is in the development of a hybrid medical intelligent information system.

HMISD, called Hybrid Medical Information System for Dizziness, is a typical HIIS for the diagnosis of vertigo diseases. It was developed as part of a research project. This system involves many activities that often happen in hospitals and doctor's offices, such as registration, medical record management, clinical diagnosis, laboratory information management, clinical research and drug data management. This complex software system consists of those components in traditional medical information systems and medical KBSs.

The HMISD software was based on the requirements of North Riding Infirmary (NRI), Middlesbrough, UK, a hospital specialising in diseases of the ear, nose and throat.

Dizziness is a common complaint and can be a symptom of numerous disease processes. These can vary from psychogenic disorder in origin to presentations of serious intra-cranial pathology. Wright describes dizziness as follows:

'Dizziness is a difficult condition, and having to diagnose and manage the dizzy patient may seem like being thrown in at the deep end when you can only just swim' (Wright, 1988).

The system developed was a hybrid medical information system that incorporated traditional medical information system and medical KBSs. It allowed patients or clerks to input medical records and symptoms as with a traditional medical record system. The system suggests the most probable disease diagnosis and gives suggestions as to the most suitable investigations.

The five major components of the system are:

• a medical record system
• a clinical decision support system
• a pharmacy system
• a laboratory information system
• a clinical research system.

SECTION 6: BUILDING A WELL-STRUCTURED APPLICATION USING AION BRE

Introduction

This section discusses how the theory we have looked can be implemented in practice, using an industry standard knowledge engineering environment (Aion BRE).

Objectives

By the end of the section you will be able to:

- understand how a well-structured application can be implemented using an industry standard tool.

Review of Theory

During this chapter we have looked at three methodologies. We have seen how, in order to aid maintenance and allow a range of knowledge representation schemes to be used, blackboard architectures promote segmented knowledge bases.

We have also seen how PSMs, and KADs in particular, promote the separation of control knowledge from domain knowledge in order to allow either to be reused.

We will now see how, based on these ideas, an ES may be structured and how this would be implemented in Aion BRE.

A Simple Example

An ES is required to recommend financial investments. Some potential users of the system will be investing their life savings and therefore the investment application should invest their money cautiously. While investing in the stock market may give better returns over a long period investing the money from these users on the stock market would be unwise as the stock market could go down as well as up. However, some of the users of the system will be wealthy customers who are planning to invest what is for them relatively small sums of money. Such customers would accept an element of risk in their investments as long as this is likely to give a higher rate of return. Therefore, the first task the ES should perform is to classify the acceptable level of risk (low or high). Having made this decision, the system should go on to recommend several good investment opportunities in order that the user of the system could make the final choice for themselves.

Looking at this application it is clear the system must make two separate decisions: classify the customer according to the acceptable level of risk and recommend investments.

It is clear that at least two separate knowledge bases are required one for each of these tasks. However, when considering investment knowledge it would seem sensible to subdivide this knowledge into two parts: knowledge of high-risk investment opportunities and knowledge of low-risk opportunities.

Having segmented the knowledge base we can now consider using different knowledge representation schemes for each knowledge base. On the assumption that for each of these we have decided to encode our knowledge using rules we can now decide whether to use forward chaining or backward chaining for each part of the decision making process.

For the first task 'classify customer' we have one clear goal to determine the level of risk (low or high). This would suggest that backward chaining would be the most appropriate method. An additional advantage of using backward chaining would be that only relevant questions are asked and thus this reduces the time spent by the user answering questions.

For the second task, recommend investments, there are multiple goals to be considered (each potential investment opportunity). This would therefore indicate the use of forward chaining. Clearly, this may necessitate the user answering numerous questions up front. For pragmatic reasons if this was too burdensome the system could be developed using backward chaining though this would limit the effectiveness of the recommendations. For the sake of this example we will presume that forward chaining has been chosen for this task.

We have now segmented our knowledge base, as theory suggests we should, and considered where we should use forward chaining and backward chaining. However, we have as yet to separate control and domain knowledge.

The domain knowledge is the declarative statements regarding the suitability of various investment opportunities and the knowledge required to classify a user.

The control knowledge is the procedural process that the expert would follow in making his or her decision that the proposed ES should mimic. In this example the process is quite simple: first the customer, or user, should be classified, then when classified the relevant investments should be identified using the appropriate knowledge and the result displayed.

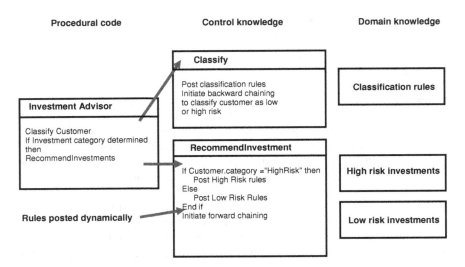

FIGURE 6.12. A structured investment ES.

An overview of a structure for such a system is given in Figure 6.12.

At the left-hand side of Figure 6.12, we can see simple procedural instructions as you would expect to see in any computer program. In the middle we can see two objects containing control knowledge. These contain procedural information but also initiate and control the inference process. The recommend investment object selects which domain knowledge is to be used when forward chaining is initiated. On the right are the three domain knowledge bases. These do not contain procedural information as it is the inference engine that decides if/when these rules should be used.

Thus we have now seen how the knowledge base within an application can be segmented and how control and domain knowledge is separated.

Creating a Benefits Advisor

In considering another example you will see how a system can actually be implemented using Aion BRE.

A knowledge base system is required to advise applicants what benefits they are entitled to—this includes child allowances, disability benefits, rent rebates and other benefits. The system should be well structured with segmented knowledge bases and use forward and backward chaining as appropriate.

Overall plan for system . . .

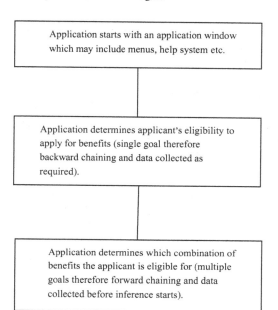

Application starts with an application window which may include menus, help system etc.

Application determines applicant's eligibility to apply for benefits (single goal therefore backward chaining and data collected as required).

Application determines which combination of benefits the applicant is eligible for (multiple goals therefore forward chaining and data collected before inference starts).

Activity 16

Following the format of the investment advisor diagram, Figure 6.12, draw a diagram to show the structure of the benefits advice system proposed. Identify on your diagram domain knowledge and control knowledge.

Feedback 16

Your diagram should look similar to the diagram below.

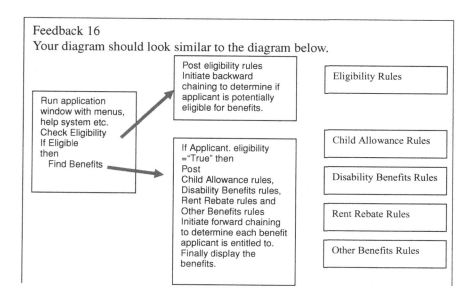

Run application window with menus, help system etc.
Check Eligibility
If Eligible
then
    Find Benefits

Post eligibility rules
Initiate backward chaining to determine if applicant is potentially eligible for benefits.

If Applicant. eligibility ="True" then
Post
Child Allowance rules, Disability Benefits rules, Rent Rebate rules and Other Benefits rules
Initiate forward chaining to determine each benefit applicant is entitled to.
Finally display the benefits.

Eligibility Rules

Child Allowance Rules

Disability Benefits Rules

Rent Rebate Rules

Other Benefits Rules

It is possible that you may not have identified the eligibility rules component. A component such as this is usually required for efficiency purposes. It may be that there are some simple requirements that must be met for all benefit applicants, e.g. being a resident in the country where you are applying for benefits. If this condition is not met then asking a lot of questions about family, financial and physical circumstances would be a waste of the applicant's time. Thus the system determines whether or not an applicant meets the basic requirements before proceeding to ask detailed questions.

Aion BRE is a modern knowledge engineering development environment and like most modern software development tools it is built upon the principles of object orientation. A full discussion of this tool is beyond the scope of this book. However, for our purposes it is sufficient to say that Aion BRE:

- supports segmented knowledge bases
- supports the separation of control and domain knowledge
- allows a combination of rule- and frame-based reasoning (not relevant to this application)
- is fully object oriented with objects (called classes) that contain procedural code (in methods), control knowledge (also in procedural methods) and domain knowledge (in rule methods).

The application as described above was implemented in Aion BRE and the following segment of code was taken from the control method used to determine an applicant's eligibility for benefits.

```
INFER                              // Start inference block
  GoalMakeUnknown(->Eligibility)   // Set Eligibility as unknown
  EligibilityRules                 // Post the rules for inferencing
  Backwardchain(->Eligibility)     // Trigger backward chaining to
                                   // deside on Eligibility
END                                // End inference block
```

The segment of code below was taken from the control method to determine which benefits an applicant is entitled to. The code is a little more complex than the code above but reading though it you should be able to follow the logic.

```
if pAppl.getEligibility = FALSE           // If they are NOT eligible
then
  messagebox("Sorry you are not eligible for any benefits")
else                                      // If they are eligible then
   pPersonalDetails = PersonalDetails.Create  // create and open dialog box
                                          // to get personal details.
  pPersonalDetails.OpenModal(age,disabled, no_of_children)

  INFER                                   // start inference block

     Childallowances                      // post child allowance rules
     DisabilityBenefits                   // post disability benefits rules
     Rentrebates                          // post rent rebate rules
     Otherbenefits                        // post other benefit rules

     Forwardchain                         // Trigger forward chaining
                                             to find the specific
                                          // combination of benefits
                                             applicant is entitled to.
  END                                     // end inference block
if pAppl.GetEligiblebenefits = ""         // Display results
then
  result = "You are not entilted to any benefits."
else
  result = "You are eligible for the following benefits" &
pAppl.GetEligiblebenefits
   end
   messagebox(result)
end                                       // End processing
                                             of eligible applicants
```

Summary

In this section you have learned how:

- a large knowledge base can be segmented
- the inference process can be tailored to each knowledge base (in this case forward or backward chaining)
- control and domain knowledge is separated
- Aion BRE implements the theoretical principles discussed in this chapter.

References

Problem-solving methods

Coelho, E. and Lapalme, G. (1996). Describing reusable problem-solving methods with a method ontology. In *Proceedings of Tenth Knowledge Acquisition for Knowledge-Based Systems Workshop*, Banff, Canada.

Marcus, S. (1988). SALT: a knowledge-acquisition tool for propose-and-revise systems. In Marcus, S. (editor), *Automating Knowledge Acquisition for Expert Systems*. Kluwer Academic Publishers: The Netherlands, pp. 81–123.

Marcus, S. and McDermott, J. (1989). SALT: a knowledge acquisition language for propose-and-revise systems. *Artificial Intelligence*, 39(1):1–37.

Yost, G. R. (1994). *Configuring Elevator Systems*. Technical report, Knowledge Systems Laboratory, Stanford University. (Edited and changed by T. E. Rothenfluh in http://camis.stanford.edu/projects/protege/sisyphus-2/s2-0.html.)

KADS and HyM

Schreiber, G., Wielinga, B. and Breuker, J. (1993). *KADS—A Principled Approach to Knowledge-Based System Development*. Academic Press: Harcourt.

Wright, T. (1988). *Dizziness: Guide to Disorders of Balance*. Croom Helm Ltd: London.

7

Uncertain Reasoning

Introduction

In this chapter we will be looking at the need to build facilities for handling uncertainty into knowledge-based systems (KBSs). We will look at one simple way of handling uncertain answers, and three different methods of dealing with uncertain reasoning:

- confidence factors
- probabilistic reasoning
- fuzzy logic.

We will briefly look at the advantages and disadvantages of each of these three methods.

The chapter consists of four sections:

1. Uncertainty and expert systems
2. Confidence factors
3. Probabilistic reasoning
4. Fuzzy logic.

Objectives

By the end of the chapter you will be able to:

- evaluate how expert systems can deal with uncertainty
- describe the use of confidence factors in dealing with uncertainty
- explain probabilistic reasoning and how to define probabilities within expert systems
- explain and use Bayes theorem
- analyse the use of fuzzy logic in dealing with uncertainty.

SECTION 1: UNCERTAINTY AND EXPERT SYSTEMS

Introduction

This section introduces the principle of uncertainty, and shows how uncertainty can be dealt with in expert system design.

Objectives

By the end of the section you will be able to:

• evaluate how KBSs can deal with uncertainty.

Introduction to Uncertainty

So far in this book, we have assumed that an event or activity either occurs or does not occur, or that a declarative statement is either true or false. While this assumption has helped us understand how an expert system works, it is not necessarily true of the real world. Many situations or events cannot be predicted with absolute certainty (or confidence). For example, it is almost impossible to say whether or not it will rain on any given day; rather a probability of rainfall is given. The same situation is true for many other events: there is a probability of occurrence, not absolute certainty or uncertainty.

This chapter describes three methods of dealing with uncertainty:

1. Confidence factors
2. Probabilistic reasoning
3. Fuzzy logic.

Before these methods are described, we need to look at the concept of uncertainty at a more fundamental level.

Reasoning with Missing Information

People cope with uncertainty and uncertain reasoning in many complex situations. Frequently, when trying to deduce the answer to a question, they will assume default or common values when precise data is unknown.

For example, when trying to design a house, it may be that the designer will assume certain things such as the layout of the path leading up to the house or where the front door should be. Based on these assumptions, the designer will design the general layout of the rooms and the internal passageways, before designing specific details within the rooms.

At some point during this design process, some of the earlier assumptions and some of the early conclusions may be proven to be incorrect. In such a case, part of the reasoning process will have to be redone, and the original solutions; i.e., internal design features, will have to be thrown away and redesigned. The term for this process is *non-monotonic reasoning*, which is a method of reasoning that sometimes needs to be built within KBSs.

Clearly, if the design of the house requires data that is missing; for example, the number of people that this house has to accommodate, then the design reached may not be perfect. The more data that is missing, the more guesses the designer has to make, the lower the quality of the final design of the house will be. However, there is only a gradual degradation in performance.

People can cope well with some items of missing data. That is, they do not fail to reach a solution just because one or more items of data are missing. In this situation, the human designer can cope with some data that is missing or information that is uncertain. Not only can they cope with missing or uncertain information, but they can still attempt to find a solution to the problem when they are uncertain of some of their reasoning processes.

However, for many problems, the process is complicated by the fact that there is rarely one correct solution. There is often a range of possible solutions, thus some solutions may be more desirable than others.

Therefore, a system designed to emulate the human reasoning process needs to be able to generate several potential solutions, and rank them in terms of their desirability.

One very simple method of building the ability of handling uncertainty into a KBS, is to allow the user to specify yes, no or unknown when answering questions. If the user answers unknown then extra processing can be triggered by the inference engine to determine an answer when a user cannot. For example, imagine an expert system careers advisor that may want to know if you have good hand/eye coordination before recommending a job as a pilot. If a user answered 'unknown' to this question the system may be able to infer an answer by asking other questions such as 'are you good at fast computer games involving combat?' or 'are you good at fast ball games such as squash?'

Another method is to use *confidence factors*—sometimes called *certainty factors*—which allow the user to express a range of confidence when answering questions, instead of just 'yes', 'no' or 'unknown'. The answer can be expressed as any number between 0 and 1, where 1 is definitely yes, 0 is definitely no, and numbers in between represent some expression of confidence that the answer is yes. This also allows uncertainty to be expressed, not just in the information, but also in the reasoning process.

Causes of Uncertainty in Expert System Design

There are two main causes of uncertainty that occur during the design of expert systems, uncertain information and uncertain reasoning.

Uncertain Information

Firstly, when answering questions posed by the expert system to solve a problem, the user (or patient in this case) may not remember some specific information such as when or whether they have had a specific disease.

Uncertain Reasoning

Secondly, the conclusion for a specific rule may not always be guaranteed to be correct. This usually occurs because the knowledge base of the expert system contains relationships that are known to be not always true. For example, it is clear from medical evidence that people with high blood pressure have a higher than normal chance of having a heart attack. However, it is also clear that not everyone with high blood pressure does actually have a heart attack. Hence, while we may be certain that a patient has high blood pressure we cannot be certain that they will have a heart attack.

An expert system working with uncertain information and using uncertain reasoning can still reach some very important conclusions. If a doctor told you that you needed to take medication to reduce your blood pressure you would be unlikely to disregard this advice just because they were not certain that you would have a heart attack.

SECTION 2: CONFIDENCE FACTORS

Introduction

This section shows how confidence factors can be used to manage uncertainty by acting as a measure of it.

Objectives

By the end of the section you will be able to:

- use confidence factors in dealing with uncertainty
- evaluate the usefulness of confidence factors as a technique for managing uncertainty in knowledge base systems.

Confidence Factors

We need to consider two kinds of uncertainty

Uncertainty in Antecedents

- based on the data supplied by the user or
- deduced from another rule in the rule base.

Uncertainty in a Rule

- based on the expert's confidence in the rule
- based on uncertainty in the data and rules must be combined and propagated to the conclusions.

Imagine we have a rule that states that if A is true, then B is true.

This can be written as:

$$A => B$$

If we are uncertain that A is true however, then clearly we are uncertain that B is true. If we are 80% certain that A is true then we will be 80% certain that B is true:

$$
\begin{array}{ccc}
A & => & B \\
0.8 & & 0.8
\end{array}
$$

However, in many situations, there is uncertainty concerning the *validity of the rule itself*. If, given A we are only 80% certain of B we could write this as

$$0.8$$
$$A => B$$

But what if we are also unsure about A?

$$0.8$$
$$A \quad => B$$
$$0.8 \quad\quad ?$$

In this situation, we can only be 64% certain of event B occurring ($0.8 \times 0.8 = 0.64$).

In other words, if we are only 80% certain that A will occur, we can only be 64% certain of B occurring, i.e., $0.8 \times 0.8 = 0.64$.

This demonstrates that as we follow an uncertain chain of reasoning, we become less and less certain that the result we obtain is accurate. The way in which confidence is propagated through a chain of reasoning is defined by *propagation rules*. In this context, 'rule' is used in a different sense to the word 'rule' in 'rule based system'.

Reasoning with Confidence Factors

When two independent pieces of corroborating evidence each imply that the result is true, clearly this should make us more certain of the result. If we are 80% certain that A implies C, and 80% certain that B implies C, then if A and B are both true, how confident are we that C is true?

Together, clearly we must be more than 80% confident that C is true, as both of these independent pieces of evidence suggests that is the case; so the answer must be higher than 0.8. But still we cannot be 100% certain, so the answer given must be less than one.

To calculate this we *invert the rules*; i.e., we take the rule A implies B and say that given A we are 20% (i.e., 100%—80%) certain that B is *not* true, and given B we are 20% certain that C is *not* true.

We then multiply these two numbers together (0.2×0.2 to give us 0.04) and thus we can say that given A and B, we can be 4% certain that C is NOT true.

Inverting this again (100%—4%) gives us that A and B together means that we are 96% confident that C is true. We therefore get an answer that shows clearly that, given these two corroborating pieces of evidence, we are now very confident, though still not 100% certain, that C is true.

Activity 1
Given that

$$
\begin{array}{ccc}
& 0.8 & 0.6 \\
A & \Rightarrow \quad B & \Rightarrow \quad C \\
0.8
\end{array}
$$

How confident are we that C is true?

Feedback 1
Our confidence that C is true is $0.8 \times 0.8 \times 0.6 = 0.38$

Activity 2
This activity introduces you to inference networks and provides the opportunity for some practice in calculating combinations of confidence factors.

Look at the following diagram:

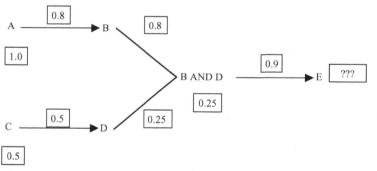

This is known as an *inference network* and illustrates a sequence of relationships between the facts A to E and the confidence factors assigned to the facts as well as the rules connecting them.

The first three equations governing the application of different confident factors and their combination as we work through the network from left to right are as follows:

$$
\begin{aligned}
CF(B) &= CF(A) \times CF(IF\ A\ THEN\ B) = 1 \times 0.8 && = 0.8 \\
CF(D) &= CF(C) \times CF(IF\ C\ THEN\ D) = 0.5 \times 0.5 && = 0.25 \\
CF(B\&D) &= \min\,(CF(B),CF(D)) && = \min\,(0.8, 0.25) = 0.25
\end{aligned}
$$

There are two separate rules being applied here to the ways in which confidence factors are combined, depending on the context. What do you think these rules are?

What justification is there for the difference in these rules?

Complete the calculation for the fourth equation:

$CF(E) = CF(B\&D) \times CF\ (IF\ B\&D\ THEN\ E) =$

Feedback 2

You should have been able to interpret the rules being applied in the equations as follows:

The first equation applies the rule whereby the confidence factors for the fact A and for the rule IF A THEN B are multiplied together to give the confidence for the fact B.

The second equation applies the same rule to calculate the CF(D).

This is appropriate since we begin with certainty (CF $= 1$) for fact A and this is adjusted for the 0.8 confidence in the rule itself IF A THEN B. Similarly, we begin with CF $= 0.5$ for fact C and then adjust for the confidence in the rule IF C THEN D.

The third equation adopts a different approach and takes the minimum of CF(B) and CF(D) since the lack of confidence in the combination of the two components can only be as high as the confidence in the weakest (link) of the two.

The fourth equation can be completed as follows:

CF(E) = CF(B&D) $\times$ CF(IF B&D THEN E) $= 0.25 \times 0.9 = 0.225$

Strengths of Confidence Factors

The main strengths of using confidence factors is that they allow us to:

- express varying degrees of confidence, which allows these values to be manipulated
- rank several possible solutions, especially *if not too much emphasis is placed on the actual numerical values generated.*

It is in this latter respect particularly that confidence factors differ from probabilities, which are calculated values.

Limitations of Confidence Factors

The limitations of confidence factors include:

- Confidence factors are generated from the opinions of one or more experts, and thus there is very little hard evidence for these numbers in practise. People are notoriously unreliable when assigning numbers to express levels of confidence.
- As well as two people finding very different numbers, individuals will also be inconsistent on a day-to-day basis on placing values on confidence factors.

Not withstanding the comment above if a doctor said they were:

- 90% confident that a patient had pneumonia
- 5% confident that a patient had the flu
- 1% confident that a patient had a common cold.

Without placing too much emphasis on the actual numbers we can see that the doctor strongly believes that the patient has pneumonia, and while we recognise that other possibilities exist, the patient should receive the appropriate care for this.

Summary

In this section you have learned about confidence factors and how these can be applied to rules in a knowledge base in order to allow meaning to be extracted from the knowledge even where uncertainty exists.

SECTION 3: PROBABILISTIC REASONING

Introduction

This section introduces the principle of probabilistic reasoning, and shows how Bayes theorem can be used to determine the extent of that uncertainty, firstly in a written example, and then using formulae.

Objectives

By the end of the section you will be able to:

- explain probabilistic reasoning and how to define probabilities within knowledge based systems
- explain and use Bayes theorem.

Bayesian Inference

Probability theory originated with Pascal in the seventeenth century. In the eighteenth century Reverend Bayes developed a theorem that forms the basis of conditional probability. Most attempts to use probability theory to handle uncertainty in KBS are based on Bayes theorem.

If enough data, of the right sort, is available, statistical analysis based on conditional probability theory is the best way to handle uncertainty. However, there is often simply not enough data to produce adequate sample sizes, or the data does not have the necessary properties, such as independence from one another.

Bayes theorem can be represented by the following equation.

$$P(A|B) = \frac{P(B|A)P(A)}{P(B)}$$

In other words, the probability (P) of some event A occurring *given that event B has occurred* is equal to the probability of event B occurring *given that event A has occurred*, multiplied by the probability of event A occurring and divided by the probability of event B occurring.

A Bayesian inference system can be established using the following steps.

1. Define a set of hypotheses, which define the actual results expected.
2. Assign a probability factor to each hypothesis to give an initial assessment of the likelihood of that outcome occurring.

3. Check that the evidence produced (i.e., the outcome of the expert system's decision-making process) meets one of these hypotheses.
4. Amend the probability factors in the light of the evidence received from using the model.

Defining the Hypotheses

The system may have one or more goals. This is the hypothesis that the system has to prove. Those goals are normally mutually exclusive and exhaustive, i.e., only one goal can be achieved.

Activity 3

This activity will help you grasp the implications of the logic underlying Bayes equation.

If:
- $P(H)$ is the prior probability of the hypothesis H being true, before we have determined whether any of the evidence is true or not.
- $P(E:H)$ is the probability of an event E being true, given that a hypothesis H is true.

Consider this in the light of an actual example:

When the base rates of women having breast cancer and having no breast cancer are 1% and 99% respectively, and the hit rate is given as P(positive mammography/breast cancer) = 80%, applying the Bayes theorem leads to a normative prediction as low as P(breast cancer/positive mammography) = 7.8%. That means that the probability that a woman who has a positive mammography actually has breast cancer is less than 8%.

What are represented by:
- $P(H:E)$
- $P(E:not\ H)$

Feedback 3

You should have been able to recognise that:
- P(H:E) is a probability of a hypothesis H (e.g. breast cancer) being true, given that an event E (positive mammography) is true, and
- P(E:not H), is the probability of an event E being true, given that the hypothesis H is known to be false.

Defining the Probabilities

One method of dealing with uncertainty is to state the outcomes from a particular system as a set of hypotheses. There is an inherent assumption within this model that one of the hypotheses will actually occur, so care is needed to ensure that the set of possible hypothesis is complete. Each hypothesis is given a probability of occurring, providing a guide to how often that outcome can be expected.

For example, the set of outcomes from throwing a dice can include the hypothesis that an even number is thrown (50% probability) or an odd number is thrown (also a 50% probability).

Similarly, a set of hypotheses can be produced for the different diseases that a person could be suffering from. Probabilities can be calculated for each disease showing how likely it is that the patient has that disease.

Checking the Evidence Produced

The accuracy of the probabilities attached to each hypothesis will be tested by collecting evidence about the outcome actually achieved. In effect, the hypothesis is proved by ensuring that the evidence actually falls within one of the expected hypotheses.

Amending the Probabilities

The idea the probabilities must be assigned to each hypothesis introduces one of the main points of Bayesian inference: *some assumption must be made concerning the initial probabilities of each hypothesis occurring.*

However, as evidence is obtained showing whether or not each outcome was determined correctly from the facts available, these probabilities can be updated to provide a better match to reality. In turn, this enables the expert system to provide more accurate answers to the problems presented to it.

Example of the Application of Bayes theorem

The hypothesis (H) is that a patient visiting a doctor has the flu. The events (E) are the symptoms that are presented by that patient such as:

- running nose
- sneezing
- high temperature
- headache.

The *prior* probability *based on previous experience* is that $P(\text{flu}) = 0.3$, or there is a 30% chance that any patient walking into the doctors surgery has the flu. This probability will be amended as information about the patient becomes known.

In this case let's imagine that the patient does have a high temperature, runny nose and is sneezing, but has no headache. How do we determine the specific probability of flu given this particular set of symptoms?

Given one symptom, then a new probability of having flu can be determined by collecting statistical data as follows.

	Probability of flu	Probability of not flu
When patient has a high temperature	0.4	0.6
When patient has a runny nose	0.4	0.6
When patient has a headache	0.5	0.5

This suggests that, of those people who have a high temperature, 40% of these have the flu and 60% don't, and so on.

Without knowing anything about a visitor to the doctor's surgery therefore, we can determine that there is a 30% likelihood that they have flu. If we discover that they also have a high temperature, we can deduce that there is now a 40% likelihood of this person having flu.

However, how do we determine the probability that they have the flu, given the fact that they have a combination of symptoms such as:

• high temperature and runny nose
• high temperature and headache
• runny nose and headache?

The probability of having flu will increase for *any one* of the symptoms but patients often present a unique combination of symptoms, and we cannot measure the probability of patients having the flu given a specific set of symptoms.

We *cannot* measure the probability of the hypothesis given event 1, and event 2, but not event 3, as this would require us collecting 100 past cases of patients that have an identical set of symptoms to the current patient. Such an opportunity is highly unlikely to exist. However, we can easily measure the *prior probability of the hypothesis*.

We can also easily measure the probability of the event, given the hypothesis for each and all of the events, or symptoms, we wish to measure. For example, if we take 100 people who are known to have the flu; for each of these, we can find out how many of them have a high temperature, how many have a runny nose, and how many have a headache.

We can also measure P(E:given not H), i.e., sample 100 visitors to the surgery diagnosed with ailments other than flu. We can look at this population, and ask, in turn, how many have a runny nose, headache or high temperature.

This data is quite easy to obtain, and given Bayes theorem, we can then calculate the probability of the hypothesis; i.e., that someone has the flu given any combination of symptoms we choose. In doing this we have changed our data collection slightly but significantly.

Instead of fixing the symptom, and then determining how many patients with this symptom have the flu, we first sample 100 people *with the flu* and determine the probabilities of the symptoms appearing. Similarly, we sample 100 *people who do not have the flu*, and determine the probabilities of the same symptoms appearing.

Imagine that we wanted to determine the probability of the hypothesis if two symptoms were evident but a third symptom was not, e.g.

P(flu: given high temperature and runny nose but no headache) = ???

We cannot measure: $P(H:E_1$ and E_2 and not $E_3)$ as this would require finding 100 previous patients with this exact combination of symptoms. At the same time we would need 100 patients with every other possible set of symptoms—and there could be an almost infinite set of combinations.

However, we can measure the probability where three different events will occur to support the hypothesis:

$$P(E_1 : H), P(E_2 : H), P(E_3 : H)$$

Also, we can measure

$$P(E_1 : \text{not } H), P(E_2 : \text{not } H), P(E_3 : \text{not } H)$$

i.e., testing that the three different events do not support the hypothesis.

Using Bayes theorem we can then calculate the probability of H given E_1 and E_2 occurring to support the hypothesis but E_3 not occurring:

$$P(H : E_1 \text{ and } E_2 \text{ and not } E_3)$$

Assume that the following data is available.

	Probability of high temperature	Probability of runny nose
When flu is true	0.7	0.6
When flu is not true	0.5	0.2

In this case, we sample 100 people *who have the flu* and determine that 70% of them have a high temperature.

In 100 people *who do not have the flu*, 50% of these have a high temperature.

Activity 4

Determine why do these two numbers (70% and 50%) do not add up to 100%.

Feedback 4

You should have been able to recognise that the two numbers do not add up to 100% because we are sampling two different populations, i.e., 100 who have the flu and 100 who do not have the flu.

Similarly, we look at the population of those people with the flu, and 60% of those have a runny nose. In a sample of 100 people who *do not have the flu* and we find that only 20% of those have a runny nose. We do the same to determine the probability of the symptom 'headache' being true, given that the hypothesis flu is true, and the probability of symptom 'headache' being true given that the hypothesis, flu, is not true. Notice that this data is not the same as shown in the previous table and that numbers do not necessarily add up to 100%.

Collecting this data is fairly simple. We merely sample 100 patients who have been diagnosed with flu, and we take 100 patients who have been diagnosed as not having the flu, and determine the probabilities of the symptoms for each of these populations of patients. We can now repeatedly use Bayes equations to calculate the probability of flu, given a range of symptoms.

Another way of writing the Bayes theorem is using the two equations below.

$$P(H:E) = \frac{P(E:H)\,P(H)}{P(E:H)\,P(H) + P(E:\text{not } H)\,P(\text{not } H)}$$

$$P(H:\text{not } E) = \frac{(1 - P(E:H))\,P(H)}{(1 - P(E:H))\,P(H) + (1 - P(E:\text{not } H))\,P(\text{not } H)}$$

The first of these equations is used to calculate the probability of a hypothesis given an event or symptom is true, the second is used if an event or symptom is not true.

Let's imagine that a patient has a high temperature, and the prior probability of the flu is 0.3. We can use the equations to calculate the probability that this patient has the flu, now that we have discovered that they have a high temperature. As the symptom is true, i.e., the event is true, we use the first equation, and calculate the probability of the hypothesis. The first equation says we calculate the probability of the event given the hypothesis, and multiply that by the prior probability of the hypothesis.

We divide all of this by the part of the equation beneath the line, which is the *prior probability of the event, given the hypothesis* multiplied by the *prior probability of the hypothesis*, plus the *probability of the event given not the hypothesis* multiplied by the *prior probability of not the hypothesis*.

The prior probability of not the hypothesis, in other words P(not H) is clearly just one minus P(H), the prior probability of the hypothesis.

Using the equations and the data taken from the table above we can now calculate the probability of flu for a range of symptoms.

Assuming 'High Temperature' is true and 'Runny nose' is false we firstly calculate the probability of flu given that high temperature is true using the first equation. Initially, we ignore the fact that runny nose is false—we take account of this later by using the second equation.

Thus we use the first equation

$$P(H:E) = \frac{P(E:H)\,P(H)}{P(E:H)\,P(H) + P(E:not\ H)\,P(not\ H)}$$

to calculate P(flu:high temperature).

Given that the prior probability of having flu is 0.3, then the equation can be completed as follows.

$$P(H:E) = \frac{0.7 \times 0.3}{0.7 \times 0.3 + 0.5 \times 0.7}$$

Therefore,

$$P(\text{flu:high temperature}) = 0.375$$

Now that the probability of having flu with a high temperature is set at 0.375, then the probability of having flu with two symptoms can be derived. As the second symptom is false we use the second equation

$$P(H:not\ E) = \frac{(1 - P(E:H))\,P(H)}{(1 - P(E:H))\,P(H) + (1 - P(E:not\ H))\,P(not\ H)}$$

to calculate P(flu:high temperature, not runny nose).

In this case P(H) is not 0.3, it is the calculated value of 0.375 as we are taking the fact that the patient has a high temperature into consideration.

Applying the probability factors from the different events produces the following.

$$P(H:not\ E) = \frac{(1 - 0.6) \times 0.375}{(1 - 0.6) \times 0.375 + (1 - 0.2) \times (1 - 0.375)}$$

This means that the probability of the hypothesis being correct with the patient having a temperature but not a runny nose can be stated as:

$$P(\text{flu:high temperature, not runny nose}) = 0.23$$

We can repeat the process above many times in order to calculate the probability of flu given any specific combination of symptoms a patient may have.

Clearly, at the same time as calculating the probability of flu we would, in parallel, also calculate the probability that the patient has a common cold and all other potential hypotheses. By determining which symptom has most effect on all of these calculations we will know which symptom is most important and thus which question the doctor should ask next. Furthermore, before asking any more questions we can determine if the probabilities could change significantly. If so then we have not yet reached a firm conclusion. However, if the probabilities will not change significantly irrespective of the answers a patient may give then we can be satisfied that we have reached a definitive diagnosis and no longer need to ask anymore questions.

Bayesian Networks

A Bayesian network (also known as Bayes net, causal probabilistic network, Bayesian belief network, or simply belief network) is a compact model representation for reasoning under uncertainty.

A problem domain—diagnosis of mechanical failures, for instance—consists of a number of entities or events. These entities or events are, in a Bayesian network, represented as random variables. One random variable can, for instance, represent the event that a piece of mechanical hardware in a production facility has failed. The random variables representing different events are connected by directed edges to describe relations between events. An edge between two random variables X and Y represents a possible dependence relation between the events or entities represented by X and Y. An edge could, for instance, describe a dependence relation between disease and a symptom—diseases cause symptoms. Thus, edges can be used to represent cause–effect relations. The dependence relations between entities of the problem domain are organised as a graphical structure. This graphical structure describes the possible dependence relations between the entities of the problem domain, e.g. a Bayesian network model for diagnosing lung cancer, tuberculosis, and bronchitis would describe the cause–effect relations between the possible causes of these diseases.

The uncertainty of the problem domain is represented through conditional probabilities.

Conditional probability distributions specify our belief about the strengths of the cause–effect relations, e.g. lung cancer does not always produce a positive (bad) chest X-ray, or a mechanical failure does not always cause an alarm to sound. Thus, a Bayesian network consists of a qualitative part, which describes the dependence relations of the problem domain, and a quantitative part, which describes our belief about the strengths of the relations.

Bayesian networks have been applied for reasoning and decision making under uncertainty in a large number of different settings. The next activity requires you to identify some applications.

Activity 5

This activity will help you appreciate the usefulness of the Bayesian approach to dealing with uncertainty in KBSs.

Search the Internet for examples of the use of Bayesian networks.

Feedback 5

You might have discovered examples of the application of Bayesian Networks to any of the following:

- *Medicine*—diagnosis of muscle and nerve diseases, antibiotic treatment, diabetes advisory system, triage (AskRed.com).
- *Software*—software debugging, printer troubleshooting, safety and risk evaluation of complex systems, help facilities in Microsoft Office products.
- *Information processing*—information filtering, display of information for time-critical decisions, fault analysis in aircraft control.
- *Industry*—diagnosis and repair of on-board unmanned underwater vehicles, control of centrifugal pumps, process control in wastewater purification.
- *Economy*—credit application evaluation, portfolio risk and return analysis.
- *Military*—NATO Airborne Early Warning & Control Program, situation assessment.
- *Agriculture*—blood typing and parentage verification of cattle, replacement of milk cattle, mildew management in winter wheat.

The Strengths of Probabilistic Reasoning

- Bayes theorem is mathematically sound so it provides a good basis for the investigation of uncertainty.
- The results of using this method have strong justification, adding value and credibility to the output from expert systems.
- Probabilistic reasoning, when compared with confidence factors (only expressions of opinion), has higher validity because the results are based on mathematically proven reasoning and statistical data.

The Limitations of Probabilistic Reasoning

- Needs statistical data to be collected from previous results, and will only work where this data is available. Furthermore, this data may not be accurate invalidating the results of the hypothesis being tested.
- Often one might have to rely on human estimates of one or more of these probability factors. But if you have to do that, it might be better to let experienced experts estimate the relevant probabilities from the start. This is the point of view of the advocates of confidence factors.

Summary

This section introduced the principle of uncertainty, and showed how Bayes theorem could be used to determine the extent of uncertainty, firstly in a written example, and then using formulae.

Self-Assessment Question

The following information is available concerning why a motor vehicle will not start. The hypothesis is that the battery is flat (i.e., not working) and so the engine will not start.

	Probability of engine turning	Probability of noisy alternator	Probability of lights working
When battery flat is true	0.1	0.5	0.3
When battery flat is not true	0.7	0.4	0.6

Assume that the prior probability of a flat battery is 0.7. Complete the Bayesian equation assuming that car lights are working but that the engine is not turning.

Answer to Self-Assessment Question

Calculate probability of having a flat battery given that the car lights are working.

$$P(H{:}E) = \frac{P(E{:}H)\,P(H)}{P(E{:}H)\,P(H) + P(E{:}\text{not } H)\,P(\text{not } H)}$$

$$P(H{:}E) = \frac{(0.3 \times 0.7)}{(0.3 \times 0.7) + (0.6 \times (1 - 0.7))}$$

$$P(H{:}E) = \frac{0.21}{0.21 + 0.18}$$

$$P(\text{flat battery:lights working}) = 0.54$$

Thus given the fact that the car lights are working the probability of the problem being a flat battery has fallen from 0.7 to 0.54. The next step is to calculate the probability of the battery being flat given that the car lights work but the engine does not turn.

$$P(H:\text{not } E) = \frac{(1 - P(E:H))\,P(H)}{(1 - P(E:H))\,P(H) + (1 - P(E:\text{not } H))\,P(\text{not } H)}$$

$$P(H:\text{not } E) = \frac{(1 - 0.1) \times 0.54}{(1 - 0.1) \times 0.54 + (1 - 0.7) \times (1 - 0.54)}$$

$$P(H:\text{not } E) = \frac{0.486}{0.486 + 0.138}$$

$$P(\text{flat battery:lights working and engine not turning}) = 0.78$$

So the probability of having a flat battery when engine isn't turning but when the lights are working is 0.78.

SECTION 4: FUZZY LOGIC

Introduction

This section provides an introduction to fuzzy logic and its use within KBSs as an approach to storing knowledge where uncertainty is a factor.

Objectives

By the end of the section you will be able to:

• evaluate the usefulness of fuzzy logic in dealing with uncertainty.

Fuzzy Logic

Fuzzy logic is a method of dealing with uncertainty in expert systems. The technique uses the same principles as the mathematical theory of fuzzy sets (Jamshidi, 1997). It attempts to simulate the process of human reasoning by allowing the computer to behave in a method that appears to be less precise or logical than activities normally ascribed to a computer.

The reasoning behind fuzzy logic is that many decisions are not true or false, black or white, etc. Decisions actually involve uncertainty and terms such as 'maybe', indicating that actions may or may not occur. The decision-making process may not, therefore be particularly structured, but involve many partial decisions taken without complete information.

Many people confuse uncertain reasoning with fuzzy reasoning. Probabilistic reasoning as in Bayes theorem is concerned with the *uncertain reasoning about well-defined events* such as symptoms or illnesses. On the other hand, fuzzy logic is concerned with the *reasoning about 'fuzzy' events* or concepts.

Fuzzy Logic Statements

Fuzzy logic allows a degree of impreciseness to be used for both inputs to, and outputs from a KBS. For example, the following statements are valid in fuzzy logic terms, but not in probability theory.

Input terms allowed:

• The temperature is 'high'
• The vibration is 'low'
• The load is 'medium'.

Outputs can be in terms of:

- The bearing damage is 'moderate'
- The unbalance is 'very high'.

Activity 6

This activity draws on examples of your own thinking patterns to help you understand fuzzy reasoning.

Consider the temperature of the room you are in at the moment, without looking at a thermometer, how would you characterise the temperature?

Consider someone you know quite well, how would you characterise their height, given that you have never measured it?

Feedback 6

The chances are you might use terms such as cool, warm or freezing to describe the room, or short or tall to describe your friend's height.

When is a person tall, at 170 cm, 180 cm or 190 cm? If we define the threshold of tallness at 180 cm, then the implication is that a person of 179.9 cm is not tall. When humans reason with terms such as 'tall' they do not normally have a fixed threshold in mind, but a smooth fuzzy definition. Humans can reason very effectively with such fuzzy definitions and in order to capture human fuzzy reasoning we need fuzzy logic.

An example of a fuzzy rule that involves a fuzzy condition and a fuzzy conclusion is:

```
IF holiday is long THEN spending money is high
```

Fuzzy reasoning involves three steps:

1. Fuzzification of the terms in the *conditions* of rules (i.e., inputs).
2. Inference from fuzzy rules.
3. Defuzzification of the fuzzy terms in the *conclusions* of rules (i.e., outputs).

Fuzzification

Using the technique of fuzzification, the concept 'long' is related to the underlying objective term that it is attempting to describe; i.e., the actual time in weeks. As an example, the term 'long' can be represented in this graph (see Figure 7.1).

The graph shows the degree of membership with which a holiday belongs to the category (set) 'long'. Full membership of the class 'long' is represented by a value of 1, while no membership is represented by a value of 0. At 2 weeks and below

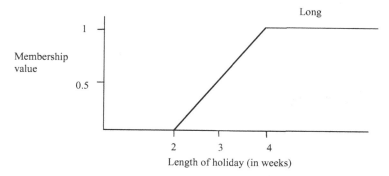

FIGURE 7.1. Fuzzy concept 'long' related to length of holiday in weeks.

a holiday does not belong to the class 'long'. At 4 weeks and above a holiday fully belongs to the class 'long'. Between 2 weeks and 4 weeks the membership increases linearly between 0 and 1. The degree of belonging to the set 'long' is called the confidence factor or the membership value. The shape of the membership function curve can be non-linear.

The purpose of the fuzzification process is to allow a fuzzy condition in a rule to be interpreted. For example, the condition 'holiday = long' in a rule can be true for all values of 'length of holiday', however, the confidence factor or membership value (MV) of this condition can be derived from the above graph. A 3-week-long holiday is 'long' with a confidence factor of 0.5. It is the gradual change of the MV of the condition 'long' with the length of holiday that gives fuzzy logic its strength.

Normally, fuzzy concepts have a number of values to describe the various ranges of values of the objective term that they describe. For example, the fuzzy concept 'hotness' may have the values 'very hot', 'hot' and 'warm'. Membership functions of these values can be shown in Figure 7.2.

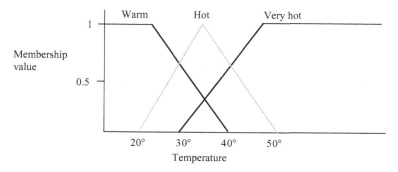

FIGURE 7.2. Membership functions for 'warm', 'hot' and 'very hot'.

Fuzzy Inference

Inference from a set of fuzzy rules involves fuzzification of the conditions of the rules, then propagating the confidence factors (membership values) of the conditions to the conclusions (outcomes) of the rules.

Consider the following rule:

```
IF (location is expensive) AND (holiday is long) THEN
spending money is high
```

Inference from this rule involves (using fuzzification) looking up the MV of the condition 'location is expensive' given the price of food, etc. and the MV of 'holiday is long' given the length of the holiday. If we, as suggested by Zadeh, take the minimum MV of all the conditions and assign it to the outcome 'spending money is high' then from our example, if 'location is expensive' had a MV of 0.9 and 'holiday is long' had a MV of 0.7 we would conclude that the 'spending money is high' with a MV of 0.7.

An enhancement of this method involves having a weight for each rule between 0 and 1 that multiplies the MV assigned to the outcome of the rule. By default each rule weight is set to 1.0.

In a fuzzy rule base a number of rules with the outcome 'spending money is high' will be fired. The inference engine will assign the outcome 'spending money is high', the maximum MV from all the fired rules. Thus from the rule above we deduced that the spending money is high with a MV of 0.7. However, given the rule below we may deduce that the spending money is high with a MV of 0.9.

```
IF (holiday is exotic) THEN the spending money is high
```

Thus, taking the conclusions of these two rules together we would deduce that the spending money is high with an MV of 0.9.

In summary, fuzzy inference involves:

- Fuzzification of the conditions of each rule and assigning the outcome of each rule the minimum MV of its conditions multiplied by the rule weight.
- Assigning each outcome the maximum MV from its fired rules.
- Fuzzy inference will result in confidence factors (MVs) assigned to each outcome in the rule base.

Defuzzification

If the conclusion of the fuzzy rule set involves fuzzy concepts, then these concepts must be translated back into objective terms before they can be used in practice.

For a rules set including the 'spending money is high' rule above, fuzzy inference will result in the terms 'spending money is low', 'spending money is medium' and 'spending money is high' being assigned membership values. However, in practice, to use the conclusions from such a rule base we may need to defuzzify the conclusions into threshold *figures* for the actual amount of spending money we would recommend someone take with them when going on holiday. To do this we need to define the membership functions for spending money as shown in Figure 7.3.

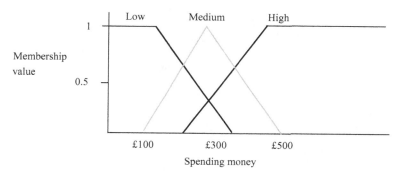

FIGURE 7.3. Membership functions for spending money.

One method of defuzzification is to place the MV generated by inference for each fuzzy outcome at the point where the membership function has its highest value. The required defuzzified value can then be calculated as the centre of gravity of the three MVs.

Assuming that fuzzy inference results in MV of 0.3, 0.5 and 0.7 for the low, medium and high spending money respectively.

The defuzzified value of 'spending money' is calculated as the centre of gravity of the three MVs (viewed) as weights placed at £100, £300 and £500 (see Figure 7.4).

The expression for the defuzzified value is:

$$\frac{(HV\_low \times MV\_low + HV\_med \times MV\_med + HV\_high \times MV\_high)}{(MV\_low + MV\_med + MV\_high)}$$

HV_low, HV_med and HV_high are the values of spending money that are recommended at the *highest membership values* for low, medium and high spending money holidays.

MV_low, MV_med and MV_high are the MV values generated by fuzzy inference for low, medium and risk of burst outcomes.

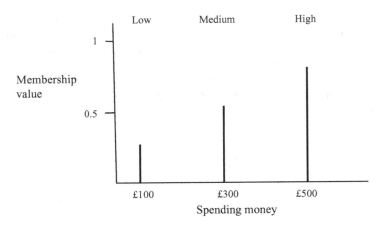

FIGURE 7.4. Membership values for spending money.

Applying the formula to the example gives

$$\frac{(£100 \times 0.3 + £300 \times 0.5 + £500 \times 0.7)}{(0.3 + 0.5 + 0.7)}$$

Thus we have a defuzzified recommended spending money value of £353.

Activity 7

This activity will help you apply fuzzy logic to an additional example.

Imagine you are trying to determine the optimum temperature for a room. There may be a range of temperatures that can apply to the room (e.g. 15°C–30°C), although some of those temperatures will give the room the 'correct' temperature, while others will be too hot or too cold.

Each one (the 'members') of the set of all possible temperatures can be assigned a value between 0 and 1 indicating how desirable that temperature actually is, or the strength of membership of that particular temperature in the overall set.

Draw a diagram to indicate a membership set for 'room temperature' where values of 19°C–22°C represent perfect room temperatures and temperatures of 17°C and below, or 24°C or above, or too cold or too hot to be considered as room temperatures.

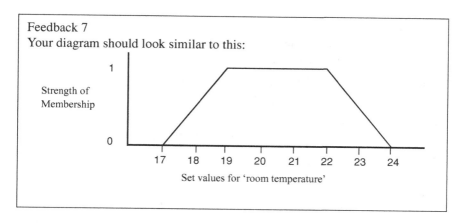

Feedback 7
Your diagram should look similar to this:

If we were to write a heating controller using normal logic we would need rules to describe what actions to take under various conditions, e.g.

If temp < 17°C turn heating on full.
If temp is 17°C turn heating to 0.75 × full.
If temp is 18°C turn heating to 0.5 × full.
If temp is ≥ 19°C and ≤ 22°C turn heating off.

We would need a similar set of rules for rooms that are too warm. Notice how the heating gradually decreases as the room becomes warmer.

Using fuzzy logic we could replace many of these rules. Assuming we have three membership sets, 'cold', 'normal' and 'hot' we could have rules such as the following:

If temp is 'cold' then heating is on full.
If temp is 'normal' then heating is off.

On first inspection you may think that according to these rules the heating would be either on of off. However, as the membership values of 'cold' and 'normal' changes gradually so would the results of the rules. Thus, 'heating on full' may have an MV of 0.8 and 'heating off' may have an MV of 0.2. Defuzzification would take these two membership values and determine an actual setting for the heater somewhere between off and full on.

When the room temperature reaches 19°C 'cold' will have an MV of 0 and 'normal' will have an MV of 1 at which point the heater would be turned off.

Note that the temperature can still move within a narrow range, and no action is required by the system. The temperature recording system displays some fuzziness that is it will accept a range of temperatures as being correct, rather than have an absolute figure showing the 'correct' temperature.

Activity 8
This activity will help you recognise the value of a fuzzy logic approach to a
simple temperature control system.

One morning you turn on the shower and someone has left the temperature dial
on a setting that is too cold for you.

Describe the difference between your response and the response that a
computer-controlled device might make to adjust the temperature appropriately.

Feedback 8
It is likely that you will make the water comfortable very quickly with little
trouble by acting without the precision that would need to be programmed into
a temperature control device. You will do this simply by turning the dial to
an appropriate position based on your experience and not worry if it is a few
degrees either way. A computer-controlled device on the other hand would
need to be told a precise range of temperatures that would be acceptable or not
acceptable and, depending on how hot or cold the water was, how quickly to
increase or decrease the temperature.

Fuzzy logic obviously requires some numerical data in order to operate, such
as what is considered significant error and significant rate-of-change-of-error,
but exact values of these numbers are usually not critical unless very respon-
sive performance is required in which case empirical tuning would determine
them.

For example, a simple temperature control system could use a single temperature feedback sensor whose data is subtracted from the command signal to compute 'error' and then time-differentiated to yield the rate-of-change-of-error. Error might have units of degrees Celsius and a small error considered to be $2°C$
while a large error is $5°C$. The rate-of-change-of-error might then have units
of degrees/minute with a small rate being $5°C/minute$ and a large one being
$15°C/minute$.

The fuzzy logic approach incorporates a simple, rule-based 'If X and Y then Z'
approach to solving a control problem based on the operator's empirical experience
rather than attempting to model a system mathematically. For example, rather than
dealing with temperature control in precise terms like

• If the temperature is $35°C$ and increasing by $3°C/minute$ then reduce the temperature to $30°C$.

Instead, something like the following would be used:

- if (the water is too hot) and (the water is getting hotter) then (turn the heating down quickly), or
- if (the water is too hot) and (the water is not getting hotter) then (turn the heating down slowly).

These terms are imprecise and yet very descriptive of what must actually happen. Fuzzy logic is capable of mimicking this type of behaviour and using fuzzy logic reduces the number of rules required in the system.

The Strengths of Fuzzy Logic

The following factors offer advantages over other rule-based approaches to KBS development:

- Fewer rules are required within a knowledge base. Rather than having a rule for all possible situations, the degree of membership of a set can be determined using fuzzy logic.
- Membership functions can be used to represent intuitive knowledge from experts. It is unlikely that knowledge can be expressed in terms of absolute values or statements. Fuzzy logic allows vague or imprecise terms to be introduced into the expert system to reflect the fuzziness of decision making in the real world.
- Outputs can be in terms familiar to humans. We tend to work with imprecise statements such as **'I think there is a good chance it will rain today'** rather than certainty (it will or will not rain). The outputs from the system are therefore more understandable.

The Limitations of Fuzzy Logic

The use of fuzzy logic is limited by the following factors:

- Fuzzy logic still requires the writing of a large number of rules—many of which are difficult to write and check due to the imprecise nature of the logic.
- Knowledge acquisition and representation problems apply, as in any KBS development. However, in this case, the knowledge engineer may find it even more difficult to elicit the required knowledge or write this in expert system format.
- A system based on fuzzy logic can be difficult to maintain and upgrade, especially as the membership of classes may need amending over time.
- As with any rule-based system, systems based on fuzzy logic are not adaptive in their pure form; additional programming in terms of feedback from example inputs will be required if the system is to automatically update the rules.

Summary

This section has provided an introduction to fuzzy logic and its use in dealing with uncertainty in KBSs. You have learned how intuitive knowledge from experts can be represented to reflect the fuzziness of decision making in the real world.

Self-Assessment Question

Which of the following could be applications for fuzzy logic?

- Autofocusing in cameras
- Regulating water temperature in shower heads
- Varying the length of time traffic lights are on green.

Justify your answers.

Answer to Self-Assessment Question

All of these activities could be applications for fuzzy logic.

In some situations, the camera may have to 'guess' which is the most important element of a potential picture, and focus on this.

The temperature of water in a shower is affected by water pressure, which in turn can vary depending on water usage in a building. Fuzzy logic can be used to maintain a constant shower temperature by monitoring water usage in other parts of the building.

The length of time traffic lights need to be on green to provide optimal traffic flow will vary depending on the number of cars approaching the traffic lights. Fuzzy logic can be used to try and determine the traffic flow in advance and therefore amend the traffic light sequence accordingly.

Current Research Issues in Uncertain Reasoning

Reasoning with Uncertainty

Association for Uncertainty in AI
http://www.auai.org/

Certainty (or Confidence) Factors

UT ML Group: Uncertain Reasoning
http://www.cs.utexas.edu/users/ml/publication/uncertain-abstracts.html

Probabilistic Reasoning

K-State KDD Lab: Probabilistic-Reasoning
http://www.kddresearch.org/Groups/Probabilistic-Reasoning/

Probabilistic Reasoning and Bayesian Networks
http://personales.unican.es/gutierjm/main/ai.html

Fuzzy Logic

FAQ: Fuzzy Logic and Fuzzy Expert Systems
http://www-2.cs.cmu.edu/Groups/AI/html/faqs/ai/fuzzy/part1/faq.html

Rule Chaining in Fuzzy Expert Systems
http://www.csee.usf.edu/~hall/papers/fuzzes.pdf

A New Environment for Developing Fuzzy Expert Systems
http://www.iis.sinica.edu.tw/JISE/1999/199901_05.pdf

MEDEX—A Fuzzy Expert System
http://www.nrlmry.navy.mil/~medex/tutorial/medex/fuzzy.html

FLINT toolkit
http://www.lpa.co.uk/fln.htm

Reference

Jamshidi, M. (editor) (1997). *Applications of Fuzzy Logic: Towards High Machine Intelligence Quotient Systems*. Prentice-Hall: Englewood Cliffs, NJ.

8

Hybrid Knowledge-Based Systems

Introduction

In Chapter 6, you encountered the concept of a hybrid system where a conventional system and a knowledge-based system (KBS) can be coupled to achieve specific aims by drawing on the features of both types of system. In this chapter we will explore the rationale behind and the implications of coupling one KBS with another KBS.

Objectives

By the end of this chapter you will be able to:

- Distinguish between symbolic systems and connectionist systems.
- Identify advantages of one type of KBS that can counterbalance a disadvantage of another KBS.
- Describe a number of classification schemes of hybrid systems.
- Describe some example hybrid systems.

Types of Knowledge-Based Systems

Throughout the earlier chapters of this book you have learned about:

- Expert systems (ESs)
- Neural networks (NNs)
- Semantic networks
- Genetic algorithms
- Kohonnen self-organising maps
- Case-based reasoning systems
- Probabilistic reasoning systems
- Frame-based systems
- Fuzzy logic systems.

Within this list, it is possible to distinguish two broad types:

- *Symbolic* systems
- *Connectionist* systems (sometimes referred to as sub-symbolic systems).

Symbolic Systems

Symbolic systems operate with symbolic representations of reality and in doing so come close to representing, in a semantic manner, human cognitive processing.

Connectionist Systems

Connectionist systems on the other hand, operate by taking advantage of often very large numbers of connections between processing nodes. Such systems might be considered an attempt to represent capacities such as skill and intuition and cannot be expressed in normal human language, i.e., these systems use an *implicit* knowledge representation scheme.

Activity 1
In the list of KBSs below, identify those which are symbolic and those which are connectionist by completing the following table:
- Expert systems
- Neural networks
- Semantic networks
- Genetic algorithms
- Case-based reasoning systems
- Kohonnen self-organising maps

Feedback 1

Symbolic	Connectionist
Expert systems	Neural networks
Case-based reasoning systems	Genetic algorithms
Semantic networks	Kohonnen self-organising maps

Note that though semantic networks are clearly networks, their content and processing are semantically explicit.

Symbolic and Connectionist Systems Compared

For each of these types of system, it is possible to distinguish advantages and disadvantages. For example, you saw how ESs require large amounts of efforts to write the rules on which they depend for their operation. Similarly, a case-based reasoning system might require a large number of cases to be written and stored in order to anticipate new scenarios and provide assistance to decision making. However, while ESs require significant development time they are expected to provide accurate output and to be able to explain how that solution was derived.

On the other hand, you also saw how genetic algorithms can solve large, almost intractable, problems but that their output can only be relied upon to be merely adequate—not necessarily optimal. For example, a genetic algorithm tasked with generating solutions to a timetabling problem, may generate many acceptable solutions but be unable to find the best possible solution.

You also saw how NNs can learn previously unknown relationships in data presented and are relatively noise tolerant. However, the knowledge is encoded as weights within a network and thus is not open to inspection by humans.

This consideration of the relative advantages and disadvantages leads to a recognition that some of the disadvantages of symbolic systems are not shared by connectionist systems and vice versa. It does not take a huge leap of inspiration therefore, to consider the possibility that by applying one or more of each type of system to a specific problem, the disadvantages of one can be cancelled out or at least reduced by the advantages of the other.

Works by Dreyfus and Dreyfus (1987) and Smolensky (1988) have highlighted additional relative advantages that can be taken into account when considering a hybrid approach.

Advantages of connectionist systems include:

• Learning capabilities
• Tolerance to missing or noisy data
• Massive parallelism in relation to processing
• Graded representation.

Advantages of symbolic systems include:

• Clarity of representation and processing
• Ease of specifying processing steps
• Processing precision.

> **Activity 2**
> Now that you have seen how the advantages of the different KBSs vary depending on whether they are symbolic or connectionist, suggest why it might be useful to combine an ES with a NN such that the combined features complement each other.

> **Feedback 2**
> You may have been able to recognise that by combining an ES and a NN, it might be possible to overcome the limitations of either.
>
> Expert systems cannot learn and cannot process sensory data. However, if we can combine an ES with a NN we can overcome both of these limitations.
>
> Similarly, NNs cannot explain their reasoning process. By combining a NN with an ES we may be able to overcome this limitation also.

An Example Hybrid NN/ES

One simple way of combining a NN and an ES is to have two separate component systems with the outputs from one system feeding into the other. If a NN was used as an input to an ES this would provide an overall system which behaved like an ES but with the advantage of being able to process, and identify patterns in, sensory data.

Imagine a scenario where an ES is being developed to monitor a patient in intensive care and automatically administer drugs where appropriate. One of the inputs is a patient's heartbeat and the ES needs to know if the heartbeat is strong or weak as this will have an impact upon the decisions it makes. However, the ES cannot process sensory data. One option to overcome this would be to write a long and complex procedural algorithm to process the heart signal and to return an answer of 'strong' or 'weak' as appropriate. Another much simpler solution would be to train a NN to monitor the heartbeat and to decide if the signal is 'strong' or 'weak', 'regular' or 'irregular'. The outputs from the NN would then feed directly into the ES (Figure 8.1).

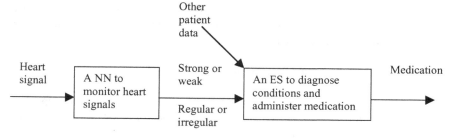

FIGURE 8.1. A loosely coupled hybrid knowledge-based system.

Having decided to integrate a NN with an ES let us consider the possibility of widening the scope of the NN component. Since the NN is monitoring the patient's heartbeat it could be decided that the NN should trigger an alarm if a sudden change is detected. Clearly, heart monitors already signal an alarm if the heart stops but using a NN an alarm could be triggered much sooner, assuming the NN could learn to distinguish important changes from normal fluctuations. However, what if the heartbeat changed in response to the medication administered by the ES? The NN could only recognise that this was an expected change if it knew what medication was administered by the ES. Thus, the NN's outputs are needed by the ES and the ES's outputs are needed by the NN (see Figure 8.2).

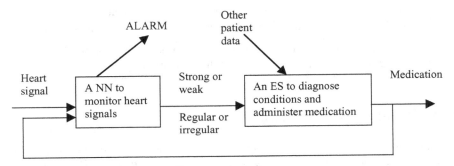

FIGURE 8.2. A tightly coupled hybrid Knowledge-based system.

We can see that the two separate component systems, in the example system above, are still clearly distinguishable. But is there a need to create a component that it is neither an ES nor a NN but has characteristics of both?

An Integrated Hybrid KBS

Consider the problem of identifying animals from photographs. This application sounds like an obvious choice for a NN system and indeed a NN could be trained to recognise a range of animals from photographs (see Figure 8.3).

However, such a network would be unable to explain its reasoning. If an ES came to the conclusion that the animal was a cat it could explain its reasoning, at least in part, by showing the appropriate rule, e.g.

If animal is small, fluffy and had four legs then animal is a cat.

A NN cannot explain its reasoning because we have no idea what concepts the nodes in the hidden layer represent. However, imagine a structure which is neither an ES nor a NN but instead has properties associated with both of these (see Figure 8.4).

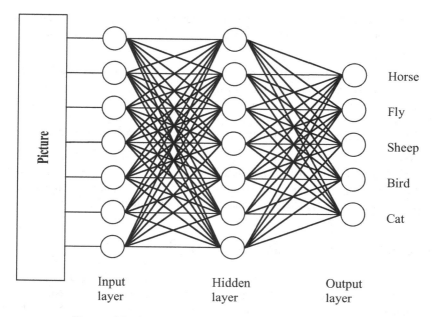

FIGURE 8.3. A neural network trained to recognise animals.

On first glance the system above would appear to be a NN. However, it is one where we know what concepts the inner nodes represent. This can be achieved by training the system one node at a time. Instead of training the whole network to recognise any animal, one node is trained to spot six-legged creatures, another to

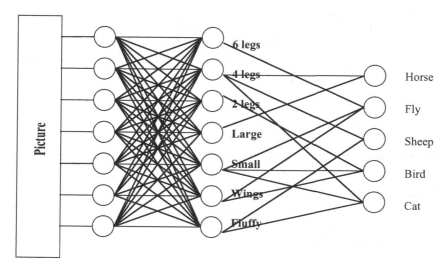

FIGURE 8.4. An integrated hybrid expert system/neural network architecture.

recognise small creatures and another to recognise wings, etc. Finally, the nodes in the inner layer are connected to the outer layer. This can either be done in one of two ways.

1. Links are made by specifying rules to represent a human expert's knowledge, as in an ES. For example, the links between fluffy and cat, small and cat, and four legs and cat (as shown in Figure 8.4) represent the rule specified earlier.
2. The links can be learnt by training the outer layer as any NN is trained.

Irrespective of how the links are made to the outer layer we now have a network that displays properties of a NN and properties of an ES. The system can be trained, can process visual data and can explain its reasoning (by identifying inner nodes that caused the output). This is an example of a fully integrated hybrid system.

Integrating Symbolic and Connectionist Systems

Having now explored some basic ideas we will now look at how to integrate symbolic and connectionist components in a hybrid architecture. Considerations when integrating symbolic and connectionist systems are suggested by Sun (2002):

- Should hybrid architectures be modular or monolithic?
- For modular architectures, should different knowledge representation schemes be used in different modules or the same representation schemes throughout?
- How do we decide whether the representation of a particular part of an architecture should be symbolic or connectionist?
- What are the appropriate representational techniques for bridging the heterogeneity likely in hybrid systems?
- How are representations learned in hybrid systems?
- How do we structure different parts to achieve appropriate results?

We will look at some of these aspects as we explore a number of approaches to classifying hybrid architectures.

Classifying Hybrid Systems

Several schemes have been applied to classifying and describing hybrid architectures. Three schemes will be explored here. These relate to:

1. the number of modules of the different components
2. the tightness of the integration between the symbolic and connectionists components themselves
3. the configuration of the modules and the conceptual understanding of the associated processing.

As always, classification schemes will display areas of overlap.

Single Module and Multi-Module Architectures

One NN coupled with one ES would be an example of a *single module architecture*. However, there may be advantages in including two or more NN modules in a hybrid system. In such *multi-module architectures*, it becomes necessary to describe whether the multiple NN modules, for example, are **replications** of a single structure or modules of **differing** structure. The former can be referred to as **homogeneous** and the latter as **heterogeneous** systems.

Integration in Hybrid Systems: Coupling

The term *coupling* refers to the degree of integration of the symbolic and connectionist components of a hybrid system. Three degrees of coupling have been described in the literature:

* Loose coupling
* Tight coupling
* Fully integrated.

Loose Coupling

A loosely coupled hybrid architecture has **separate** symbolic and connectionist modules. The control flow is **sequential** in the sense that processing has to be finished in one module before the next module can begin. Only one module is active at any time, and the communication between modules is **unidirectional**.

An architecture illustrating very loose coupling has been described in a model for structural parsing within the SCAN framework. First, a chart parser is used to provide a structural tree representation for phrases or sentences. Triples of 'noun relationship noun' are then used as input for several feedforward networks which produce a plausibility measure of the relationship. Based on this connectionist output, a symbolic restructuring component changes the original tree representation if the semantic feedforward networks indicate that this is appropriate.

This system has a loosely coupled hybrid processing architecture since there is a clear division between symbolic parsing, connectionist semantic analysis and symbolic restructuring. Only if the preceding module has finished completely, will the subsequent module begin processing (Wermter, 1995).

Tight Coupling

A tightly coupled hybrid architecture contains **separate** symbolic and connectionist modules, and control and communication are via **common** internal data structures in each module that allow **bidirectional** exchanges of knowledge between two or more modules. Processing still takes place in a single module at any given time, but the output of a connectionist module can have direct influence on a symbolic module (or vice versa) before global processing is complete. Feedback between two modules is therefore possible.

A tightly coupled hybrid architecture allows multiple exchanges of knowledge between two or more modules. Tight coupling has the potential for more powerful interactions. Such architectures however, need more complex interfaces in order to support the dynamic control between symbolic and connectionist modules.

Fully Integrated

In a fully integrated hybrid architecture—the most advanced of the hybrid processing architectures—there is no discernible *external* difference between symbolic and connectionist modules, since the modules share an interface and are embedded in the same architecture. The control flow *may be parallel* and the communication between symbolic and connectionist modules is via messages. Communication *may be bidirectional* between many modules—though not all possible communication channels need to be used.

Unified, Transformational and Modular Hybrid Systems

The third classification scheme (McGarry *et al.*, 1999)—categorises hybrid systems as being either *unified*, *transformational* or *modular.*

Unified Hybrid Systems

Unified hybrid systems are those where all processing is implemented by NN elements, i.e., though the system is a hybrid, the components are all *different* NNs.

Transformational Hybrid Systems

Transformational hybrid systems have the ability to insert, extract and refine symbolic knowledge within the framework of a NN. This is achieved by the use of both symbolic and connectionist components working to achieve a specific task.

Modular Hybrid Systems

Hybrid systems that are modular in nature and as such might contain more than one type of each component. In this way, if additional processing is required of a type that can be done by a NN, additional NN modules can be added to the hybrid until the desired level of processing is achieved.

Examples of KBS/KBS (AI/AI) Hybrid Systems

MACIE

The earliest *neural expert system* was MACIE (**MA**trix **C**ontrolled **I**nference **E**ngine) developed by Stephen Gallant as long ago as 1988.

Neural expert systems attempt to reduce the disadvantages of the *implicit* knowledge representation in pure NNs. They enrich NNs with heuristics which analyse NNs to cope with incomplete information, to explain conclusions and to generate questions for unknown inputs. This means that NNs are endowed with other functionalities so that they have all the required features of ESs.

MACIE is based on a feedforward NN, in which neuron outputs are spin values (± 1) produced by applying a threshold to the weighted input sum. In addition, hidden neurons coincide with output neurons so their purposes are application specific. The inputs to the system represent user's answers to questions which may have only 'yes' or 'no' answers, encoded by 1 or −1 respectively. An unknown state is encoded by 0. The neural knowledge base is created from training patterns which compute relevant weights. All states of neurons (including hidden neurons) in the feedforward network need to be prescribed because the algorithm works only for a single layer of neurons. In the case where all inputs are known, MACIE computes all the outputs. If some input facts are unknown, MACIE can still reach a conclusion and determine whether there is a chance of an output value change, should unknown inputs become known.

MACIE can also provide a simple justification of inference by generating IF-THEN rules. If the user asks for an explanation about the particular value of an output neuron, the network looks for the minimal subset of the unit's incident neurons which ensure its state, regardless of the remaining ones.

fSC-NET

In fSC-Net, a distributed connectionist representation of cells connected by links is used to represent symbolic knowledge. Rules may be directly encoded in the connectionist network or learned from examples. The learning method is a form of instance-based learning in which some of the individual instances in the training set are encoded by adding structure to the network and others cause modifications to weights.

Learning in fSC-Net only requires a single pass through the training data and it is therefore a true incremental learner. New hidden units are automatically recruited and the need for parameter tuning can be eliminated. Rules can be extracted after processing and loaded back into the system, thereby creating a system capable of supporting knowledge refinement.

KBANN

KBANN (Towell and Shavlik, 1990), integrates propositional calculus with neural learning. A set of rules designates a domain theory which is partially correct. This set is integrated into a NN as training material, thus refining the rules. Finally, the rules are extracted from the network—though this final step is not an official part of the KBANN algorithm.

The authors of KBANN have established a correspondence between the domain theory and a NN which appears in the following table.

Domain theory	Neural network
Final conclusion	Output units
Intermediate conclusions	Hidden units
Supporting facts	Input units
Antecedents of a rule	Highly weighted links

KBANN has been compared to empirical learning systems, i.e., those that learn only from data or from theory and data. KBANN has been claimed to generalise better than other empirical-based methods but exhibits the following limitations:

- It cannot handle rules with variables or cycles.
- There is no mechanism for handling uncertainty in the rules.
- The symbolic meaning of the initial NN is ignored by KBANN, which results in long training times.
- There is no mechanism for dynamically changing the topology of the NN.

Activity 3
Search the Internet for the following examples of hybrid systems and note what different KBSs they incorporate in their hybrid structure as well as the knowledge domain in which they are used.
- GANNET
- SCREEN
- CPD (Connectionist Deterministic Parsing)
- GFMM (General Fuzzy Min Max)

Feedback 3
You should have been able to find most of the following:
- GANNET uses a combination of genetic algorithm and neural network approaches in the context of *information retrieval.*

GANNET performs concept (keyword) optimisation for user-selected documents during information retrieval using genetic algorithms. It then uses the optimised concepts to perform concept exploration in a large network of related concepts through the Hopfield net parallel relaxation procedure. Based on a test collection of about 3000 articles, GANNET helped identify the underlying concepts that best describe user-selected documents.

However, you may also have located: Hancock, P.J.B., GANNET: Design of a neural net for *face recognition* by Genetic Algorithm, Proceedings of IEEE Workshop on Genetic Algorithms, Neural Networks and Simulated Annealing applied to problems in signal and image processing, Glasgow, 1990.
- SCREEN was developed for exploring integrated hybrid processing for spontaneous language analysis.

One main architectural motivation is the use of a common interface between symbolic and connectionist modules which are externally indistinguishable. In SCREEN, the many connectionist and symbolic modules have a common interface and can communicate with each other in *many directions*. From a module-external point of view it does not matter whether the internal processing within a module is connectionist or symbolic. This architecture therefore exploits a full integration of symbolic and connectionist processing at the module level.
- CDP is a system for connectionist deterministic parsing in language analysis.

While the choice of the next action is performed in a connectionist feedforward network, the action itself is performed in a symbolic module. During the process of parsing, control is switched back and forth between these two modules, but processing is confined to a single module at a time. Such a tightly coupled hybrid architecture has the potential for feedback to and from modules.
- GFMM– a **G**eneral **F**uzzy **M**in **M**ax neural network for decision support for the operational control of industrial processes.

You will find many more examples on the Internet of hybrid systems that have been applied to a huge range of sophisticated problems.

Summary

In this chapter you have seen how obtaining the full benefits of the use of KBSs can be achieved by a 'using the right tools for the job' approach and mixing and matching them as the application dictates. Hybrid systems, in which both symbolic and connectionist approaches are combined can be particularly effective where the combination overcomes the limitations of individual approaches.

Self-Assessment Question

Look at the following diagrams and label them appropriately as either:

- Full integrated transformational
- Tightly coupled unified
- Loosely coupled modular

NN = Neural Network
ES = Expert System

Diagram 1

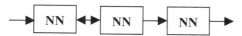

Diagram 2

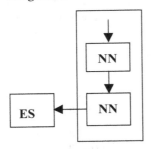

Diagram 3

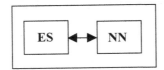

Answer to Self-Assessment Question

You should have been able to recognise that:
Diagram 1 represents a tightly coupled unified hybrid system.
Diagram 2 represents a loosely coupled modular system.
Diagram 3 represents a fully integrated transformational system.

References

Dreyfus, H. and Dreyfus, S. (1987). *Mind Over Machine*. Free Press: New York.
Gallant, S. (1988). Connectionist expert systems. *Communications of the ACM*, 31(2):152–169.
McGarry, K., Wermter, S. and MacIntyre, J. (1999). Hybrid neural systems: from simple coupling to fully integrated neural networks. *Neural Computing Surveys*, 2:62–94.
Smolensky, P. (1988). On the proper treatment of connectionism. *Behavioral and Brain Sciences*, 11:1–74.
Sun, R. (2002). Hybrid systems and connectionist implementationalism. In *Encyclopedia of Cognitive Science*. Nature Publishing Group (MacMillan): London, pp. 697–703.
Towell, G. and Shavlik, J. (1991). Interpretation of artificial neural networks: mapping knowledge-based neural networks into rules. In *Advances in Neural Information Processing Systems (NIPS)* MIT Press: Denver, pp. 977–984.
Wermter, S. (1995). *Hybrid Connectionist Natural Language Processing*. Chapman and Hall: London.

Bibliography

Darlington, K. (2000). *The Essence of Expert Systems*. Prentice-Hall: London England.

Ginsberg, M. (1993). *Essentials of Artificial Intelligence*. Morgan Kaufmann: Los Altos, CA.

Gruber, T. R. and Olsen, G. R. (1994). An Ontology for Engineering Mathematics. *In Proceedings of the 4th International Conference Principles of Knowledge Representation and Reasoning*, Gustav Stresermann Instutut, Bonn, Germany, Morgan, Kaufmann.

Kelly, G. (1955). *The Psychology of Personal Constructs*. Norton: New York.

Tansley, D. S. W. and Hayball, C. C. (1993). *Knowledge Based Systems Analysis and Design* (A KADS handbook) Prentice Hall: Hemel Hempstead.

Turban, E. and Aronson, J. E. (1998). *Decision Support Systems and Intelligent Systems*. Prentice-Hall: London, England. (See chapter 16 for alternative system development approaches.)

Wielinga, B., Schreiber, G. and Breuker, J. (1993) Modelling expertise, In Schreiber, G. Wielinga, B. and Breuker, J. (editors), *KADS: A Principled Approach to Knowledge-Based System Development*, Academic Press, San Diego.

Yeates, D. and Cadle, J. (1996). *Project Management for Information Systems*. Prentice-Hall/Pearson Education: London, England.

Index